JANE LYNCH grew up on the South Side of Chicago and currently lives in Los Angeles. She married Dr Lara Embry in 2010, and was lucky enough to get two daughters in the deal.

From the reviews of *Happy Accidents*:

'[A] frank, engaging, and at times uproariously funny autobiography of a roller-coaster life'   *Vogue*

'Lynch is, for once, not going for laughs; she's going for something remarkably close to wisdom … look[s] back over a life that would drive many memoirists to hyperbole if not histrionics with astonishing perspective'   *LA Times*

'Lynch's candour and comfort with self-revelation, as well as her knack for self-depreciation, are all on show in her excellent and often surprising autobiography'   *Guardian*

'Lynch deserves credit for honesty and for seriously handling subjects that could have been melodramatic minefields, with a lightness that doesn't drag the reader into a morass of therapeutic psychobabble'   *Washington Post*

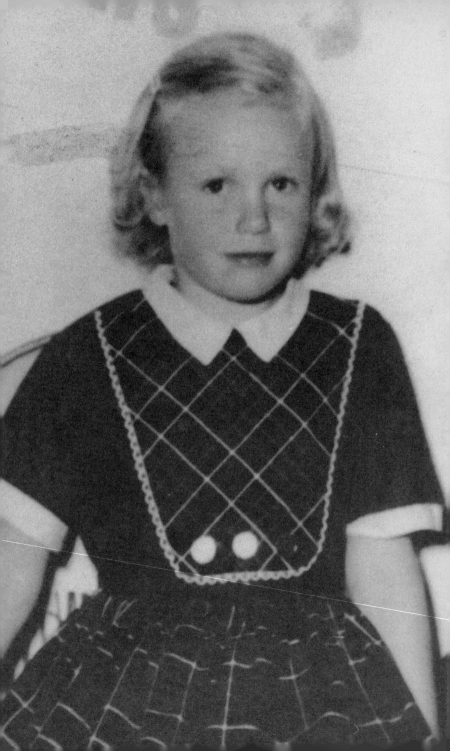

Happy Accidents

Jane Lynch

FOURTH ESTATE • *London*

Fourth Estate
An imprint of HarperCollins*Publishers*
77–85 Fulham Palace Road
Hammersmith, London W6 8JB

This Fourth Estate paperback edition published 2012
1

First published in the United States by Hyperion in 2011

A catalogue record for this book is
available from the British Library

ISBN 978-0-00-744758-9

Photos are courtesy of Jane Lynch, except: Page 152: Jeannie Elias; page 198: Courtesy
of Universal Studios Licensing LLC; page 203: *For Your Consideration* © Shangri-La
Entertainment, LLC. Licensed by: Warner Bros. Entertainment Inc. All rights reserved;
page 215: Timothy Norris/Stringer/Getty Images Entertainment/Getty Images; pages 223 and
224: Courtesy of Universal Studios Licensing LLC; page 234: Reuters/Fred Prouser/Landov;
page 237: (Patrick Ecclesine)/FOX; page 250: Trish Tunney; pages 270 and 271: Guy Shalem;
page 277: FOX; page 286: Frederick M. Brown/Getty Images Entertainment/Getty Images;
page 290: Dana Edelson/NBC; page 293: (Justin Jay)/FOX; page 296: FOX.

Book design by Ralph Fowler/rlfdesign

Printed and bound in Great Britain by
Clays Ltd, St Ives plc

MIX
Paper from
responsible sources
FSC™ **FSC** C007454
www.fsc.org

FSC™ is a non-profit international organisation established to promote
the responsible management of the world's forests. Products carrying the
FSC label are independently certified to assure consumers that they come
from forests that are managed to meet the social, economic and
ecological needs of present and future generations,
and other controlled sources.

Find out more about HarperCollins and the environment at
www.harpercollins.co.uk/green

For Mom and Dad

. . . and every kid out there mustering up

the courage to answer the call of their

own hero's journey

Contents

Foreword

I FIRST BECAME AWARE OF JANE LYNCH WHEN I SAW the movie *Best in Show*.

I had turned into a Christopher Guest junkie after seeing his brilliant comedy *Waiting for Guffman*. He created an atmosphere of sheer mirthfulness. I loved the wonderfully talented group of actors he put together. He let his players run with their characters without the benefit of a formal script. They were not only actors but also writers and improvisers. He trusted them, and they were hysterically funny. I couldn't wait until his next movie would be released.

That turned out to be *Best in Show*. Along with his regular group of actors, there was a new face, and I thought she was terrific. I looked for her name at the end of the picture: Jane Lynch. I hoped she would become one of the rep players in Christopher's future movies. She did.

Next came *A Mighty Wind*, followed by *For Your Consideration*. In each of these films Jane played an entirely different character, with hilarious results. Later, I was bowled over by her scene-stealing role opposite Steve Carell in *The 40-Year-Old Virgin*. These aren't Jane's only credits by any means, as you'll learn when you read her down-to-earth, heartwarming (and sometimes, heartbreaking) life story.

I finally had the pleasure of not only meeting her but getting to work with her in a little-known movie, *Post Grad*, starring Michael Keaton. I played her mother-in-law, and most of my scenes were with Jane. The main thing I took away with me from that experience is how much Jane made me laugh even off camera. She sees the "funny" in everything.

And then came *Glee*. I loved the show from the get-go. I asked my agent to call the producers and let them know I'd be willing to carry a spear, or whatever, if they'd only allow me to get into their sandbox and play . . . preferably opposite Jane. My wish came true. I was cast as Jane's mother, who was a former Nazi-hunter . . . (excuse me??). We got to sing, *"Why, oh why, oh why, oh—why did I ever leave Ohio?"* from the Broadway musical *Wonderful Town*. Did I mention that Jane has a great singing voice? Twice, I jumped up and down in front of the TV set in my living room when she won the Emmy and a Golden Globe for her portrayal of Sue Sylvester.

I remember once many years ago when I was doing *The Garry Moore Show* and the brilliant vaudeville comedian Ed Wynn was the guest star that week. Sitting at the writers' table one afternoon, Ed was regaling us with tons of wonderful stories about the icons he had worked with and known throughout his illustrious career. Among those he mentioned were Bob Hope and Jack Benny. He gave us his definition of comedians, which I never forgot:

"Comics say funny things [Bob Hope] and comedic actors say things *funny* [Jack Benny]."

Jane is cut from the same cloth as Jack Benny. She doesn't need a joke to get a laugh. What's funny about her is her "take" on any character she's playing . . . and I might add, because she's a wonderful actor, she plays the character very seriously, thereby making it that much funnier.

I was honored when she asked me to write this foreword. Her story is fascinating, and she relays it without holding anything back. It's all here, warts and all. She has gone through a lot in her life (good times and bum times) and tells about it with courage and honesty. She has come out on top as a performer and as a human being.

I'm happy to call her my friend.

—Carol Burnett

Happy
Accidents

Pontifical

F I COULD GO BACK IN TIME AND TALK TO MY
twenty-year-old self, the first thing I would say is: "Lose
the perm." Secondly I would say: "Relax. Really. Just relax.
Don't sweat it."

I can't remember a time when I wasn't anxious and fearful
that the parade would pass me by. And I was sure there was
someone or something outside of myself with all the answers. I
had a driving, anxiety-filled ambition. I wanted to be a working
actor so badly. I wanted to belong and feel like I was valued and
seen. Well, now I am a working actor, and I guarantee you it's
not because I suffered or worried over it.

As I look back, the road to where I am today has been a series of happy accidents I was either smart or stupid enough to
take advantage of. I thought I had to have a plan, a strategy.
Turns out I just had to be ready and willing to take chances,
look at what's right in front of me, and put my heart into everything I do. All that anxiety and fear didn't help, nor did it fuel
anything useful. Finally releasing that worry served to get me
out of my own way. So my final piece of advice to twenty-year-

old me: Be easy on your sweet self. And don't drink Miller Lite tall boys in the morning.

. . .

I DON'T KNOW WHY, BUT I WAS BORN WITH AN EXTRA helping of angst. I would love to be able to blame this on my parents, as I'm told this is good for book sales. But I can't.

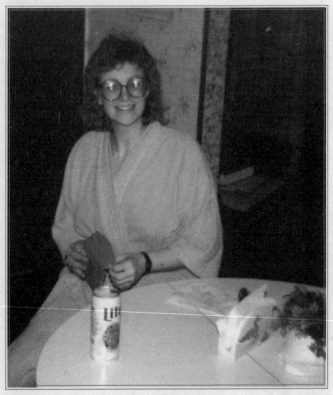

Enjoying a Very Merry Breakfast, Christmas 1980.

I grew up in a family that was pure Americana. We lived in Dolton, Illinois, one of the newly founded villages south of Chicago created to house the burgeoning middle class. We were like the subject of a Norman Rockwell painting, except it was the 1960s and '70s, so he would have had to paint us with bell-bottoms and a stocked liquor cabinet. I didn't settle into myself as a child, but the family I had around me was entertaining and embraced the life we had.

My dad, Frank, was a classic Irish-Catholic cutup. He was always singing a ditty, dancing a soft-shoe, or cracking wise while mixing a cocktail. He was almost bald by the time he was nineteen, and every day he'd smear Sea & Ski sun lotion on top of his naked head, then slap a little VO5 onto his hands and smooth the ring of hair around the sides with a flourish. "How do you like that?" he'd say to himself in the mirror, and sing under his breath, "*I've got things to do, places to go, people to see.*" And after that daily Sea & Ski ritual, damn if he still didn't end up getting skin cancer on his pate. However, it would be lung cancer that took my dad from us in 2003, and I miss him every day.

I can remember my dad, when I was really young—so young, it's like Vaseline over the memory—dancing with me in the living room. "Do you come here often?" he'd ask, twirling me around and singing along with Sid Caesar: "*Pardon me miss, but I've never done this . . . with a real live girl . . .*"

My dad also did a bang-up Bing Crosby. I loved it when he sang, and we never had to wait very long for it. He'd sing while putting sugar in his coffee, while buffing his shoes, or for no reason at all. He'd make up songs about us, the more ridiculous the better: To the tune of "*Val-deri, Val-dera,*" he'd sing "*Jane-*

eree, Jane-erah." My nickname became simply *Eree-Erah*. He added *–anikins* or *-erotomy* to the end of anyone's name. My older sister was Julie-anikins, my younger brother, Bob-erotomy. One of his favorite joyous exclamations was "Pon-TIFF! Pon-TIFF!" from the word "pontifical," which was his way of saying "fabulous." And "My cup runneth over" was boiled down to "My cup! My cup!" Speaking of cup, coffee was *coffiticus*, my mom was *L.T.* (Long Thing, because she was tall), and the phone was the *telephonic communicator*. We would roll our eyes or feign embarrassment—but we all wanted to be the subject of Dad's silliness, to be a part of his joy.

Each day, when Dad came home from his job at the bank, the first thing he'd do was put his keys and spare change into the saddlebags of the little ceramic Chihuahua that sat on his dresser. Then he and my mom would indulge in their nightly cocktail ritual with their favorite drink, Ten High Whiskey. Dad had his with ginger ale and Mom had hers with water, and they'd toast with the words "First today, badly needed." Dad would say, "L.T., let's get some atmosphere!" and they'd dim the lights and start singing something from *My Fair Lady*, Dad harmonizing perfectly to my mom's melody.

Banks were closed on Wednesday, and my dad loved his day off. It started at Double D (Dunkin' Donuts) because he loved their coffiticus and the chocolate cake donut. Wearing his blue elasticized "putter pants," he would check off items on his to-do list. He was forever singing something goofy under his breath; "*liver, bacon, onions . . .*" was a favorite. He wanted us to be as

OPPOSITE: *The Lynch family in red, white, and blue for the 4th of July, circa 1964 (I'm on the right).*

[5]

Dad goes after Mom with our new electric knife.

enthusiastic as he was about his accomplishments. If Wednesday's lawn work went unnoticed for its superior greenness, he'd plead, "Rave a little! Rave a little!"

My mom, Eileen Lynch (nee Carney), was, and still is, gorgeous. Tall and blond, with navy blue eyes and beautiful long legs, she never failed to turn heads. She always had a nice tan in the summer. And she's a clotheshorse who never pays full price . . . ever . . . unlike her middle kid. To this day (and she is now in her eighty-second year) she puts on an *outfit* every morning. She's classy down to her socks. She would kill me if she saw the comfort shoes I sneak under those long award-show gowns, especially because we have been known to watch hours and hours of *What Not to Wear* together. I share her love of fashion— I just don't have her eye, or the figure to look fabulous in anything off-the-rack like she does.

Mom is half-Swedish and half-Irish, but the Swedish tends to win out. She can get sentimental, but for the most part, she's strong and independent and doesn't suffer fools, show-offs, or braggarts, and of course I'm nothing if not a foolish bragging show-off. Somehow, she manages to love me anyway.

But when Mom opens her mouth, she's hilarious, though mostly she doesn't mean to be. She's a bit spacey, and her synapses don't fire as fast as the rest of ours. She has always been unperturbed by her oblivion—and barely fazed when she finally gets the joke.

Her eyeglasses were always full of fingerprints, smudges, and pancake batter. I'd take them off her head, wash them with dish detergent, then put them back on. "Wow!" she'd exclaim, seeing what she had been missing.

She is absolutely frank with her opinions and literal in her interpretations. In our family she was the perfect "straight man" to the hijinks.

Our house ran like clockwork. All five of us sat down to dinner at the same time every day, after which Mom would have another cocktail, and maybe another. Dad would watch the news, and at 10 P.M. he'd eat a Hershey bar with almonds and settle in for Johnny Carson's monologue. After that, it was time for bed.

My parents truly loved each other, and almost always got along. If you ask Mom now about their life together, the only negative comment she'd come up with is "Sometimes he'd bug me." She had to have at least one criticism; she's Swedish. Dad, on the other hand, had no criticism of my mother. And for a man in the sixties, my dad really *got* women—he understood and loved them. Once, when he had to go buy my mom Kotex

Apparently my mother was unaware that witches don't have vampire teeth or wear sunglasses. With Dad and first grandbaby, Megan.

at the store, the guy at the counter, embarrassed, slipped them into a paper bag. He started to carry them outside, so my dad could take the bag where no one would see, but my dad just laughed. "It's all right," he said. "I don't need to sneak out the back door."

He also liked women's company more than men's. For a number of years when I was a kid, we went on vacation to summer cottages in Paw Paw, Michigan. The guys would all go play golf while the women sat on the beach. My dad would stay with the women, sitting under an umbrella in his swim trunks, with Sea & Ski slathered all over his pasty white body, chatting the afternoon away.

. . .

THOUGH WE WERE ONLY TWO YEARS APART, JULIE AND I were totally different. From the moment I was born, she was looking to create her own family because she now wanted out of ours. She loved dolls, little kids, and telling people what to do. She was thin and pretty, with long blond hair—the Marcia Brady to my Jan.

But Julie had a great sense of humor—we all did, thanks to our parents, who taught us by example that being the butt of the joke is a badge of honor. Julie was the space cadet, so we Lynches would mock her in a high-pitched dumb-blonde voice that made her giggle. We were not a thin-skinned people.

And although Julie and I fought like crazy, we insisted on sharing not only the same room but the same bed the whole time I was growing up. I still don't know why. I mean, we *hated* each other. When I recently asked her what was up with that, she had no answer either. On the same ironic note, we also wrote words to *The Newlywed Game* theme song about how much we loved being sisters. "*Everybody knows who we are / We're not brothers, you're a bit too far / We are sisters by far!*" I shared the writing credit for this masterpiece with Julie, but in truth, I wrote it all by myself.

My brother, Bob, was the much-awaited son. Dad was ecstatic when he came along two years after me, thinking he'd finally get to partake in the classic American father-son ritual of playing catch. But Bob was shy and not athletic, and he couldn't have cared less about classic American rituals. I, on the other hand, was a huge tomboy and wanted nothing more than to play baseball from sunup to sundown. I would have killed to play Little League baseball, unlike Bob, who dutifully put on his little uniform every Saturday but just hated it. My dad did enjoy throwing the ball with me, but I always felt like he'd rather have played with Bob.

Unlike me, Bob was quiet, and he did everything he could to avoid getting any attention. Even when he was little, he refused to wear clothes that matched because he didn't want it to look like he'd tried. He just wanted to blend into the background, which I, the family ham, did not understand *at all*. Dad would clap him on the back and say, "That's my *boy!*" which only caused Bob to shrink in embarrassment. All I could think was *I'll be your boy!*

I always felt like I got the middle-child shaft. My parents had their hands full with whatever Julie was demanding at the moment, or they were worried about why Bob was hiding in his room listening to Led Zeppelin. I was the easy one, and I thought that would get me something. I kept offering myself up to occupy the space Bob kept turning down. But I just didn't have a place. So, of course, the frustration would build and build until I finally pitched a fit: "No one pays attention to ME!" For them it seemed to come from nowhere, and they'd look at me like I had ten heads. I just wanted a little attention.

There was never much discipline in our family, not to mention academic supervision. I'd bring home my report card, and no matter what my grades were, Dad would barely glance at it and then sign it with a flourish and say, "That and a quarter will get you a cup of coffee." Mom might occasionally throw her hands up and say, "How come nobody brings a book home? Nobody studies around here!" We wouldn't answer, and she'd forget about it as we all went back to watching *Gilligan's Island*. Six months later, she'd say it again: "How come nobody brings a book home?"

On my first-grade report card, my teacher wrote, "Jane does not take pride in her work. She spends too much time talking and visiting." My mother wrote back, "I spoke to Jane about this and she has promised to do better." I'm sure that never happened. I could no more stop myself from talking and cutting up than I could stop the earth from turning.

Whether at home or at school, I'd do anything to get laughs or attention. When the phone would ring, I'd rush to it and answer in a baby-talk voice that cracked the family up—"*Well hellooooo, who's calling, please?*" Once, when I was about eight, my mom got on the phone after I'd answered it, and I could tell she was defending me. "Well, that was my daughter. . . . She's eight. . . . I *beg* your *pardon*!" And she slammed down the phone. I am pretty sure the person on the other end asked if I was developmentally delayed.

TO THE PARENTS:

The purpose of this report is to give you the teacher's estimation of the kind of work your child is doing in school. In order that a closer cooperation may be developed between parents and our schools we have provided space for comments by the teacher or the parent when necessary. We will welcome any suggestions or comments that you may care to give us and we want you to feel free to talk to us at any time.

You can help your child and the school by following these practices: 1. Be keenly interested in your child's school work. 2. Avoid comparison of his work with that of other children. 3. Do not use his report card as a basis for reward and punishment. 4. Consult your child's teacher when you desire more information than the report reveals.

Please sign the card and have it returned to the school by the following Monday after it is sent to you. Cards may be kept by the pupil at the end of the third grading period.

ALBERT TILENDIS, Superintendent.

COMMENTS FROM TEACHERS	COMMENTS FROM PARENTS
First Report *Jane does not take pride in her work. She spends too much time talking and visiting*	*I spoke to Jane about this & she has promised to do better.*
	Parent's Signature *E. Lynch*
Second Report	
	Parent's Signature *Mrs. E. Lynch*
Third Report	

My sister was embarrassed by my antics, but my brother, the quiet one, would be smirking in a corner. He was supremely dry in his humor, and because he was so shy, it snuck up on you. He'd come up with a particularly witty youthful retort like "someone's got their panties in a wad." I'd watch him walk away so pleased with his little quip that he'd relive the moment by mouthing it silently.

Once, again when I was about eight, my brother was listening to his transistor radio. He kept switching the earpiece from one ear to the other, which I thought was his idea of a joke. "You can't do that," I said. "You can only hear out of one ear."

"No, I can hear out of both," he answered. And that was how I discovered I was deaf in my right ear. I really thought that everyone could only hear out of one ear, because for as long as I could remember, that had been true for me.

I told my mother that I couldn't hear out of my right ear, and she took me to the doctor to get checked out. Turns out I have nerve deafness, probably a result of a high fever when I was a baby. My parents had taken me to the hospital, where I was put on ice to bring the fever down, but the right ear must have been already damaged.

I didn't think too much of it, since I'd been doing fine all this time. But I could hear my mom saying to the doctor in a hushed tone, "Will she live a *normal life*?" I think this was my mom's constant concern for me, reflecting her Midwestern priority list, on which "normal life" came right after "food" and "shelter." But I was thrilled with the diagnosis, because I was *finally* special—and getting some attention.

It came in handy, too—when I wanted to take revenge on a bully in elementary school. I was a safety patrol officer, which meant I wore an orange vest and helped kids cross the street. When one boy whacked me in the head as he crossed, I pretended he had deafened my one good ear. I made a big deal out of it, holding my head and looking scared, and they called the kid's mom in. Someone yelled, "CAN YOU HEAR ME?" while I just shook my head and flailed my arms. That kid was in trouble.

. . .

AS MUCH AS I JOKED AROUND, AND AS LOVING AS MY parents were, I still always felt a weird, dark energy bottled up inside. Even as a very young kid, I had a sense I was missing out on something. My body was filled with a buzzing nervous tension that constantly threatened to erupt in what my mother came to call "thrashing."

Whenever the pent-up energy got to be too much, I'd throw myself to the floor and pitch a fit. I'd flail my arms and kick my legs, rolling around like I was possessed. It wasn't even that I was angry or upset—it was just that I couldn't take the built-up pressure. I had to release that energy somehow, and the only way that I knew was to have a total spazz-out on the floor.

"Get up! Stop thrashing!" Mom would shriek. She had absolutely no idea what I was doing or why. But I couldn't get up or stop—not until I'd spewed out whatever was bottled up inside me. It never lasted very long, as I wasn't really that upset. It was more like this was something my body needed to do—a sudden physical cataclysm, like a violent sneeze.

The problem was, I just never felt quite right—in my body, with my family, in the world. As much fun as I had with my parents, sister, and brother, I still felt like an outsider, like no one understood me at all.

These feelings scared me, so I would joke about them. "I know you adopted me," I'd announce gravely to my mother. "I know I came from the Greens, down the street." There were no Greens living on our street, but that was part of the joke. I didn't belong anywhere, to anyone. I was alone.

I not only felt out of place in my family, I also felt out of place in my own body. Growing up, I didn't feel like the other girls seemed to feel. I wanted to be a boy. I loved Halloween, because I could dress up as a guy—I was a hobo, a pirate, a ghost who wore a tie, and one year I was excited to dress as Orville Wright for a book report on the Wright Brothers. I went bare chested in the summers until I was eight and my mom finally pulled the plug on that. She grabbed me off my bike and sent me into the house. "Put a shirt on!!" Watching Disney movies, I wanted to be the heroic prince—not the weak, girly, pathetic princess who always needed rescuing. I had no interest in being saved by a guy on a white horse.

Whenever I could get away with it, I'd sneak into my dad's room and put on his clothes. I loved everything in his closets— his suits, his button-down shirts, his ties, his shoes. I'd dress myself up, fill his martini glass with water, and look at myself in the mirror, sipping my "cocktail" like the quintessential sixties man I longed to be. It was very *Mad Men*. (This past year I went trick-or-treating as Don Draper. Some things never change.)

I embraced the melodramatic potential of all these feelings clashing around in my body. "No one understands me!" I would cry, hurling myself onto my bed in tears. As I saw it, there was only one person in the world who ever understood me, and he had died on my fourth birthday. My grandfather.

I actually have no idea if Grandpa understood me at all, but this was a useful notion for an emotionally overwrought child to cling to. The family lore was that whenever I came over, he would shout, "Here comes the house wrecker!" He adored me, a truth that seemed obvious enough in one of the few surviving photographs of us together. It was taken in June of 1964, just

Grandpa beams adoringly at me. Oh, and Julie's there, too.

before my fourth birthday. My sister and I are wearing matching dresses and playing near my grandfather, who is beaming at me with a look of pure love.

The fact that he died soon after that picture was taken and on my birthday only added to the mystique, and for years afterward, whenever I felt sad or alone, I'd think to myself, *If only Grandpa were alive. He would have appreciated me.*

I just wanted to believe that someone, somewhere, understood me. And since Grandpa wasn't an option, I went for the next best person: Mary Tyler Moore. I watched a lot of television and loved *The Mary Tyler Moore Show*. Soon, I began imagining myself as a character in it. I'd write scenes for myself, where I'd go to Mary for advice, and she'd look into my eyes and say, "Jane, you are so *special*." In my scenes, Mary and I had a very sweet, tender relationship. She *got* me.

When I was twelve, the feeling that I was odd and misunderstood jumped to a whole new level. That was the year my friends the Stevenson twins gave a name to another feeling I'd been having.

Jill and Michelle Stevenson were in my class at school, and every year during spring break they went with their parents to South Florida. They told me about a weird thing they'd seen there. "Sometimes," Jill said, "you'll see boys holding hands with *each other* on the beach, instead of with girls. It's because they're *gay*."

They could already procure a tone of scandal and disgust, as if the subject were the sexual proclivities of circus freaks. I just stood there in shock.

Oh my god, I thought, *that's what I have. I'm the girl version of that.*

No sooner had this thought burst into my head than another followed: *No one can ever, ever know.* I may have only just learned what being "gay" meant, but I knew instinctively it was a disease and a curse. I'd always had crushes on girls and hadn't really thought too much about it. But watching the Stevenson twins' mortification about the South Florida boys told me everything I needed to know: being "gay" was sick and perverse, and if you had the misfortune of being that way, you'd better hope no one ever found out.

2

Grand Delusions

LIKE ANY GOOD, CLOSETED YOUNG LESBIAN OF THE seventies, I developed a raging crush on Ron Howard.

Not a well-known fact, but many young lesbians have gay boyfriends, or crushes so safe they might as well be gay. *Happy Days* was my favorite TV show, and Ron, who played all-American boy Richie Cunningham, was cute, boyish, and asexual—all Mayberry and apple pie. I thought Anson Williams, who played Potsie, was cute, too, but less so. As I wrote in my scrapbook, he was just "pretty good foxy."

Ron and Anson came to town in the summer of 1974, just after I turned fourteen, to promote *Happy Days*. When they were on WGN, the big talk radio station in Chicago, I called in and said, matter-of-factly, "Hi, I'm fourteen and I want to be an actress." I don't remember exactly what Ron said, but it was something sensible like "Stay in school, be in plays, and then when you get out of college, if you still want to do it, you should come to Los Angeles." Then, Anson Williams piped up: "Jane, here's what you should do," he said. "Go downtown to the Screen Actors Guild, get a list of agents, and start writing to them."

RONNY HOWARD

ANSON WILLIAMS

My desirability assessments of the stars of TV's Happy Days.

This was stupid advice to give to a fourteen-year-old girl in Chicago—especially one whose entire acting résumé consisted of a couple of school plays and a sixth-grade talent show where I pretended to play the guitar. But I didn't know that. I decided Anson was right, so not long afterward, when I was downtown with my parents, I made sure we stopped by the Screen Actors Guild office so I could get a list of talent agents in Chicago. An office assistant made a copy on mimeographed paper for me, and I went home and wrote them all letters. Our family had visited Universal Studios on a vacation to California the previous summer, so I sent a letter off to them as well. I watched the credits of *The Brady Bunch*, to see who cast the show, and wrote them a note of my availability while I was at it. I think I even sent a school picture.

Needless to say, the talent agents and studio executives did not come knocking. But one afternoon, maybe six months later, I finally did get a reply. It was from the office of Monique James, the head of casting for Universal Studios.

Okay, so it was from Linda, *assistant* to the casting director, who perhaps was taking this opportunity to feel better about her assistant status by crushing the dream of a young girl in suburban Chicago. And . . . she spelled my name wrong. And . . . it was just about the most unencouraging letter she could have possibly sent.

An observant child, or maybe just one who wasn't completely delusional, would have felt dismissed by this. But I was over the moon—it was on Universal letterhead! Yes, they got my name wrong, but Jamie is such a cute name! I was never a fan of my name anyway. I was so buoyed by the letter that I put it in my scrapbook. Linda Abbott and Monique James might have

The answer to my
letter

UNIVERSAL CITY STUDIOS, INC. AN MCA INC. COMPANY

October 7, 1974

Ms. Jamie Lynch
15451 Sunset Drive
Dolton, Illinois 60419

Dear Ms. Lynch,

Thank you for your letter expressing interest in Universal Studios.

Even though you feel you have the ability and a natural talent for
acting, professional training is a requirement in our search for
talent. Because the production schedules are limited and the budgets
high, the performers used in our TV programs and features have to be
knowledgeable in film. We do not have the luxury of training young
actors who are in the learning stage when we are working under such
demanding professional conditions.

If you decide to study and become a trained actor or when you have
gained some professional film acting experience, please feel free to
contact our office again.

Sincerely,

Linda Abbott

Linda Abbott,
Assistant to Monique James

LLA:km

100 UNIVERSAL CITY PLAZA · UNIVERSAL CITY, CALIFORNIA 91608 · 985-4321

thought I would never come to Hollywood, but in my mind I was trying to figure out travel plans.

I had known early on, almost out of the chute, that I wanted to be an actress. My first theatrical experience happened at the age of about five, when my parents took me to see a school play one of the neighborhood kids was in. I remember going into the dark theater, and when the lights came up, there was this *whole world* that came out of nowhere. It was alive and bright and you could see that everyone had makeup on.

We were sitting very close to the stage, and as part of the play, there was a little kid in a cage, playing a bird. I remember thinking, *Let the bird out of the cage, let him out!* That is how real it was to me. I was transfixed by the whole experience, as if I were watching magic happen right in front of me.

My folks loved to sing and perform themselves, and even more so with an audience. This was post–World War II cocktail culture, and Rodgers and Hammerstein weren't the only ones exploring the world through song and dance. Our parish church, St. Jude's, put on a show every year called *Port o' Call*, and this was the highlight of my parents' performing lives. The various schoolrooms at St. Jude's were transformed into McGinty's Irish tavern, full of revelers, or a Hawaiian luau with grass-skirted hula dancers, or a risqué German cabaret for which the neighbor ladies donned fishnets, eliciting hoots and howls. The audience would go from room to room, taking in various spectacles from other ports of call. I was there with my parents every night until the final bow was taken. I was absolutely riveted by the frenzied backstage energy of putting on a show. I remember the smells and the sights, the thick pancake makeup, and how they all dropped trou in full view of one another in the tiny cloakroom

Dad sings "Look to the Rainbow" in the Irish Room, St. Jude's Port o' Call show.

that served as the dressing room. All the adults were so focused and engaged when they put on these shows. And I was literally beside myself with elation to be among this business called show.

But to my parents this was something you did for fun, not for a living. My mom was not on board with my plan to become an actress. As I wrote those letters to agents at our dining room table, she asked, "Who are you writing to?" When I told her, she spoke to me in that flat voice of Midwestern reality.

"Janie, you know, people can't always do what they want to do," she said. "And it's probably not realistic to think you'll be a Hollywood star." To her, my saying I wanted to be an actress was a little like saying I wanted to be an elf. "Well, honey," she'd have said, "you can dress up as one, and you can have fun as one, but you're not gonna *be* one."

I'm sure that to Mom, this was just realistic motherly advice, like telling me to stay out of traffic. She wanted to convince me to dream a little less big, to protect me from heartache—but of course her words just made things worse. Sitting there at the dining room table, I started to cry from the depths of my soul, feeling my life was over before it had begun.

My mother felt terrible. She tried to console me, saying she wanted me to be the best actress I could be, but that I should be careful of aiming too high. Years later, she'd tell me that until that moment, she'd had no idea how dead serious I was about being an actress. But that realization didn't change her message. She would reluctantly support me in the years ahead, but she still wanted me to have a backup plan, which usually involved learning to type.

About five months after getting the Universal letter, I got a reply to a fan letter I had sent to Vicki Lawrence, a star of *The Carol Burnett Show*, a program I so loved and wanted to be on that it hurt just thinking about it. She sent me an autographed photo, a soft-focus headshot of her gazing meaningfully into the camera, her hair gently feathered. It came with a form fan letter printed on blue paper, but at the bottom she'd written a

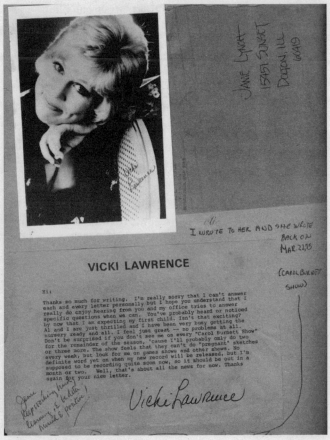

Vicki Lawrence wrote me back!

note: "Janie, Keep working hard, learning, & be determined & positive!"

I knew that Vicki had gotten on *The Carol Burnett Show* because of a fan letter she'd written to Carol. So, of course, I had the fantasy that my letter to Vicki would produce the same result. The fact that it didn't was of no consequence to me—I'd received a *personal* note from Vicki Lawrence. And she'd even spelled my name right.

These snippets of encouragement were huge to me—my bubble was now un-burstable. I pasted Vicki's letter and photo into my scrapbook, along with the Universal letter and my Ron Howard photos, and continued forward.

. . .

SPEAKING OF MY SCRAPBOOK, I DUG IT OUT RECENTLY and was delighted to find it was a proud monument to absolute mediocrity.

Included are my report cards (mostly Bs and Cs), in addition to other cherished mementos of averageness:

- An "Award for Achievement" from Vandenberg Elementary School—the award they gave to kids who didn't win an award.

- A handwritten schedule for my basketball team, the Dirksen Junior High "B" team, showing a final record of three wins and eleven losses.

- Ribbons for third-place finishes in a 1975 swim meet.

I appear to be greatly amused by my own mediocrity, writing silly notes in the margins throughout the scrapbook:

- Beside my basketball numerals, which were awarded to benchwarmers (starting players received letters), I wrote in all caps: "AGAIN! HA HA!"

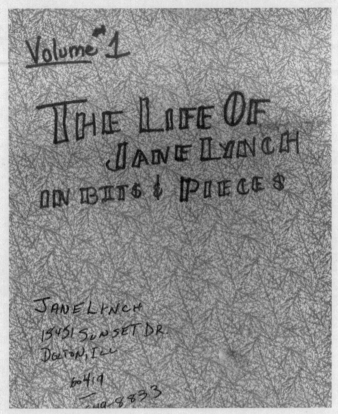

There is no Volume #2.

- Next to a note from my seventh-grade teacher,
  Mr. Gerson, that read "Mr. & Mrs. Lynch, Jane has put
  forth much more effort recently. She is doing better work
  and behaving better. I hope this continues," I scribbled:
  "It didn't! HA!"

- Beside the letter from Universal, in which my name had
  been misspelled, I wrote: "Jamie, Ha ha! I think I'll keep
  it." On the next page, I pasted the envelope the letter had

Hi,

Thank you for your interest in me. I appreciate having you as a fan, and I will do my best to perform, for you, in the best tradition of the theater.

I do like to hear from my fans, so please drop me a note. It will be most welcome. My personal mailing address is . .

Box 3375, Burbank 91504

Hi JANIE:
GOOD LUCK IN YOUR ACTING CAREER. I'm SORRY IT'S SO LATE IN ANSWERING BUT JUST GOT MY MAIL FOR THE LAST 6 MONTHS.
ON 3-4-75 I'LL BE SINGING ON HAPPY DAYS. IT WOULD BE A BIG HELP TO ME IF AFTER THE SHOW YOU & YOUR FRIENDS WOULD WRITE TO:
PARAMOUNT STUDIO'S
C/O HAPPY DAYS
MARATHON ST
HOLLYWOOD CAL 90038
SAYING - I LIKE ANSON'S SINGING. WHEN WILL HE SING AGAIN.
THANKS A MILLION
LOVE
anson

I did not like his singing. I did not write a letter asking when he would sing again.

come in, highlighting its return address of the "New Talent" department. I wrote, "New Talent! That's me!"

Of course, not everything in the scrapbook was a monument to mediocrity. There was also a photo postcard from Anson Williams, who kept writing me for some reason, with a handwritten note on the back.

As I recall, when Anson sang he sounded like a Lawrence Welk baritone. Not my cup of tea, so I never did his bidding. (Besides, he was only "pretty good foxy.")

. . .

DURING FRESHMAN YEAR IN HIGH SCHOOL, I WAS CAST as The King in a one-act production of *The Ugly Duckling* (the beginning, incidentally, of a lifelong pattern of being cast in roles originally intended for men). I was thrilled out of my mind—this was what I wanted to do with my life! This was my dream, and now I was officially taking the first step toward fulfilling it.

My name appeared in the school newspaper, *The Bagpipe*, along with those of the rest of the cast, and by all appearances, I was on my way. But when we started rehearsals, I found myself paralyzed with fear—the fear of blowing it. So . . . I quit the play and joined the tennis team instead.

I don't think anyone understood why I had quit. I'm sure I didn't. I know now it was out of pure terror. I was face-to-face with my destiny and I walked away from it rather than risk failure.

In my scrapbook, I pasted the article about *The Ugly Duck-*

ling, then right next to it, I pasted another article about the tennis team. Underneath, I wrote this: "Had to drop out of play because of tennis, but mostly because I couldn't get my character. Darn!" Obviously I had either read something or heard someone talk about the importance of "getting your character," and I used that to feel better about what I had done. My poor little fourteen-year-old self had no idea how to process this.

But deep down inside, I knew I had killed the thing I most

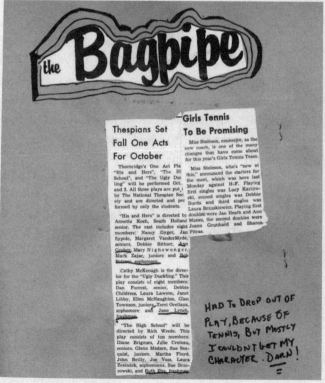

My poor little conflicted self!

wanted in the world. I couldn't stand to stay away, though, so I signed up to work on the stage crew. Stage crew—when I could have been *in* the thing! In the official program for the evening of one-acts, I made little check marks next to all my friends who were in the cast and crew—and I put a little star by my own name. I was putting on a brave face, but inside I was crushed.

Making things even worse, I was now officially branded a quitter. In the spring of my freshman year, I tried out for another play, but I didn't get chosen. One girl who got a part told my sister, Julie, it was because I'd quit *The Ugly Duckling*. When the same thing happened with *Man of La Mancha*—I was even passed over for the chorus!—I realized with dread that at age fourteen, my acting career was already over.

One night, as my parents sipped their "first today, badly needed" cocktails, I poured my heart out to them at the kitchen table. I cried as I explained why everything was ruined, and my mom tried to soothe me. "You made one mistake, Janie," she said. "It doesn't mean your life is over."

But I was inconsolable. I started having dreams in which everyone I knew had gotten a part in a play, and I was the only one who was left out. All these years later, I *still* have those dreams. And when I wake up, I hug my Emmy.

. . .

MEANWHILE, MY SISTER, JULIE, MADE THE POM-POM Squad. Julie was a big eye-roller, especially with me. She was always bugged by my corny jokes and goofy faces at home, but when I was about to be a freshman in the high school where she was a junior, she was wracked with fear that I would embarrass her. She was skinny and cute and looked like she just walked out of the Sears catalogue. I was clumsy and silly and had a belly. At the breakfast table, she'd say, "Okay! Get all the goofiness out now, before we go to school. Now! Get it out! Get it out! Get it out!"

My sister and I couldn't have been more different. She went through a neatness phase where, every morning, she'd make the bed—but because I slept later than she did, I was usually still in it.

"Just slide out!" she'd say. "Don't mess it up!"

I was a slob, so she didn't want me touching her stuff or wearing her clothes. And she was right—I don't know if it was the oil in my hands or what, but I had a way of ruining anything I touched. Everyone would get the same paperback math books at the beginning of the year, and somehow, by the end, mine would be completely destroyed—smudged black, dog-eared, bent cover. Everyone else's was pristine, while mine looked like I'd taken a bath with it.

So my sister, sensibly enough, wouldn't let me wear her clothes. "Don't even touch them!" she said. "You'll ruin them, or stretch them out, or both." She even went to the trouble of locking her favorite pair of jeans to the hanging rod of our closet, through the belt loop. Which meant I had no choice but to cut them off. When she saw me strutting down the hall wearing them, she shrieked aloud. As I passed her, she mouthed, "I'm going to kill you." I'm pretty sure I didn't care one way or another about those jeans. I simply enjoyed tormenting her.

I tormented her in other ways, too. She wanted nothing more than to be able to sing, but the family musicality eluded her. So when I caught her in the downstairs bathroom pouring her heart into a pitchy rendition of "Edelweiss" into a tape recorder, I had to play it for all her friends.

Yet my goofiness and ability to woo with humor worked in Julie's favor, too. There was a group of "cool girls" that she wanted so badly to hang out with. She was invisible to them. Despite the fact that she was blond and pretty, her shyness could be paralyzing. She wanted me to come to the rescue.

Two members of this cool group of girls were Carol, the good-time party girl, and June, the wholesome sweetheart who reminded me of Julie Andrews. They were both in my second-semester Algebra I class. I had barely passed the first and was hanging on by a thread as the second semester began.

When I told Julie that these girls were in my class, she instructed me on how to win them over for her: get them to laugh at me so they'd ask me to go out with them one weekend. I would then bring Julie with me. I said, "What am I, your clown?" This question didn't really need an answer.

By the second week, the class was lost for me as far as the algebra was concerned. I obediently became the class clown and a pain in the teacher's ass. I remember Carol and June doubled over laughing at what I'm sure were my hilarious shenanigans. They invited me to hang out with them one Friday night and I brought Julie with me. We hopped into several cars, cracked open beers, and drove around town. This was a huge group of girls, about fifteen of them. And they were a delightful mix of personalities: some were cheerleaders, some were popular, some not so much, some got straight A's, some loved to party (my sub-group). What we all had in common was we loved to laugh and hang out. We had our own language and inside jokes. We'd scream from car windows as we drove by the boys hanging out in the St. Jude parking lot, "What's your *gimmick*?!" This would just crack us up. I'm still not sure why we found this so funny.

I had started drinking in my freshman year of high school. At first, it was just a little Boone's Farm or a beer here and there, but by my junior year, I was drinking every night. And now my new friends and I would party hearty on weekends together. We went to football games and Flings (school dances). We'd have keggers at one another's house. There was no drinking behind my parents' backs, though: it was all in the open. It was a drinking culture all round in this neck of the woods in the late 1970s. Our house was the place to go for singing and drinking. We'd sit around the kitchen table, and Mom and Dad would tell stories and sing songs from their youth. My favorite was their two-part harmony rendition of "Coney Island," a peppy 1920s tune. My new friends adored my parents and couldn't get enough of them.

My parents were creatures of their era—they loved to drink and throw parties. As soon as I was old enough to think of it, I'd sneak downstairs after everyone had gone and take sips out of the leftover drinks. I also liked relighting the cigarette butts that people had left behind, so I could practice smoking. Once, when my dad caught me lighting up outside (I was about twelve, and I had literally picked up a butt out of the gutter in front of our house), I overheard him proudly telling Mom in the kitchen, "She's out there smokin' like a pro!"

When my mom would have a few drinks, she might get a bit sloppy and sentimental, and my dad would gently prod her upstairs to bed. But no matter what she drank the night before, she never, ever had a hangover. She'd be up at five in the morn-

To the manner born.

ing, bright-eyed and ready for the day. So drinking just seemed like a lot of fun. And with this new group of girlfriends, I was starting to do it for real, with the sole aim of getting wasted.

My friend Peggy Quinn's house was another fun place to party. Unlike the Lynches, the Quinns were good Irish Catholics who dutifully produced a tribe of redheaded children with saint names. What made their house the best place in the world, as far as I was concerned, was that Mr. Quinn had a keg in the basement. I don't remember that we were allowed to drink from it, but I was captivated by the idea of it. He had a keg . . . in his *basement*.

I remember Big Jim Quinn sipping a glass of his Special Export out on his front porch and me out there with him, shooting the breeze upon a summer's evening. I guess I felt comfortable enough to tell him the secret I had only ever told my mom, Ron Howard, and Anson Williams: I wanted to be an actress. I think he was the first grown-up who took me seriously. Instead of telling me to learn to type or some other surefire way to make a living, Mr. Quinn said, "You get out there and do that, Jane. And be sure to thank me when you get that Academy Award."

I flunked that second-semester Algebra I class, by the way, but the class wasn't a total loss. I had successfully pimped myself out for my sister and got us both into one of the popular cliques. But even in the midst of all the parties and goofing around, I still had that feeling that I was on the fringes of life and not genuinely a part of the world around me. Much of it had to do with my big gay secret and the fantasy life it spawned. I was noticing a different girl every week, but the one I fixated on most was in that same Algebra class, and she was deaf. I imagined romantically rescuing her from her alienated existence and making her feel that her thoughts and dreams were understood. I realize now that I wanted so desperately to be rescued that I projected it all on to her. But to a high school freshman that was irrelevant. I would blissfully slip into daydreaming about sweeping her off her feet whenever the teacher started writing equations.

What I didn't know was that soon I would meet someone with whom I would feel connected and understood—my own unlikely version of Prince Charming.

3

Refuge

CHRIS AND I FIRST SPOTTED EACH OTHER ACROSS the crowded floor at a dance at St. Jude's the beginning of our sophomore year. How I missed noticing him all of our freshman year at Thornridge High, I don't know. But there he was: smaller than the rest of the guys, hair dyed bright red, and extremely fey. I was taken aback, yet attracted at the same time.

He seemed to see something in me, too. He sidled over to where I was standing, scanned me up and down, and said, "Hmmm . . . we're going to have a lot of fun together."

My friend Josephine, who was standing with me by the door, giggled. She thought he liked me and wanted to go out with me.

But I knew that wasn't what he meant.

What he meant was that we had found a soul mate in each other, and he was right. We quickly became inseparable best buds. We even gave each other nicknames—he was "Gwiz" and I was "Trix"—just because we thought nicknames were stupid, and it was fun to make fun of stupid things.

Like me, Chris was not your typical teenager from Dolton, Illinois. But unlike me, he couldn't have cared less.

Chris had a big mouth, and when I say this I don't just mean he was loud (although he often was). I mean his mouth was enormous. Mine was nothing to sneeze at either. We talked about lots of things with those mouths of ours, but the fact that we were both gay was not one of them.

I had been a pretty solid rule-follower prior to meeting Chris. Chris lived to ignore or, if possible, destroy all rules. He reveled in questioning those in authority and throwing the ridiculousness of their rules back at them. Yes, he stuck out. But he just

"Jane is fine. Chris is fine. But Jane and Chris are trouble."

walked through the world exactly as he was—a goofy, funny, quirky guy. For the first time in my life, I felt like I'd found a kindred spirit—even if my spirit was not as fully exposed. I could look at him and see something of who I was reflected back.

Chris seemed to live to make me laugh. I would be walking down the stairs between classes at Thornridge High School, and suddenly, a few steps above me, a guy would trip and tumble down the stairs, arms flailing wildly and books flying past. He would land with a thud at the bottom, then look up at me, all Cheshire cat. It would be Chris, throwing himself down the stairs to crack me up. Again. My own private Stooge.

He loved to make prank phone calls, which gave me anxiety. He was sly and could be snarky and loved to shock people, especially adults. They never knew what hit them. Once, he said to our Spanish teacher, "Your hair is such a beautiful shade of red—why do you dye the roots black?"

On Sundays, he was the organist at St. Jude's. For most of the service, he would play standard church fare, but if you listened closely to his incidental music after Communion, you would hear the dulcet strains of something like "Afternoon Delight," played in minor chords. He'd catch my eye and solemnly mouth the words: "Gonna grab some afternoon deliiight . . ." No one mocked piety like Chris.

He was also immune to Catholic guilt, despite St. Jude's doing everything in their power to break his defiance. He had been in school there from first to eighth grade, and the one person who seemed to be on his side was the hip young priest we all loved because he related to us kids. And it turns out, he did, but not in the way we thought. We later discovered this priest was actually a pervert (the extent of his misdeeds have only recently come to light when he was removed from public ministry in 2005). He'd targeted Chris at one point: when he was in seventh grade, the guy had tried to show him his underwear drawer at the rectory, asking him, "Have you ever seen a grown man naked?" (hopefully unintentional in his quoting of Peter Graves's line in *Airplane*). Before he could get any further, Chris said, "If you touch me, my father will kill you," whereupon young Chris was sent on his way. Christopher John Patrick would not be intimidated by anyone.

My whole family adored Chris, but no one more than my sister, Julie, who loved it when he made fun of her dumb-blonde ways. She *begged* him to mock her. He had heard the tape of her attempting to sing "Edelweiss" and was merciless in his imitation of it. She loved it. "Do it again!" she'd plead. She also loved that he colored his hair and cared about how he looked, and he played it up for her. A few years back, my dad was battling that awful lung cancer and we were all so devastated. But Chris called and said, "Tell Julie I had a full face-lift." She belly laughed hard for the first time in a long time. He knew just what to say. (He lied. He'd actually only had a partial one. . . .)

One Ash Wednesday, Chris convinced me to cut choir, my favorite class, and go with him to the Chicken Unlimited across the street. Over Cokes and fries, we used cigarette ashes to make crosses on each other's forehead, intoning, "You are dust, and to dust you shall return." When we got back to school, we told the campus cop we had been at Mass. Nothing was sacred.

On the flip side of this disregard for our family faith, Chris had a love, a reverence even, for the pageantry of the Catholic Church. On Friday nights, when most of Thornridge High was

John Carr hearing confession in Man of La Mancha.

drinking itself silly at a kegger, Chris and I, plus our pal John Carr, would do what we called a "church tour." John was another sly and witty fellow, soon to come out of the closet. His other big secret was that he wanted to be a priest.

Back in the late seventies, some churches kept their doors unlocked because they were supposed to be a place of refuge, a place you should be able to enter at any time to escape whatever was chasing you. We knew which ones on the city's south side were kept open, and we high school snots snuck in. We were usually drunk and doing poppers and giggling our heads off, but there would always come a moment when it got absolutely serious. We would perform the Mass, and we'd mean it. If

Chris could unlock the organ, he'd play the entrance hymn, and if not, he'd hum it solemnly. My role was to lead the imaginary congregation in song. John would play the priest, making his ceremonial walk up the aisle toward the altar, kissing the good book and performing all the other ritualistic gestures, and begin the Mass.

If we could get into the confessional booths, we would take turns playing priest to the others' confessor. We would mostly goof around pretending to be people from our own parish. We had them coming clean on ridiculous sins like having VD or something. Chris told me that John would actually confess to him. Of course, Chris wasn't really a priest, so he told me everything. John told him that he was afraid he was gay; that he missed his dad, who'd died when he was a kid; that he feared he wouldn't get into the seminary because his grades were so bad. John Carr was a bright light—funny and smart—but not a fan of school or studying. He died of AIDS in 1996.

On some level, I knew Chris was gay. It became harder to ignore once he started driving into Chicago for the weekends, not so secretly going to gay bars and hooking up with guys there—but I still somehow managed to deny it to myself. He lived like there was no tomorrow—smoking, drinking, doing drugs; generally doing whatever he wanted. Chris couldn't help but be himself. He has always been constitutionally incapable of anything else.

And he never felt shame about anything he did. Chris's attitude was *The world just needs to catch up with me*. In this way, he and I were very different. I really wanted to fit in, *wanted* to want to have a boyfriend, *wanted* to want to have kids. I wanted to want what every other girl in the world seemed to want. I did not want to admit, to myself or anyone else, that I did not.

I tried to act like the straight kids, but I couldn't even fake it. I went out on a couple of dates with guys, but it was a struggle the whole time. I'd be deep in my own head, thinking, *This should be nice. I should want to kiss him right now.* I knew how I was supposed to act, how I was supposed to feel, but no matter how hard I tried, I couldn't be that person.

Chris was a lifeline, because with him I could be myself. It was also hard to be worried with so much laughing and goofing around, and his self-acceptance was contagious. As awkward as I felt around others, I felt like myself with Chris.

Choir was where we really flourished. We both loved to sing, so we never cut this class (except that one Ash Wednesday at the Chicken Unlimited). We'd even sing on the way there. It helped that we had to go through a breezeway with awesome acoustics that ramped up our harmonies. Then we'd spend the first fifteen minutes of the choir hour in the girls' bathroom, smoking with any boy or girl who wanted to share a hot-boxed Marlboro.

But the real joy was singing in that choir, with so many different voices coming together. District-wide integration meant that black kids were bused into our white neighborhood for high school. This had caused riots in our school, and cops patrolled the hallways to keep the peace. The choral room in A Building was one of the only places at Thornridge High School where integration worked effortlessly. Black and white kids, football players, cheerleaders, nerds, and wood shop guys all lifted their voices in song together in this room. It was an idyllic setting, not unlike the version in *Glee*. Our differences seemed to disappear as our voices were raised in song, and the harmony lifted us beyond ourselves. For Chris and me, it was a refuge.

The other times I felt at ease were when I drank. My drinking self was good and had nothing to fear or be ashamed of. If I was drinking *and* with Chris, the good fired on all cylinders. Dolton was right next door to a suburb called Hegwisch, a blue-collar area with a famous record store and more bars per capita than any other burg outside Chicago. Al Capone had loved the prairies and heavily wooded landscape of this place and was said to have hidden out there a lot. For us, the winding roads of Hegwisch led to cash-strapped taverns more than happy to sell drinks to teenagers doing poppers. I used to love going with Chris to this one real dive bar called Jeanette's, a place filled with toothless old men. One obese and gummy guy called "Uncle Frank" would sit immobile in a dark corner and yell at us. "I love you kids!" he'd slur. At those moments, I loved him right back.

Chris introduced me to a few new things, too. The first time I smoked pot was with him, during sophomore year. He failed to tell me that he'd laced it with angel dust, so I began to hallucinate at Pizza Hut and was so out of my gourd that I had to spend the night in his garage.

Pot scared the hell out of me, with or without angel dust. I panicked when I smelled it. If I went to a party where someone was smoking it, I expected the cops to swarm the place, and judgment and paranoia must have been written all over my face. I began to be known as "the Narc," and I started to notice that I wouldn't be invited to certain parties. It hurt my feelings, even though I continued to feel that pot smoking was evil. I was, however, very happy to get loaded on booze.

. . .

IF YOU LOOK BACK THROUGH MY HIGH SCHOOL scrapbook, you'd think I was one of the popular kids. I was involved in a million activities—speech team, girls' choir, basketball, tennis, theater guild. And despite earning the "quitter" label after *The Ugly Duckling*, I even managed to get small roles in a couple of plays my sophomore year, playing a male police officer (go figure) in *Arsenic and Old Lace* and a tomboy (ditto) in *The Brick and the Rose*.

But it wasn't until my senior year that something transformative finally happened. That was the year my theater arts class put on *Godspell*.

Somewhere in the back of my head I was aware that *Godspell* was based on a Bible gospel—we sang "Day by Day" at guitar mass at St. Jude's—but I didn't care. I just wanted to put on a show! I loved the music, and we wouldn't have to try out; if you were in the class, you were in the play. Chris and I listened to the original cast album over and over.

We also went downtown to see the show live at the Drury Lane Theater. Chris, our friend Ed (another soon-to-be-gay musical theater lover), and I went at least ten times. That professional cast added some funny bits and one-liners that we claimed for ourselves and brought home to Dolton. We were obsessed.

Our production played one Friday night only. Everyone in my family, extended and otherwise, came. We thespians were beside ourselves with excitement. We put everything we had into this thing and made a plan to drink real wine during the final betrayal scene that closes the play. We wanted to be crying real tears, and we were pretty sure we couldn't unless we were tipsy.

Ed played Jesus, Chris was John the Baptist/Judas, and along with being in the ensemble, I played the hussy who sang "Turn Back, O Man."

I was now a part of the magic that had so mesmerized me when I was a kid seeing my first stage play. I actually lost my balance I was so excited—I almost fell over several times the day of the show—and I smelled funny. I would have this smell many times in the future and would come to know it as the pungent odor of pure, unadulterated fear. But because it was mixed with pure, unadulterated joy, I survived.

We were all swept up in the electricity of putting on this show. We were more focused, disciplined, and committed than we had ever been in our young lives. We had all pitched in to build the set together, and showed up after school for rehearsals. When we finally performed, no one missed a line or a cue. We were a team, and we supported one another. Being a part of this group of fellow actors, feeling needed and valued and there for one another, was a high I would chase for the rest of my life.

We were playing pretend, but we were sharing the experience. I had always felt so different and thus "less than" my peers. I remember thinking that even if I, Jane Lynch, wasn't worthy of friendship, then at least I knew the character I was playing *was*. In everyday life, I second-guessed myself relentlessly. But in a play, my difference was hidden and I was worthy. I was needed. Because it's written—it says, *I am*.

And that was the heart of the matter: on stage, playing a role that was written in black and white—*I could not be rejected*. The only place I felt safe from that possibility was on stage, and

I loved it. In fact, I still get joy from it, even today. In any movie, TV show, or play that I'm in, I'll still have that fleeting thought: *These people might not want to be my friend after this, but for the next 8.2 seconds, they're all about me and I'm all about them.*

Finally, I had found my place.

But unfortunately, right in the middle of this transcendent, fantastic experience, disaster struck. Jesus and John the Baptist, also known as Ed and Chris, started spending all of their time together, without me. I didn't know what was happening—or didn't want to. All I knew was that now I was the odd man out.

In response, I acted as cold and mean as I could. With this, I was starting a pattern that I would rely on for far too long in dealing with what felt like rejection. My hope in acting this way was that the person I felt had wronged me would ask what he'd done wrong. Chris didn't, of course—I'm not sure he ever even noticed. My mom noticed, though, and she became worried that I had fallen in love with Chris—not a surprising conclusion, since I was acting exactly like a jilted lover. One afternoon, she finally gave voice to the fact that I was still too stubborn to admit.

"Honey," she said, "I don't want you to get your heart broken. But I think maybe Chris likes boys. Don't you think that maybe he and Ed are boyfriends?"

"No, no, no!" I snapped. "Chris isn't gay."

It was getting harder to deny it to myself, though. I mean, even my mother knew. It was hard to miss. My wild and free-spirited Chris had always stuck out in our little suburb, but by the time we were seniors, he was taking it to a whole new level, with an afro and parachute pants. It was the late seventies, but still: to say he stood out is an understatement. But I still didn't want to acknowledge that "gay" existed. Now it was right in front of me. Chris and Ed were having an affair. Chris even wrote "I will love Ed forever" in *my* yearbook.

In the pain of feeling dumped, I wrote Chris a scathing letter telling him that he looked like a freak and *I* didn't want anything to do with *him* anymore. I was a stereotypical closet case, rejecting him for his open homosexuality that got him a boyfriend and left me alone. I pushed him away for what I was afraid of in me. Maybe I was also afraid of guilt by association, that other people would think I was gay, too. Whatever it was, I felt that he needed to be punished for flaunting his gayness. Didn't he understand you were supposed to keep it under wraps?

But also, deep down, my heart *was* broken. I felt rejected on a soul level. In some ways, Chris was my first true love. I trusted him like I trusted no one else in the world, and I showed him parts of myself that no one else saw. Now he was gone. All that had been good in those final months of my senior year of high school was suddenly buried under despair.

After graduating from high school, I reluctantly set off for Illinois State University, which at that time was where the B and C students in Illinois went to college. I had absolutely no academic curiosity or drive, and I didn't particularly want to go to college, but that was what people did. With my impressively low ACT score ISU was the only school that admitted me, so I packed up my things and headed for Normal, Illinois (of all places).

I was assigned to a room in an all-girls dorm, and at any given moment, I had at least three very severe crushes: I was obsessed with the ladies of Hamilton Hall. Perhaps getting out of Dolton and away from my family allowed me to admit these feelings . . . sort of. I still put them in a mental file labeled "intense feelings of friendship," managing to continue to ignore the pounding refrain of "You're gay!" knocking on my psyche's door.

Before I left Dolton, my mother had said, "Jane, don't major in Theater. Major in something *like* Theater but where you can get a job, like Mass Communications." In her mind, a general smear of media would satisfy my need to trod the boards. I desperately wanted to be an actress, but wanting also to please, I followed my mom's advice.

Unfortunately—or, really, fortunately—when I tried to register for Mass Comm 101, all the classes were closed. So instead, I started taking acting courses on the sly. It was truly luck that the one state school with low enough standards to admit the likes of me had one of the best undergraduate theater departments in the country. Several original Steppenwolf Theater ensemble members had been recent graduates, including Laurie Metcalf and John Malkovich. The professors were treated as minor celebs themselves and managed to inspire both respect and fear in their students. Freshmen weren't allowed to audition for shows during their first semester, but as soon as second semester started, I tried out for *Lysistrata*, a very cleverly updated musical adaptation of Aristophanes' classic about the Peloponnesian War.

The play had been rewritten with a Southern theme: the Athenians were *Gone With the Wind*–style upper-crust Southerners, the Spartans a big old tribe of hillbillies. I managed to land a speaking role, which was a huge coup for a freshman.

I'm sure there was nothing subtle about the way I played the country bumpkin Karmenia of Kornith, but I also added a minor twist to her character—one that, in retrospect, seems a bit odd, considering how deep in the closet I was. I made her an open lesbian.

There was a line where the lady warrior from the Isle of Lesbos said something like "You know, we women hang very close on Lesbos," intimating that island's Sapphic past (as if the name of the island didn't make that clear enough). So I thought it would be funny to be super-obvious and ad-lib, "You told me weren't gonna say nothin' . . ." When I first delivered the line, the director cracked up. Which I guess wasn't surprising; there was a lot of whispering that she was a closeted lesbian herself.

As far as I can recall, there was only one open lesbian student in the theater program. She was burly, with a deep voice and hairy legs and armpits: the perfect stereotype of a butch lesbian. She also had a chip on her shoulder and a demeanor that said "Fuck you. This is who I am, take it or leave it." Looking back now, I can appreciate how brave she was.

Our theater department was full of closeted homosexuals. We were too afraid to look at this aspect of ourselves, so of course we marginalized the one person who had the courage to be who she was. Needless to say, I didn't want anything to do with her.

I was so excited to be a part of the cast of *Lysistrata*, which was a huge production featuring all the big department stars. (It was like in the old days of Hollywood, when MGM would do a movie like *Grand Hotel* and the entire roster of studio talent would appear in it.) I was always taking a look from outside my body and marveling that I was now one of them. A few of the women were so talented and such bright lights that I worshipped them like they were movie stars. The comedy was very pithy and smart. The music was inventive and fun. I was over the moon.

Sophomore year, I auditioned for *Gypsy*. The list for principal cast went up before the chorus list, and I almost didn't check it because I was pretty sure that if I got anything it would be chorus. But there it was: my name on the principal cast list. I was gobsmacked. I was cast as Electra, one of the three strippers.

I had always loved singing, which is perhaps not surprising given how musical my parents were. Our whole family sang together almost every day, mostly Christmas carols and show tunes—*Funny Girl, Man of La Mancha, The Sound of Music*. In fact, we were mildly obsessed with *The Sound of Music*. When it was playing at the River Oaks Cinema, my mom dropped me, my sister, and the Climack girls off for the first showing of the day, and we never left our seats. We watched it over and over until she picked us up later that evening.

Gypsy would be my first time really singing a solo on stage, and although I was terrified, I proceeded to "act as if" I could do it. I also had no reason to believe anyone in their right mind would ever buy my baby-dyke self as a stripper. Obviously the director thought I could do it—he had given me the part—but I was afraid that what he saw wasn't really there, that I had somehow fooled him. Looking back, I can see that I couldn't give myself credit for anything, like I felt obliged to bow to the altar of my fears and trepidations. Maybe it kept the bar low, expectation-wise. But unlike my reaction to this kind of inner challenge when I walked away from *The Ugly Duckling* in high school, it never crossed my mind to quit.

The big show-stopping burlesque stripper number in *Gypsy* is called "You Gotta Have a Gimmick." My character, Electra, had the gimmick of electricity: she "did it with a switch," an actual electrical switch on her costume that lit her up. "I'm electrifying and I ain't even trying!" she squealed. I worked my butt off rehearsing, and suddenly I found this full, robust chest voice I'd never had before. It felt wonderful, like massaging my soul. And even though I was über-critical of myself at this point in my life, I was flushed with victory. I'd walk through the quad with a giant inner smile, thinking, *I'm in the school musical.*

Unlike the other shows I'd been in, *Gypsy* was practically a professional production. The auditorium was state-of-the-art, and we had top-notch sets, lights, costumes, and a full stage crew. I imagined that this was what it must be like to do a show on Broadway.

. . .

MY PARENTS, TRUE TO FORM, WEREN'T TOO CONCERNED about what grades I was making in college. They were more interested in whether I was happy and making friends, and whether I needed money. (My dad would periodically mail me $20, with a note saying, "Here's some green for the scene, teen." He also sent $1 rebates for Ten High Whiskey to my dorm room, because you could only cash in one per address.) When I changed my major to Theater Arts, I was pretty sure they wouldn't notice, and they didn't. The Theater Arts Department had talent-based tuition waivers, and I auditioned and got one. My parents learned of my new major when they received the tuition bill marked "paid." "Hey! Good for you!" Suddenly, being a theater major was pretty cool.

I loved my acting classes, and I even loved my theater history class. I actually started to get good grades because I gave a hoot about what I was learning.

One Christmas break, I was particularly excited to go back to Dolton because I wanted to show off a new skill I'd been developing. In one of my acting classes, I was learning to speak in what is called American Standard English, which has the objective of neutralizing speech to get rid of obvious regionalisms. I not only took to this process, I loved it in the way only a pedantic, overcompensating, insecure young person could. I practiced and practiced and decided I would speak American Standard English all the time. When I went home for the holidays that year, I launched right into showing off my new skills at the family Christmas party. "I had an in-ta-view lahst week," I declared haughtily, as my sister rolled her eyes. My mom had a squinty "say what?" look, and our neighbor, impressed, said, "Gosh, Jane, you sound just like you're from Boston!"

But sounding haughty was only the beginning. With my newfound success in the theater, I suddenly discovered—and unleashed—my inner diva. The more comfortable I got and the more empowered I began to feel, the more I tried to force my genius on others. If something in a production I was in wasn't to my liking or up to my standards, I'd pitch a fit. I never hesitated to tell everyone exactly what they were doing wrong, in the most condescending tones possible. After someone poured their heart into a scene, I'd protest with "I didn't believe you at all." And for some reason I was surprised that this behavior seemed to alienate people. . . .

Looking back, I can see I was a repressed, judgmental adolescent who mistook my newfound adequacy as brilliance. As with most overcompensating virgins, my puffed-up ego would soon be deflated by a heavy crush.

4

Normal

IT WAS IN MY JUNIOR YEAR AT ILLINOIS STATE THAT I became mentally and emotionally consumed by a full-on crush. This was beyond the vague feeling of dread that I'd had since the Stevenson twins' revelation. My "gay" now had a focus, and she was a petite, spritely professor with perfect handwriting. That she was straight didn't matter. I wasn't thinking I would ever actually win her love. And when I daydreamed about kissing her, I imagined myself as a handsome boy, so I still wasn't entirely on board with the whole "gay" thing.

But nonetheless, the intensity of my obsession was almost overwhelming. Seeing her for class on M/W/F wasn't enough, so I used to walk by her office just to smell the patchouli. I still hadn't done anything about being gay, but the fantasy was awesome, and gay was getting good.

And then, suddenly, she left. She got a job somewhere else, and for the whole of that summer break home in Dolton, I couldn't even get up in the morning. For the first time in my life, I understood what depression was. In order to get through it, I turned it into something noble, heroic almost. I even gave it a soundtrack. I was depressed to the song "Another Grey Morning" by James Taylor. I am pretty sure for him it's a song about heroin addiction, but for me it was about the loss of a fantasy. And I grieved this loss like the death of a loved one.

> *Here comes another grey morning*
> *A not so good morning after all . . .*

Oy gevalt, the drama.

. . .

HAVING TASTED THE THRILL OF A FIRST CRUSH, I WAS primed for another. After the great summer of mourning, I returned to Normal for my senior year on the hunt for love. I found another teacher, but at least this time I picked an actual gay lady. She had spiky hair, unshaven legs, and a low, butchy voice. She didn't rock my world, but there was enough projection on my part to get the crush going.

My initial reaction to her was shock, though. She was obviously a dyke, which made me extremely uncomfortable. But then I got to know her, and I really started to like her. She loved to party, and she loved to hang out with us undergrads, and we just thought that was so cool. Yeah, she was a professor, but she was only ten years older than we were, which at my age was just enough to make her seem wise and alluring. And she was out and proud about who she was, unlike so many of us Midwestern theater majors who were still firmly encased in our shells. Normal, Illinois, had not seen anything like her, and I found myself positively intrigued and excited. We began to flirt. She started it. But I followed. We'd sit too close, let our eyes linger too long, and brush our hands together. It was the first time I had ever flirted with anyone.

But we went back and forth with it. We'd flirt, but then one of us would pretend nothing had happened. Maybe the image of herself as a professor chasing a slightly unhinged undergrad in and out of happy hours was just too much for her. As for me, I was titillated and then terrified, with no in-between. I felt like if I went forward there would be no going back—I'd be for-real gay, not just in-my-head gay. Then one night we greased the wheels with a few dollar pitchers of beer, and things got interesting.

We were at a party and she was dancing to a Devo song with full punked-out abandon. I walked up to her, looked her straight in the eye, and put one hand through her spiky hair. I walked away, like a bold idiot, knowing that I had just made the first move. We ended up back at my apartment, drunk, and we fell asleep on the living room floor. In the middle of the night, someone rolled over, and just like that, we were kissing.

As we were making out, I thought, *Oh my god, so this is what kissing is*. I had kissed a few boys, but never felt anything and never understood what the big deal was or why people bothered to kiss each other at all. But for me, kissing a woman was different. It was the point of no return.

The next day in her apartment, I helped myself to her journal. Why would I do a thing like that? Because it was there, she was not, and I have no impulse control. In a fresh entry, written that morning, she asked of our night together, "Have I opened Pandora's box?" After I went to the library and found out who this Pandora was (remember, I'm still a C student), I had to answer, "Yes, she has."

Our relationship proceeded as smoothly as you'd expect between a teacher and a self-hating student who's having her first-ever homosexual experience. I pulled her close, then pushed her away, then threw myself at her, then despised myself for doing it. I couldn't stand to see her, and I couldn't stand not to see her. I was tormented, guilt-ridden, ashamed . . . and out-of-my-mind excited. And I had no clue how to handle any one of those emotions, much less all of them together.

I hung out in Normal for the summer of my final year at ISU to marinate in the drama of the push and pull of love. To support myself, I got a job detasseling corn with migrant workers in the endless cornfields outside town. I wanted to do something physical and be outside so maybe I could get a tan. What I got was cuts all over my arms because I went sleeveless.

At the end of the summer, I reluctantly left Normal to start an MFA program at Cornell in upstate New York. I had auditioned for a bunch of grad programs earlier in the year, and to my absolute surprise, Cornell had offered me one of their six graduate positions. Cornell wasn't Juilliard or Yale in terms of actor-training-program gravitas, but they wanted me! I got a free ride and the promise of two more years doing what I loved in the safety of academia. And seeing as I had projected every last ounce of neediness onto the gay teacher lady, I would imagine my exit came not a moment too soon for her.

Now that I had broken my relationship cherry, I finally got the sense to call Chris. It had been four years since I'd sent him the cruel letter that had ended our friendship. At home in Dolton over Christmas break, I got out my folks' Harveys Bristol Cream, poured myself a mugful, and dialed Chris's number.

"I'm sorry about that letter," I told him. "I miss you. And I'm gay now, too."

"I know," Chris replied. And just like that, he forgave me. A fan of late sixties easy listening music, I felt such a joy to hear his familiar sign-off before hanging up: "Don't sleep in the subway, darling." I had my friend back.

. . .

MY MOM ALWAYS SAID THAT IF SHE COULD BUY ME A town, it would be Ithaca. It was perfect for me—woodsy, contained, and quaint. I arrived there via train and bus in the late summer of 1982. Ithaca is a lovely little place, full of old hippies and smarty-pants students. Every street is a steep hill, and all the students had wonderfully toned legs. I would have a pair of my own in short order. I had grown up feeling fat next to my bony brother and sister. They effectively taunted me, calling me "ub"—short for "tub-o-lard." I had tried all sorts of tricks and fads to become slim and therefore happy. But now that I was finally losing weight, I still felt miserable. Once again, I could hardly get out of bed in the morning. Not only did I have that damn gay secret, but the fact that I had just come from the buckle of the corn belt had never been more obvious. Way out of my element, I made social gaffes at every turn. I actually tried to take out a priceless first-edition book like it was a regular library book. I had never eaten a taco or had Greek food. I had never had a bagel, much less a Jewish friend. Cornell was teeming with Jews, Greek food–eaters, vegetarians, and New York City types who kept hurting my feelings. Unlike these kids, I didn't give two hoots about grade point averages, and how much I knew about anything was not a point of pride for me (yet). I was very alone and felt stupider than everyone else.

Even though it had a middle-tier graduate acting program, Cornell was an elite Ivy League school. Some kids who had been high school valedictorians found themselves at the bottom of the class when they got there. There were many incidents throughout the years where really good students jumped to their deaths into the gorges that tore through the landscape of this otherwise delightful little hamlet. They couldn't take their own perceived failures. It was called gorging out. I understood their pain.

I was all on my own here. I had made my decision to travel across the country for grad school by myself and for myself. I didn't consult my parents; I just sort of presented it to them. I had a long-running fantasy of someone magically appearing to hold my hand and guide me through the building of a life and a career. However, this fantasy was up against a harsh reality: I was going to have to dig deep to find the gumption to make things happen. I had zero belief in myself and would have loved to have been saved from the work of it.

One particularly tough morning, when I was doubled over in existential angst, I called in to school sick and the secretary said, "No one calls in sick to this program. It's not done. You get yourself in here." I stayed home anyway. For a self-identified good girl and rule-follower this was an outrageously rebellious act. I spent that day obsessively straightening my bed and blowing and reblowing my hair dry. My insides might be a mess, but damn it if my outsides would be. That night, I called the campus gay and lesbian hotline. I think somehow I knew that I had to feel okay about who I was in order to feel like I fit anywhere, or to make anything of my life.

"I need to talk to somebody," I said. They told me to go to the Apple Blossom Café, and a volunteer named Alice would meet me there. I loved the ABC Café. It was full of dirty vegetarians and hairy lesbians, so of course I was both attracted and repulsed.

And so I went to the ABC Café to meet Alice. She showed up, and I recognized her—she was a graduate student in the directing program. "Oh, hi," she said. "I had a feeling you were gay." We talked, went out and got drunk, and slept together that night. (For a volunteer, she clearly went above and beyond.)

This might have ended up being a happy story of finding new love . . . but it wasn't. I liked Alice okay, but she committed the cardinal sin of liking me more. I couldn't deal with the attention—it made me want to punish her.

So I did. I ignored her phone calls, acted cold when we saw each other, and generally pretended that first night had never happened. It was like the old Groucho Marx maxim: never belong to a club that would have you as a member. I saw her a couple of weeks later, and she was with someone else. I was still a mess.

. . .

I LOVED THE CONSERVATORY-STYLE TRAINING AT COR-nell. For a depressed person in her early twenties like me it would become the perfect remedy: up at the crack of dawn with fencing or dancing, working until late at night on rehearsal for whatever play we were doing.

I forgot about myself and I focused on the characters I played.

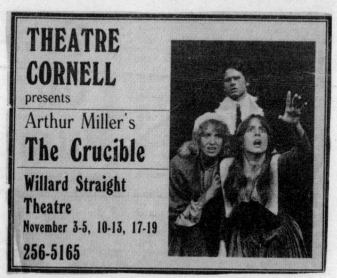

Seein' witches as Mary Warren in The Crucible.

I discovered one of the great, unexpected gifts of learning to act: all the characters ever written are already inside you. It's just a matter of accessing them and bringing them forward. And having no fear of the dark side.

Case in point:

Stuart White was an amazingly talented guest director from New York City. I met him early in my first semester. He came to Cornell to direct a Reynolds Price play called *Early Dark*. He cast me as Rosacoke Mustian, a young girl who loses her virginity when the man she loves violently rapes her. On stage.

This blew my mind. This character was nothing like me. I had never fallen in love with a guy, never slept with a guy, never been thrown around by anyone. I didn't know what it was like to live in the South during the Depression. I had no idea what it was Stuart White thought he saw in me to make him say, "Yep, she's the one." This was also the very first time I had been given the role of a character whose emotional arc was the center of the play. This experience would push me further than I'd ever been pushed.

Stuart probably knew all of this, but he could probably also see the vulnerability I was always trying to hide from the world: my fear of failure and not being good enough. This lined up nicely with Rosacoke's fear of being stuck in the generational poverty and pain of her world. He believed that if I could dig deep enough, I could tap into what I needed to bring this young girl to life.

Stuart knew what he was doing. He would take me for long walks, and we would talk. I started to confide in him, and when I told him I was a virgin (I hadn't been with a guy, so I thought the term still applied), he almost cried. "That is so sweet!" He was from the South and these were his people. Stuart urged me to see that depth and virginal innocence in me as something I could use creatively. I just had to be strong enough to allow myself to be vulnerable. Great lesson. For art and for life.

The whole time Stuart was directing us in *Early Dark*, he was sick. "I can't seem to shake this cold," he'd say, just about every week. I didn't think anything of it until one night when I mentioned it to Chris on the phone.

"Oh my god," Chris said. "He may have AIDS."

At that time, the early 1980s, AIDS was this mysterious new illness. It was the first I'd heard of it, though it wouldn't be long before it would decimate the gay male community.

About a year later, when I heard the news that Stuart had

died from AIDS-related complications, I was devastated. What a loss.

· · ·

I DID A LOT OF DRINKING DURING THIS TIME. I HAD company, because we all did. But at least to me, in my own private Idaho of pain, my drinking was different. Unlike the social drinking my friends did, getting to my "first today, badly needed" was compulsive and all-consuming.

I had all four of my impacted wisdom teeth taken out while I was at Cornell, and I couldn't drink for a while after the surgery because I was wiped out. I realized then that I had boozed it up every single day since my senior year of high school. I drank specifically *to get drunk*. I'd think nothing of tossing back a six-pack of Miller Lite—anything to get that merciful buzz. Although sometimes the buzz wouldn't come and I'd just feel bloated.

I wanted to feel good. I just wasn't sure how to make myself happy, and I wished someone else would get me there. I started spending a lot of time with another grad student, named Hugh. He was a smart, self-deprecating, easygoing guy. We'd go out for dinner at the ABC Café, and he'd look over the vegetarian menu and then order a "rib eye, medium rare." The humorless vegetarians and bearded lesbians didn't find it funny. But Hugh cracked me up.

We'd go out to bars and drink, or we'd drink at home, or on some nights, we'd do both. Hugh had some culture, so I started drinking more exotic beers like Heineken, smoking Turkish cigarettes we rolled ourselves, and drinking flavored coffee. No

*Hugh in the blue shirt I wish I'd kept. It looked
better on me. With Beth, my roommate.*

more Folgers. Hugh was a wonderful friend, and I told him
everything, including about my relationships with women. He
was cool with it.

My roommate was moving out, so Hugh moved in. We became inseparable and even started wearing each other's clothes.
I loved spending time with him, but when he started to fall for
me, things changed.

I didn't really want a physical relationship with Hugh, and if
it had been just up to me we'd have stayed close friends. He had
reasonable heterosexual expectations and was moving our relationship toward sex. I was curious enough, and in need of affection, that I moved with him. We started having sex, which led
me to fear I was pregnant every two seconds. An unreasonable
fear since we used protection. No matter what we did (or didn't

do) the night before, the next day I was always convinced I was pregnant. Once, Hugh laughed and said to me, "You'd have to be a goddess of fertility to be pregnant after what we did last night."

Hugh was as sweet and kind as he could be, so I soon found myself despising him. He never gave voice to these feelings, but I knew he was falling in love with me. How did I know? Because I had helped myself to his journal (yes, it's a pattern). I'd push him away, but he'd just wait patiently for me to come back, which I always did. I needed the comfort and companionship.

Then I became a real asshole. I started pushing away anyone who showed me kindness. That inner diva who had first reared her ugly head at Illinois State reappeared with a vengeance. I was the worst person to have at critiques. No one could do anything right as far as I was concerned, and I made absolutely sure they knew it. In the haughtiest of tones, I'd demand, "What the hell was that?" "How dare you demean Molière in that way!" "Why are you making that face?" "You're just showing off!" Everything everyone did was wrong, and I couldn't let anything go. I was undoubtedly an absolute joy to have around.

Thus began my phase of assholatry, a period that would go on for some years. I just felt like something within me was fundamentally broken. In true Psychology 101 fashion, the crap I spewed at them was the crap I wanted to spew at myself. I was scared to death that I didn't have what it took. Everyone started to steer clear of me, except for Hugh.

I was at one of my lowest points, and Hugh took the brunt of it. I even came to hate his accent, not that he really had one, having grown up in Southern California. He was like a puppy, loyal and loving, which I found pathetic. How dare he love me? What was wrong with him?

I should say that while all of this suffering was unnecessary, it did make for some good comedy. Years later, with lots of distance, I saw my young self in one Sue Sylvester. Hell-bent on revenge and out to crush the dreams of the innocent, Sue is always looking for the next fight. "Get ready for the ride of your life, Will Schuester. You're about to board the Sue Sylvester Express. Destination horror!" I was awful in those Cornell years, but I hadn't yet figured out how to make my ridiculousness funny.

In the midst of my turmoil, I had one teacher—a visiting instructor, actually—who saw what I was doing and tried to help me. Her name was Jagienka Zych-Drweski, and I barely remember anything else about her, but I've never forgotten what she said to me.

She shook her head with a mix of pity and frustration and said in a thick Polish accent, "Jane. You *have* to learn to let things roll off your back!"

I wanted to, but I didn't know how. Unfortunately for me (and anyone else within earshot), it would be years before I'd figure it out.

Eventually I pushed even Hugh away, but shockingly, we stayed friends, and to this day we call each other on our birthdays.

. . .

WHEN I GRADUATED FROM CORNELL, MY MOM AND dad and Aunt Marge picked me up for a little family vacation. I was twenty-four, with an overbearing perm and an attitude to match. We were making our way to New York City, where I was hoping to ply my trade in theater.

We drove all up and down the East Coast, sightseeing, the four of us sharing small hotel rooms. I was in a terrible mood the whole time. I was critical of everything and rolled my eyes so frequently I gave myself vertigo. Soon, everyone had had enough of me. Things came to a head in Boston.

My dad wanted to do the Freedom Trail, a walking tour of historical sites in Boston that's supposed to be a fun, easy way to learn New England history. But we kept losing the trail. We wandered through Boston with Dad saying, "Where's the goddamn Freedom Trail?" as I let my parents know exactly how stupid I thought the whole thing was by complaining at every turn. "Oh my god, we walked all that way for this?"

The next morning, I opened my eyes to find my mother sitting at the foot of my hotel bed. "You're ruining my vacation," she said quietly. I behaved a little better after that, but my inner bitch was only temporarily muzzled.

When the Goddamn Freedom Trail vacation was finally over, they reluctantly left me at my new home in the West Village, on Christopher Street. It was the day after the Gay Pride Parade and it looked like a cyclone had hit it. In 1984, New York was not the clean, friendly wonderland it is today. Times Square was a giant porno shop, people got mugged on the subway, and Central Park wasn't safe after dark. I was living in a one-bedroom sublet apartment with a Chinese graduate student from Cornell, so we had to take turns sleeping on the couch because there was only one bed.

The sublet was across the street from the gay leather bar Boots & Saddle, and just around the corner from the Duplex, a

Dad, Mom, Aunt Marge, and me on the Goddamn Freedom Trail trip.

piano bar where musical theater wannabes and enthusiasts would sing until the wee hours. Being near the gay bars was a double-edged sword: when I was happy, it seemed like a great place to be; when I wasn't, it felt decadent, dark, and lonely.

I got a job at a friend's father's advertising agency called Creamer Incorporated, which had acquired a PR division called

Glick & Lorwin. I had no business being in PR—had no nose for it and no initiative, and basically sat at a desk all day trying to look busy. But for some reason, Boris Lorwin and Ira Glick, the two wonderful older guys who ran it, loved me.

They'd walk by my desk and wave at me and say, "You're doing a great job, Janie!" To this day I don't know what I did to make them like me so much, because the one project they gave me, I completely screwed up.

I was supposed to plan a luncheon at a hotel, so I took Boris over to meet the people who were going to throw it. They wanted us to go to the kitchen for a tasting of the planned meal, but it turned into a scene from *This Is Spinal Tap*. We kept walking through the basement and turning right, then turning left, and wondering, "Where's the kitchen? Where's the kitchen?" Boris got more and more frustrated, until he finally barked, "Just forget it!" and we somehow found our way through the labyrinth and back out of the hotel.

I thought Boris would fire me, but instead he just said, "Janie, I love you, but we won't put you in charge of anything again." So I just worked on accounts at my little desk—the Crest account, whose reps went into schools and stained innocent children's teeth to show them cavities, and the Crayola account, for which my job was to cut and paste press clippings onto pieces of paper. I'd take the clippings in and show them to Boris and Ira and say, "Look at all the great coverage we got." And they'd say, "Good work, Jane!"

But as sweet as Ira and Boris were to me, the rest of New York kicked my ass.

I didn't have an agent, so getting auditions of any kind was out. I bummed around in a few off-off-Broadway shows, doing things for free with little theater companies—such as a production of *Macbeth* helmed by an acting teacher who had "disciples" rather than students. She put an ad in the paper, and a few of my Cornell pals and I responded and got cast as spear carriers and the like. But the rehearsal process was so ridiculous and demeaning that all the self-respecting people kept dropping out, leaving us with principal roles. I was one of the three witches, and I almost came to blows with another one who kept pronouncing "hover" as "hoover." Appropriately, the show closed after about two nights, as most of the audience left before intermission.

Not only was I unable to find a professional home, I couldn't even find a literal one. When my sublet in the Village ended, I bounced around to four or five other places, always getting kicked out after a few weeks or months, whereupon I would have to move myself and all my stuff on the subway. In one place, the landlord knocked on the door and said, "You know, this is an illegal sublet. You're not supposed to be here." So I panicked and packed my two suitcases and headed out. The guy I was renting from actually followed me down the street, saying, "What are you doing? You don't have to go—he does that to everybody!" But I was a rule-follower from way back, plus that guy had threatened my sense of home and safety. I didn't have the constitution to withstand that, so I was out of there. I felt rejected and alone.

The roughness of New York City's streets seeped in everywhere. At that first sublet, my Chinese roommate had invited home some guys who were rumored to be connected to the Chinese Mafia, and they ended up ransacking the place. Another time, a friend of mine named John brought a trick home, and after I'd left for work and John was passed out, the guy rummaged through my stuff, took some cash and my boom box, and for some reason cut the sleeves off my sweatshirts.

Then there was my roommate in Chelsea. He and I shared bunk beds, and late one night he came into the bedroom all excited. "Hey, Jane," he said, "I just got four hundred bucks for giving a guy a blow job!"

Wide-eyed and shocked, trying not to look like a Midwestern bumpkin, I just smiled and said, "Hey, that's more than I make in two weeks!"

. . .

THE WHOLE TIME I WAS IN NEW YORK, I DRANK NON-stop, gained weight, and felt unsafe everywhere I went. Everything about the city felt hostile to me; it was as if New York itself were screaming, "Get out!"

The Duplex was the only place I was happy. During prime evening hours, the regulars, all of them Broadway musical theater performers, either chorus members or understudies, performed. They were fantastic singers, and I envied how close they were, how witty. I wanted to be one of them.

By around 4 A.M. I'd finally get my chance at the mike. With no awareness of the irony, I chose "I Don't Know How to Love Him" as my signature song. It massaged my soul to warble it (drunkenly, I'm sure). Then the bar would close, and I'd stumble home to wherever I happened to be living that week.

One night, about nine months after I'd moved to New York, I was fast asleep in a big apartment in Brooklyn that housed an unknown number of other roommates, when two of them came home, drunk. They stumbled into the apartment and turned all the lights on, yelling, "Get out! Get out of here!" Startled by the shouting, I emerged from the bedroom, bleary-eyed, and freaked out.

"Get the fuck out, bitch!" one of them yelled. "Now!" They obviously were not good with my living there.

"But I have no place to go!" I said, panicking. I didn't know anyone in Brooklyn. I didn't even know where to catch the subway. This was my fifth sublet in nine months, but my first in Brooklyn—which in the mid-eighties wasn't the charmingly gentrified place it is today. It felt scary and dangerous, like a no-man's-land. I was always worried about my physical safety in New York, so putting me out on the street in Brooklyn at three in the morning might have killed me from fright, if nothing else.

The guys kept yelling, and I kept begging not to be thrown out, and eventually they stumbled drunkenly back out the door. It was the cherry on top of the horrible sundae that was New York for me.

The next morning, I got up, dressed for work, and walked to the subway to catch my train. Somewhere between Brooklyn and Midtown, I started feeling sharp pains in my stomach, like I had food poisoning. By the time I got to my stop at 50th Street, it was so bad I was doubled over.

I walked to Glick & Lorwin, but because I was early as usual, no one was there. I didn't have a key to the office, so I just sat down on a box of paper outside the door, slumped over in pain. I thought my appendix might have burst, so I straggled back to the subway and got on a train heading for the Village, where St. Vincent's Hospital was.

On the train, hunched over in the worst pain of my life, I suddenly thought, *I have to leave New York. I have to get out of here.* And my stomach relaxed. I got to 14th Street, stood up, and thought, *I'm all right.* The pain was gone.

I took the subway straight back to Brooklyn, packed up my two suitcases, and called my mom. "I'm coming home," I told her. I would miss Boris and Ira (who acted like they were mad at me for leaving and wouldn't make eye contact). But I couldn't wait to get back home.

5

The Call of Comedy

I WAS NOW TWENTY-FIVE YEARS OLD WHEN I WENT back home to Dolton, back to the house where I grew up, on Sunset Drive. When I walked into my old bedroom, still with its green-and-yellow shag carpeting and bedspread, there was a big "Welcome Home Jane!" banner, with balloons and everything. I turned to my mom and, half-joking, half-serious, exclaimed, "You *can* go home again!"

Mom was happy to have me home as well. "Look, Jane—I organized your books," she said, waving her hand at the shelves.

"By author or title?" I asked.

"By height." And there they were, perfectly arranged from smallest to tallest.

My mom's excitement was short-lived, though. The balloons in my room hadn't even lost their helium when she started urging me to apply for a regular job, to start my backup career. "You could work as a secretary," she said.

My mom had been working at Arthur Andersen for years. She was an old-school secretary: she typed an outrageous number of words per minute and knew shorthand. I was a college graduate with an advanced degree; I considered myself vastly overqualified for secretarial tasks. I had no interest in working at Arthur Andersen.

But even with my inflated sense of self, I knew I needed a job, so I called and got an interview. Dressed in one of my mom's suits and looking like a young Janet Reno, I went downtown to their offices. I took the English test that they gave all new submanagement employees . . . and failed. Yes, I was college educated and I even had a master's degree, but I didn't know the first thing about the proper form for business letters.

My mother was so embarrassed.

Since I had been deemed unqualified to be a secretary, I sent my résumé to an employment agency, this time for receptionist work. Within a week or two, they found me a job answering phones at the Civic Opera House in Chicago.

I loved it—after all, I was working in a theater—but I also kept trying out for acting gigs. Before long, I got a part in a new Shakespeare company's outdoor production of *The Comedy of Errors*.

On the morning after I was cast in the play, I came bouncing into the office, all excited about my good news. "I got a part in *The Comedy of Errors*," I told a girl I worked with. "But it's gonna be over the summer, so I'll have to quit my job here." I didn't think twice about telling her. She, in turn, didn't think twice about going straight into my boss's office to tell *her*.

What I didn't realize was that, having paid a fee to the employment agency to find me, my boss wouldn't be too happy about my leaving so soon. So she fired me on the spot. Even though I had been planning to quit, I felt humiliated, as if I had been personally rejected. I was in agony over it.

I called Chris, so upset I could hardly get the words out. "They fired me," I said, near tears.

"Well," he said, "you weren't going to stay anyway. So who cares?"

In my place, Chris sure wouldn't have. He'd have just gone on his merry way, acting in the play and never giving the Opera House a second thought. But I couldn't let things roll off my back like he could. I had halfheartedly surrendered to my mom's idea of a backup plan, but I had failed. I couldn't even get into the club I didn't want to be a part of, and I took it as affirmative evidence of my uselessness. At that time in my life, if I had an opportunity to suffer, I seemed to have to take it.

To get me to forget about it and move on, Chris took me out that night and we hit the bars from Rush Street all the way up to the Closet, a gay bar in Boys Town. We called this kind of night "drinking our way north." Our "First today, badly needed" toast was usually "Cheers to queers," but tonight, since it was clear we would be downing one Long Island iced tea after another, we simply clicked our glasses and said "Bye-bye."

. . .

THE COMEDY OF ERRORS WAS STAGED OUTSIDE, IN LIN-coln Park, with the sparkling waters of Lake Michigan as the backdrop. On opening night, the park was packed. Everybody came—my parents, sister, brother, cousins, friends. Nobody had seen me act since high school, so this was a big moment for me. And I had a big role: Adriana, the wife who fears her husband is cheating on her, only to find it was a "comedy of errors."

While at Cornell, I had accumulated a huge bag of acting

techniques and methods, and I employed every one in my "process" of creating Adriana. So complete was the backstory I invented for her, I even gave her an astrological sun and moon sign. I could barely walk and talk at the same time for all my training.

In spite of my meticulous overpreparation, I had a blast out there on that stage, performing the immortal words of the Bard under the stars. It was a beautiful night and I felt incredibly lucky to be there.

Afterward, everyone was fawning over me: "Jane, you're an actress! We didn't know you had it in you!" I drank it all in, so happy to feel validated in the dream I'd been chasing for so long.

And then my mother said, "You know, Jane, I still see you teaching."

I turned to her and said sternly, "Mom, you cannot ever say that to me again."

I knew she was only trying to protect me, but now, at age twenty-five, I just didn't want to hear it anymore. I would not, and could not, pretend to want the life she wanted for me. To Mom's credit, she finally got it. She just said, "Oh, okay," and never mentioned it again.

The combination of being in a Shakespeare company and having an MFA from Cornell turned me into an even bigger, more impossible pain in the ass than I'd been before. I was sure that I knew more than anybody else in the company, considering my "classical training." I was displeased with my cast mates about 90 percent of the time and made a point of letting them know it. Some of my criticisms were valid, but I didn't have to punish people for what, in my opinion, were their failings. But some of it was me still not knowing how to let things roll off my back. I couldn't just focus on my own work and let people make their own mistakes.

They would speak their lines, and I'd be certain they had no idea what they were talking about. "You have no respect for the language!" I would splutter. "Why bother doing Shakespeare at all?" To which people would respond by rolling their eyes. "Oh, Jane's on her 'why are we doing Shakespeare' kick again."

I would criticize details that were in no way germane to my job as an actor in the company, even complaining about a paint color on the set. "Who chose *this*?" I demanded, infuriated. As I child, I had thrashed on the floor to release my pent-up dissatisfaction. As a pissed-off adult, I made myself completely unappealing by spewing it at others.

I could not seem to stop myself from being such a bitch. As my mom would call it, I was acting like "Madame Full Charge." The following behavior by this band of players always served to take me around the bend: to make sure the audience understood Shakespeare's language, or to be certain they got a joke, the actors would literally use finger quotes or cheap and stupid gestures while performing. Bunny ears around Elizabethan dialogue . . . While I will admit the paint color was none of my business, I found this absolutely galling.

I just wanted the experience of acting in a Shakespeare company to be the Shakespeare company experience I had in my head, but instead of accepting the gig for what it was and finding what I liked and leaving the rest, I fought it so hard that no one liked me anymore. There was no "going with the flow" for Jane Lynch. So I took control of the one thing I could. I pulled the ultimate "diva" and quit.

One night, as I was putting on my makeup before a performance of *A Midsummer Night's Dream*, I announced to the cast in a war-weary tone, "After this show . . . I am done with the company."

You could almost hear the collective sigh of relief. No one said anything for a moment, until one guy quipped, "You'll never get a gold watch that way."

No one chased after me and begged me to stay, and at first that pissed me off. Then it really hurt my feelings. The thought did cross my mind that I had gone too far . . . and that, in fact, I had been the one who rejected them . . . but still, the old "I have been rejected, no one wants me" pity party began again.

. . .

MY CAREER AS AN OFFICE WORKER WAS A NONSTARTER, but I still needed to make money. Fortunately, I was able to take my prodigious Shakespearean talents to a new, more challenging, venue: *America's Shopping Place*.

It was 1987. *America's Shopping Place* was one of the first home-shopping TV shows in the country, part of television's new retail frontier. It stayed on the air into the wee hours of the morning, with live hosts describing products and taking phone calls from insomniac shoppers. I showed up at the studio for what I thought was an audition. It turned out their idea of an audition was to throw me into makeup and put me on the air. There I was with a pretty young woman named Kendy Kloepfer in front of two huge cameras waiting for the red light to come on. Kendy was a sweetheart and exactly the kind of girl they wanted on the air—feminine, adorable, and good on her feet. I was not as feminine or adorable as they wanted, but I was good on my feet.

Kendy and I would stand in front of the cameras, talking about whatever we were supposed to be selling—cubic zirconia jewelry, electronic flea collars, grandfather clocks. I didn't know it at the time, but it was the best training in the world for an improv actor. Television home shopping was uncharted territory, so we had to fly by the seat of our pants and make things up as we went along. We'd smile into the camera and do our pitch. "Flea season is upon us!" or "Now, this bracelet is a delightful way to say 'I love you'!" Then they'd switch to a close-up shot of the product so we could read the product specifications out of a wire-bound notebook. Then the camera would suddenly be back on us, and we would have to be ready with a big smile and a clever line.

I loved everything about the job—being on camera, improvising, bantering with Kendy. The problem was that the producers did not love me. They wouldn't even look up at me when I came into the studio chirping "Hey, everybody!" They never fired me, but they never told me I had a job either. I would get a call a few hours before I needed to be there. I'd drop whatever I was doing to show up to do the graveyard shift of *America's Shopping Place*. Did I mention *I loved this job*?

But it was all to no avail, because no matter how good I was at improvising my enthusiasm for jewelry and housewares, I was not feminine and adorable enough. I was no Kendy Kloepfer, and the producers tried to replace me as quickly as possible. They actually auditioned my potential replacements on the air with me. These young and inarticulate pretty girls were always half my height, so the producers would pop an apple box next to me for them to stand on. But they would still come up no farther than my ear. I had to show these girls the ropes, knowing that if I trained them well they would take away the first livelihood I had enjoyed. I did so as cheerfully as I could, hoping the producers would notice how magnanimous I was and change their minds and let me stay.

I remember one poor gal was completely out of her league and unable to say anything interesting about anything. While she was selling a cubic zirconia tennis bracelet, the director had prompted her through her earpiece: "Tell them who they can buy this for." She intoned, dead-eyed and flatly, "You can buy this for your mother. You can buy this for your sister. You can buy this for your aunt. You can buy this for a girl cousin . . ." The director begged into my earpiece: "Jane, stop her!!!" And I heroically saved the day.

Sadly, we had to stop taking live calls after some drunk guy got on the air, slurring lustily about what he wanted to do to Kendy. Honestly, I am surprised it hadn't happened earlier. We *were* on in the middle of the night. What do you expect at 3 A.M.?

While the producers were working feverishly to replace me, I was thrilled to have a job on television. For several weeks they failed to find another Kendy, so they kept putting me on the air—at $200 a pop. This was good enough money to allow me to rent a Pacer from Rent-a-Wreck so I could drive from my new apartment in downtown Chicago to the studio in Glenview, a northern suburb. I'd work all night, then hop in the Pacer at 6 A.M. Having picked up a six-pack of Miller Lite on the way in, I'd pop open a cold one for the drive home. I'd finish the six in front of the TV, watching a VCR tape of myself on *America's Shopping Place*. Steady, sane, healthful living.

At around the same time, I auditioned for The Second City, an improv comedy theater. I'd sent my headshot and résumé to pretty much every professional theater in Chicago. I remember you had to call the theater's audition line, dial and redial, and hope that one time you'd be lucky enough not to get a busy signal and your call would go through. This would net you one audition spot among the hordes who would be ushered through like so much human cattle. Everyone got about two minutes to perform a monologue from whichever script was being produced. These general look-sees rarely got anyone anything, but I rarely snagged one in the first place.

I wanted desperately to get an audition at the Goodman Theater or the Body Politic, but I also sent my stuff to The Second City improv theater. I was surprised when I got into one of their big open-call auditions.

Improvisational theater scared me. It required basically making something out of nothing. You had to be quick on the draw and get right to the punch and somehow be consistent with your metaphors. There were no set rules for an improvised scene other than to accept everything that comes at you (called "yes and" in the parlance). There were no parameters, no structure to work within. Basically, one would need to enjoy freefalling. I needed the certainty of the script. I was not one to "go with the flow."

At the time, I failed to see that this was what I had been doing all along on *America's Shopping Place*. I just didn't see improvising as one of my strengths. And at that time, I had my sights focused elsewhere. I was a *serious theater actress*. . . .

But there I found myself, auditioning on the stage at The Second City, making stuff up. I don't remember being funny or even particularly inventive, just that I had fun goofing around. Out of nowhere, I was cast as one of the two women for a new touring company. I honestly had no idea why I had been cast, but I was just thrilled. I had a paying gig and I was going on tour! I threw my whole self at and into it.

Although the form is commonly referred to as "sketch comedy," at The Second City we spoke of performing "scenes." At their best, these scenes were grounded, human, and very real. The pathos was wrapped up in some sociopolitical context, with themes that were liberal and envelope-pushing, like gays or Vietnam. Someone might wear an occasional wig or funny glasses, but otherwise there was no big gimmicky shtick. It pleased me so much. I just loved it and took to it immediately.

I didn't have to face my fear of performing improv, because we did set scenes on the road—the touring show was a "best of" past Second City scenes, scenes that had started as improvisation in Chicago and had been reworked and cultivated for the main stage before finally being sent out on the road. The heavy lifting had been done for us, and we just had to perform the finished product.

Being part of this ensemble in which I played a bevy of different characters in one performance, singing a song here and there, was a brand-new high for me. Where had this been all my life? A whole new world opened up. I loved and enjoyed the heck out of my fellow cast mates and delighted in traveling from burg to burg with them. Plus, I was touring to exotic locales like St. Louis and Kansas City via a twelve-person van, which, despite sounding horrid to me now, was enormously exciting at the time.

This work also scratched my itch to be a part of a greater

whole. We were an ensemble and we had to work together for it to work at all. We were a pretty selfless group in that regard. I remember everyone being very supportive of one another, and I think we may have been unique in that way. (I have heard horror stories about members of past companies devouring one another.)

Once again, I had had a fixed idea of how things were supposed to go, but this time, instead of trying to control everything, I let things happen, and The Second City popped up out of nowhere into my life. Suddenly I was in a whole new place and ensconced in a whole new way of creating, and I felt like I had found my people: people who lived to laugh and find the funny. I showed my classically trained, uptight self the door.

Steve Carell, Stephen Colbert, Amy Sedaris, and Tim Meadows were all touring with The Second City when I was there. I got pulled off the road and onto the main stage in Chicago when they needed someone to step in for Bonnie Hunt when she got married. I stayed on as an understudy for the main stage show, usually stepping in for Bonnie or Barb Wallace. I was quite diligent with my understudy duties. I went to the show every night and sat on the bench in the back of the house where I could watch for free. I was up on everything that went on: I knew every line and every move of the current revue, and I went over and over the songs and the choreography. When they called, I was ready, and you'd never have known I hadn't been in the show for the whole run. I felt so proud of myself I thought I would be rewarded for my good work by getting a spot of my own in the cast.

That was the plan, but no one was taking the bait, so I would pop into the office to see Joyce Sloane, The Second City's pro-

JANE LYNCH

ducer and den mother, from time to time and say, "You know, Joyce, I'd love to be in the main stage company. If there's ever an opening, I'd love to have that chance." I had heard that this was how you campaigned for yourself. There was no more auditioning at this point. You either got moved up, or you didn't.

"I know, Jane, I know," she'd say. And nothing would happen.

One afternoon, I walked into her office and started my pitch again. "You know, Joyce, I'd still love to—"

"Jane," she said, looking up, "you will never be on the main stage. It's just not gonna happen for you here. I'm sorry."

I turned and walked out, stunned. I had gone above and beyond for them and I got no love. That was it—I wasn't going to make myself available for understudying anymore.

What I didn't see at the time was that, as at *America's Shopping Place*, I had gone to great lengths to please people who never had any intention of pleasing me back or giving me what I wanted. In my mind, I had been racking up brownie points and undying admiration, and it was true that everyone at The Second City was aware of my excessive effort and devotion. But sometimes I would do this to the point of disrespect for myself, and then, when the appreciation I thought I deserved didn't materialize, I'd get resentful and entertain fantasies of revenge. I'd become famous one day, and they'd regret this . . . yadda yadda yadda . . . Sometimes I'd even daydream that terrible things would befall them, but then, because I was still a knee-jerk Catholic girl, I would feel terrible.

It wasn't until after I turned on my heel and left The Second City that I started to have the tiny beginnings of awareness that this was becoming a vicious, miserable pattern. I started to see that I had been expecting the fulfillment of promises that had never, in fact, been made. It would still be a while before I would be able to see that doing things for the adoration of others, rather than for my own satisfaction, would always feed this pattern.

In the end, there were no hard feelings on either side; years later, The Second City sent me a huge floral arrangement after I won the Emmy (adoration that I do appreciate).

Though I did not enjoy feeling discarded by The Second City, it was only because my work with them ended that I was able to benefit from yet another happy accident: I was cast by the Steppenwolf Theatre in one of a series of late-night short plays. Steppenwolf was a storied theater created by actors for actors; it is safe to say that every actor in Chicago aspired to work there. It had always seemed unattainable, so much so that it wasn't even on my radar of places to audition. Steppenwolf housed its own resident ensemble of incredibly gifted actors but would also cast outside of it when necessary. A girl I had gone to college with at Illinois State was the assistant to the artistic director and had recommended me for an audition for a short play to be performed in a late-night slot. When I came home to a message on my answering machine telling me I'd been cast, I was so excited I spilled wine on the cassette tape, garbling the recording. The story of my frantic call explaining what had happened and asking "Where do I go, and when?" must have made the rounds, because after I started, the director asked me if my answering machine was still drunk.

My first part at Steppenwolf was the principal in *Terry Won't Talk*, a comedic one-act play about a little boy who refuses to speak. Wouldn't you know it: I'd be playing a man's role. My performance led to an understudy gig in the next season's series for *Stepping Out*, a comedy about English adults taking a tap dancing class. I covered five of the actresses, diligently highlighting my script with five different colors for each character, learning the lines and blocking for each. Completely unable to get my feet to tap, I learned the arms only. One night, an actress I covered got laryngitis. Through the gift of adrenaline and preparedness, I sailed through the two-hour show in what felt like five minutes. Apparently no one noticed I was just dancing the arms. Or at least that's what I was told. This time, my über-prepared and thorough self would be rewarded. I got cast in their next play, Craig Lucas's dark comedy *Reckless*, with Joan Allen and Boyd Gaines.

My career was morphing into a legitimate gig. I was doing theater and had been getting work doing voice-overs for a while, and then I started to get cast in TV commercials. I was finally making a living doing what I loved, partly because I was willing to take just about any job.

In fact, during my whole time in Chicago, I can only remember one audition I wouldn't do. I was about twenty-five or twenty-six, and there was a new agent in town we all were trying to sign with. He showed up roaring drunk at a performance of *A Midsummer Night's Dream*, the very same performance that would become my Shakespeare Company swan song. Bleary-eyed and inappropriately touchy-feely, he told me to come down to his office that next Monday. Red flags noted and ignored, I was only too delighted. On that Monday he directed me to an appointment. "There's this calendar shoot, at a garage. They're doing a look-see for models."

As he talked, I realized he was sending me to audition for one of those cheesecake calendars that hang in auto body shops, where buxom women smile as they wash cars in tube tops and cutoffs. "Go on down there," he said, "and wear something sexy." I was young, so if you looked at me in the right way, I could be somewhat fetching. I almost went to the audition, but in the end, I couldn't. It wasn't a moral thing—if I had been a girly girl, I wouldn't have hesitated for one second. I even picked out an outfit that morning, but I just couldn't make myself put it on, feeling like I couldn't pull it off.

More evidence that I would do close to anything was the 1988 movie *Taxi Killer*. An Italian production company came to Chicago to shoot the film, which would star Chuck Connors. Back in the day, Connors had starred as *The Rifleman* on TV, and he had been in classic movies like *Old Yeller*. Now that he was in his late sixties, this super-low-budget thriller was apparently his last hurrah.

I auditioned with about a hundred other actors and managed to get cast as one of the taxi drivers. The plot (such as it was) involved female taxi drivers taking revenge on a gang of young punks that had raped one of them. The producers cast actors of all ethnic stripes from all over the world—Polish, Russian, Italian, you name it. I think they just planned to overdub the whole thing at the end. The entire production had a tacky, chaotic feel to it. But I knew that when the Italian director shouted, *"Accione!"* I'd go all-in for *Taxi Killer*.

My first day, the makeup person did her thing, but there was no mirror, so I couldn't see what she'd done. Driving to the location, I looked in the rearview and gasped. I looked insane, with orange lips and brown smears all over my face. Ironically, the makeup was better done than the ridiculous and highly improbable script, in which I was to say, "My comrades and I tire of the abuses by men." I was pretty sure this film was going to suck and that I would be glad there was no distribution deal for the U.S.

After a week or two of shooting, the filmmakers blew town without paying us. The Screen Actors Guild fought for us and eventually got us a few cents on the dollar, but it was basically a wash. Ultimately, and to the benefit of humanity, the movie never got made. But for me personally, as a first movie experience, *Taxi Killer* wasn't so bad. Chuck Connors was a doll and had played sixty-six games at first base for the Cubs in 1951. I was a huge fan of those "lovable losers." We had lots to talk about.

The Rifleman and me.

. . .

IN 1990, MY FRIEND FAITH SOLOWAY ASKED ME TO join a new show. I had met Faith when she played the piano for our Second City touring company. She doesn't read a note of music but can play just by ear and intuition. She is a master of parody and sees the goofy in everything. She and her sister Jill, who is a great writer, were as obsessed with television as I was, so they ended up creating an homage to the greatest of seventies sitcoms (and our favorite show of all time), *The Brady Bunch*.

Our friend Mick Napier had just rented a huge, filthy storefront on the 3700 block of North Clark Street. He was calling the space The Annoyance. He offered it to the Soloway sisters on Tuesday nights to do what they would. The opener for the night was a mock-live game show called *The Real Live Game Show*, created by another friend, Eric Waddell. Audience members would come up on stage as contestants and compete for real prizes. The headliner was a live performance of one *Brady Bunch* episode each week in a stage show called *The Real Live Brady Bunch*. Jill created the script by watching tapes of the original TV show, rewinding constantly, and typing every word. Our stage rendition was verbatim. Faith would play all the music live on the keyboards, including the instantly recognizable incidental music. We closed the evening with our own "Alice the maid"–inspired rendition of Jefferson Airplane's "White Rabbit" (a long drug reference that conveniently included the words "Go ask Alice") as we Bradys tripped out in a psychedelic, drug-crazed nightmare. Instead of seats, the audience would sit on old ratty couches so it felt like you were watching television in your living room. Smoking and drinking were not only allowed, but encouraged.

Faith asked me if I wanted to play Alice, the maid, or Carol, the mom. I chose to play Carol, who was played by Florence Henderson in the series, because I felt I would be a natural what with my hair color and all. I told them that my friend Mari could play Alice, because not only was her hair color correct, she actually looked like Alice. So much so that she ended up becoming a bit of a sensation. After a couple of different Mikes, Andy Richter would settle in to play Carol's beloved husband. I had just turned thirty, and all the adults playing the kids were in their late twenties and on the chubby side. Our costumes were threadbare seventies clothes and smelly wigs from thrift shops. I fashioned a Florence Henderson shag with a few wispy pieces of blond wig hair attached to a piece of thick yellow yarn. A couple of painted plywood cubes served as our set, and we used only a few props.

We drank beer and ate pizza during our first rehearsal and laughed our asses off as we spoke those familiar Brady lines. We figured that only our friends and maybe a few other Brady fanatics would show up to see our show. And though ecstatic to be revisiting a favorite childhood show long gone, we were pretty half-assed with our preparation. On the opening Tuesday night, we had a last-minute run-through with light cues and music, got a bunch of pizzas and beer, and were sitting on the roof of the theater. All of a sudden we were shocked to see people gathering down below. There was a line snaking from

OPPOSITE: *A lovely lady. Me as Carol Brady.*

A bunch of Real Live Bradys.

the front door, down the street, and around the block—all to see *The Real Live Brady Bunch.*

The place was packed. It was a hot early summer evening and there was no air-conditioning. The converted storefront reeked of beer, smoke, and BO. As we stood in our places waiting for the show to start, I could hear my own heart pounding. When the lights came up on that first scene and we were revealed in all our Brady glory, the place went wild. I looked wide-eyed over to Mari and she gave me her best Alice smirk. I gave her a beatific Carol smile in return as the Brady kids chortled in idiotically.

At seven bucks a ticket, the show was sold out every night and we had to turn people away. Soon we started doing two shows each Tuesday, at seven and nine, and still both performances sold out every single week. The show became a sensation and started getting national press in magazines like *Rolling Stone*, *Newsweek*, and *People*. Everyone was happy, except Sherwood Schwartz, the creator of *The Brady Bunch*. When he heard about it, he had a cease and desist order sent to The Annoyance claiming copyright infringement—which was valid. It looked like he wanted to shut us down.

Me as Carol, Pat Towne as Greg, and Florence Henderson.

Faith and Jill Soloway.

One Tuesday night he showed up, unannounced, in Chicago, at the dumpy Annoyance. And bully for him, he was going to see for himself what all the fuss was about before he shut us down. It was the night of the Johnny Bravo episode, where Greg Brady signs a record deal and lets fame go to his head. Sherwood Schwartz stood in the back as people were screaming out the dialogue before the show had even started. Word got out that he was in the house, and the audience starting chanting "Sher-wood, Sher-wood!" and bowing in his direction and saying "I am not worthy."

We brought him up to the stage and introduced him, and the place went nuts. He told a reporter for the *Chicago Tribune*, "It was the most incredible experience I've ever had. I felt like a rock star—at my age!"

Seeing the show changed Schwartz's mind. He decided we were doing it with love and respect. He declared that he would charge us only a dollar a week as a token royalty. The show would go on.

Soon after that, much of the original Brady family would come to see our show, including Florence Henderson (Carol), Barry Williams (Greg), Christopher Knight (Peter), Susan Olsen (Cindy), and Eve Plumb (Jan). Robert Reed (Mike) came to see us when we did it at the Village Gate in New York City. A very good sport, he was also a contestant on *The Real Live Game Show*.

Davy Jones of the Monkees, who appeared in a 1971 episode of *The Brady Bunch*, not only came to see the show but played himself thirty years later in our live stage version of the episode he'd been in. He sang "Girl," let Marcia pursue him again, and took pictures with all of us. True to form, my mother, upon pasting a photo of him and me into my scrapbook, labeled it "With Billy Joel."

Actually, it's Davy Jones.

6

Compulsion

I REMEMBER BEING ONSTAGE AT THE ANNOYANCE doing *The Real Live Brady Bunch*, looking at my fellow performers all decked out in their Brady wear and wigs, their faces earnest and committed, and thinking *Can it get much better than this?* I was loving life in the big city, loving performing with these people. We all laughed so much, and I felt like that laughter was healing the part of me that had always felt broken and out of place.

Plus, every performance was a group catharsis, with all of us, actors and audience alike, sharing in the dirty secret that this TV family was the family we wished we'd grown up in. Where else but in the Brady household could you pitch a fit, storm off to your room, slam the door behind you, and then hear a gentle knock, followed by, "Honey? Do you want to talk?" It was the relationship we wished we could have had with our parents, and we just couldn't get enough of that show.

After years of a nodding acquaintance with my brother, Bob, we were finally bonding and really enjoying each other. We were living in the same building on Surf Street on the near north side. Every week, he and I would go out to dinner at a little basement shack of a restaurant called the Half Shell. We did this not only to catch up with each other but also to revisit the hilarity of that week's episode of a new TV show called *The Simpsons*. We'd wolf down their specialty, "steer and prawns," and drink beer after beer after beer. After the food and *The Simpsons* recap, we'd stumble around the corner and across the street to a tavern called the Gaslight and drink some more.

In the midst of the lighthearted hilarity and camaraderie of *The Real Live Brady Bunch* and my growing relationship with my brother, I became absorbed in the much more serious pursuit of figuring something out about myself in this world. It was spurred by the absolutely transcendent experience of reading a book called *The Seat of the Soul* by Gary Zukav. All my life, I'd felt I was at the mercy of people and circumstances; I'd had the sense that life was happening *to* me. This book presented the jaw-dropping idea that I had the power to consciously choose how I see the world and the people around me, and that my life could be different if I made more powerful choices. That thought blew my mind, and opened my heart.

I bought a copy of the book for Chris. He had the same powerful experience, so we each bought several more copies to give to our friends. We became evangelists for this book.

Realizing the power of my own choices led to a moment of reckoning that I wasn't at all eager to have. I had tried to deny it, to ignore it, to tell it to go fuck itself, but it wouldn't go away, and it was shouting at me now: I drank far too many Miller Lites. I had a problem. But whenever I entertained the idea of stopping drinking, I would panic. As the reckoning creeped its way into my conscious mind, it felt like my best friend was dying.

I'd been an everyday drinker since the end of high school. I never got crazy or out of control—I worked, I paid all my bills and taxes, and always showed up for everything not only on time but early—but I was starting to get sloppy. Some mornings, I'd wake up and shuffle to the bathroom to find vomit from the night before. I had absolutely no recollection of how it got there, and that freaked me out.

My *Brady* boozing had put me over the edge. Every performance promised a big and crazy night that I couldn't wait to get to, but every time it would kick my ass. In spite of how the night always ended, it always began for me with gleeful anticipation. With a bounce in my step, I'd hightail it to the theater at 5 P.M.-ish and initiate that first beer run so we could get it going at the run-through before the show. I'd drink during both shows and would be inebriated by the final bow. Afterward, we'd move on to the Lakeview, a tavern across the street from the theater. I was usually still there when it closed at 7 A.M.

The hangovers were debilitating. I remember "coming to" many a morning feeling like I'd been beaten up or poisoned. I remember, too, my delight in telling my friend and roommate Mari of my discovery of a surefire way to avoid hangovers: Nyquil! "It puts you right to sleep and you wake up in a soft cotton place." But soon enough, even the Nyquil lost its power and I once again started to wake up with a pounding head.

One day, in the midst of this endless alcohol-and-hangover cycle, I decided I needed to "cut back." Instead of every day, I would let myself drink just two nights a week—on my night out with brother Bob and also on Tuesday nights before, during, and after the show. But the overachiever in me kicked in and I drank enough on those two days to make up for the other five.

I finally came to terms with the idea of quitting drinking on a winter night in 1991, when I was on the phone with Chris. He was living in New York then. After years of doing drugs and being a huge boozer, he had been sober for a few years and was working out and eating well. He was healthy. He had always been a more prodigious drinker than I, and we proved the old AA adage of "he spilled more than I drank." His level of tolerance for emotional and physical discomfort was also much higher than mine, but even he had reached his limit.

As we were talking about nothing in particular, I poured myself some red wine into a big green glass goblet I used to drink from. I looked at it, then went to the sink and poured the whole thing down the drain. "That was my last drink," I said to Chris. Though I had been aware of how destructive my drinking was for me, I hadn't conceived of giving it up. The resolve felt like it came out of nowhere, and all of a sudden I couldn't be a person who drank anymore. I was "struck" sober.

"Cheers to queers," he said, and then we just kept talking and didn't mention it again. And that was the last drink I ever had. I never really drank wine, so it's kind of sad that I didn't go out on a Miller Lite, just for old time's sake.

The very next night, Steppenwolf was having a party to celebrate the opening of its new state-of-the-art theater space on Halsted and North Avenues, and when I got there, the free booze was flowing. I looked around and thought, *Well . . . maybe I'll start this sober thing tomorrow.*

But then another thought popped in my head: *If not now, when?* Because I knew tomorrow there would be another party, and I'd want to say, "You know what, maybe I'll start tomorrow." There would always be another party. I had to just stop. I also remembered something in *The Seat of the Soul* about how every time you say no to your addiction, you fund power for yourself. I decided to fund my account starting that night. Turning away from the drink in that moment was made rather effortless by that thought.

The night I poured that wine down the sink something changed, and I have never really wanted to drink since. I don't know what happened. It's as if something in me just shifted, or maybe lifted, and I no longer had that particular compulsion.

Robbed of the promise of a boozy reward at night, I began creating a delicious fantasy life. All that compulsive energy had to go somewhere, and I was a long-standing fan of a good delusion. Love relationships in the real world were not happening for me. People always said, "You're just so focused on your career!" but actually I was just so focused on my fears, my insecurity, and my lack of worthiness and entitlement that I had no room for intimacy. Intimacy was revealing, emotionally sticky, and made me feel goofy—and it certainly wasn't something I was ready to do sober. I remember getting very close to kissing someone at around this time and literally feeling like I was going to throw up.

So, like any rational person would do, I fell in love with a dead person.

I had discovered Greta Garbo on April 16, 1990, the day after she died. The obituary in the *Chicago Tribune* printed a picture of her in *Camille*, and I was enraptured. It was love at first sight. I raced off to the video store and rented every Greta Garbo movie they had, and I spent the next several months watching them over and over. But it really got bad after I stopped drinking. She was elusive and mysterious and so misunderstood. In my

As close to Greta Garbo as I'll ever get.
Me with Greta's star on Hollywood Boulevard.

somewhat obsessive, though chaste, musings, I was her love, the
one person who "got" her. So real were my fantasies that they
seeped into my actual day-to-day existence. If someone asked
how I was and I happened to be in mid-reverie, I would sigh
and say, "I'm wonderful! Just wonderful!" I was in a dopamine-
fueled bliss—based on a fantasy—about a dead person.

In addition to the gift of the black-and-white romantic film
starring me and Greta Garbo running in my head, being a non-
drinker transformed my day-to-day experience. For the first
time in my adult life, I was brushing my teeth and washing my

face before going to bed. I awoke every day at the crack of dawn and was thrilled not to have a hangover. I drank pots of coffee all day long. I found myself eating about a gallon of chocolate ice cream daily to replace the copious amounts of sugar my body was used to from my daily beer intake.

I did, however, continue my habit of taking Nyquil before bed. I wanted oblivion. Though no longer drinking Miller Lite, I was still in need of something to soothe me. The fact that Nyquil had alcohol in it was not something I acknowledged at all. I still considered myself on the wagon.

. . .

AROUND THIS TIME, JILL SOLOWAY MASTERMINDED A deal with theater producer Ron Delsner to bring our production of *The Real Live Brady Bunch* to the Village Gate in New York City. This was not an obvious place to stage a TV parody. Over the course of its thirty-eight-year history, the Village Gate had been home to the likes of Dizzy Gillespie, John Coltrane, and Nina Simone. The nightclub must have been on its last legs when it agreed to book our crazy show, because it closed just a few years later.

Jill's deal for us was a nonunion one that would pay us $900 a week, far more than the union, Equity, was paying. I was the only one in the cast who was a member of Equity, so I used a false name—Greta Wesson—to do the show. "Greta" was a tribute to my beloved, and "Wesson" was for the cooking oil Florence Henderson was hawking on TV. Someone turned me in (I think it was an ex-agent), and Equity wanted me to come before some board of members and plead my case for why I shouldn't be thrown out. "And let me tell ya," some union rep warned me, "we will not have much sympathy for you." Given those odds, I resigned from Equity.

Nine hundred dollars a week was a lot of money to us—more than any of us had ever made. Living in New York City wasn't cheap, so everyone got places together . . . except for me. Truth to tell, no one asked me to bunk up with them. Yes, I was newly sober-ish (still taking Nyquil) and they were not. But I think the real reason they didn't invite me to share an apartment was that I still viewed myself, and thus made myself, separate and outside. I could have piped up and asked, but I felt unable to deal with the possible rejection and humiliation of asking and being turned down. If I had really been using all that new information I was gleaning from *The Seat of the Soul*, I would have seen that my feelings of being alienated and alone were of my own making. But I just couldn't make the leap to reshaping those beliefs.

No one in this group of Brady people was excluding me, and if you were to ask any one of them how they viewed me at this time, they would probably be shocked to learn that I had felt so alienated. They probably thought I just wanted to keep to myself.

So here I was, back in New York. I could only hope this time would go better than the last. My first order of business was to make sure I had a rock-solid, secure place to live. I wanted my own bed, in a place where I wouldn't get kicked out by screaming men in the middle of the night, and where my cohabitants wouldn't make more than me by giving blow jobs. The West Village, where I had lived and suffered over myself, felt heavy and menacing, so I stayed away.

I went down to the Parkside Evangeline house, a "ladies only" residence on Gramercy Park, run by the Salvation Army, where they rented rooms by the week. You had to be interviewed, so I sat down with an old woman who kept referring to "the General" as she told me the rules.

"Now, the General doesn't allow gentleman callers past ten o'clock," she said, like a 1920s schoolmarm. "And not past the second floor after eight P.M. You can get three squares a day down in the cafeteria. And pay your bill on time, on the third floor."

It was as close to a convent as I would ever get, and it was perfect.

My room was tiny and really did remind me of a monk's cell, with just a sink and a twin bed. But I had my own bathroom, which a lot of people didn't, and I had a lovely view of Gramercy Park. The building housed mostly old women who had been there since the forties and could have been Eve Arden in their former life. There were also a fair number of Asian exchange students who were going to NYU. I, as usual, was in a subset all by myself. Rent came out to be a little over $600 a month.

The Real Live Brady Bunch ran for ten months at the Village Gate, and I was miserable the whole time. New York City is packed with people, but I had never felt more alone. When I stopped drinking, I stopped self-medicating and had no way to dull the edges of my anxiety or my loneliness. Though the Nyquil helped at night, the days were empty for me and dragged on. To pass the endless hours before I could leave for the show without being ridiculously early, I'd close the drapes of my tiny room, take a swig of Nyquil, toast with a simple "Bye-bye," and go into a deep sleep.

On a freezing Sunday night in January after our last show of the week, about six months into our run at the Village Gate, we booked the back room of a restaurant in Soho for a private soiree. A couple of people rolled joints and passed them around. Just as in high school, the smell alone made me fear the cops would bust in at any moment—I had smoked pot maybe ten times in my whole life, and it never did anything but make me feel paranoid. But because I was just so tired of being the outsider, I took a puff when the joint was passed my way. I was that desperate to be a part of the group. I also wanted to feel altered. Or maybe I just wanted to feel anything other than what it felt like to be me.

I smoked myself into oblivion that night. I never even felt "high" but went straight to a place of even more severe loneliness and isolation. I hoped someone would notice when I just got up and walked out, but I made it all the way back to the Parkside without anyone catching up to me and asking me if I was okay. The real world wasn't the Brady Bunch. I crawled into bed, just despondent. I had blown my year of sobriety, and for what? I still felt like crap, and even lonelier than I had felt before.

So the next morning, I got up, called Alcoholics Anonymous, and found a meeting. It was January 20, 1992. I was thirty-one years old.

. . .

I DON'T REMEMBER MY VERY FIRST AA MEETING, BUT I do know that I didn't mess around when it came to working the program. To my relief, there was a recipe, rules to follow called the 12 Steps of AA. We all know how I love me some rules. I was no fan of the gray area. So I got the Big Book, I got busy, and I worked all twelve steps in about an hour and a half and said, "Okay, I'm ready to do some service."

I adored going to meetings. Because of the Irish DNA dancing in my person, I've always been drawn to storytelling. The hero's journey that Joseph Campbell talked and wrote about has always fascinated me. In the rooms of AA, I was captivated by the courage and the extraordinary effort it takes to face an addiction and come out the other side transformed. What is facing an addiction and getting sober if not a hero's journey? I ate those drunkalogues up. They inspired me. I was convinced that in these meetings, the real stuff of life was going on and being talked about. The emotional honesty and good humor blew me away. I was all ears.

I did sometimes have a bit of drunkalogue envy. Had I known that in AA one of the things you do is tell your drinking story over and over, I would have made mine much more interesting. My own story was unmistakably bland. First, I drank only Miller Lite. Second, many of my contemporaries drank far more than I and were fine with themselves and their lives. They did not suffer it the way I did. In AA there would be one dramatic story after another, with people losing everything to drugs and booze. And here I was with my Miller Lite and morning hangovers and some occasional unremembered vomit in the bathroom. Some of the stories I heard in the rooms of AA were so endless, horrible, and tragic that I would have to stop myself from screaming at them "At what point did you hit bottom?!" I guess what I'm saying is: when I stopped, I had reached *my* limit. I knew that my mind, body, and spirit had just had it.

Despite being a girl looking for excuses to feel different, unworthy, and separate, my not-so-exciting drinking backstory did not prevent me from feeling a kinship. I felt the very same feelings many of the people in AA spoke of: alienation, self-contempt, and obsession. I felt like I'd come home and I couldn't wait to get to a meeting every day, and sometimes I'd hit two.

I also experimented with a new version of myself. I wanted not just to try on a different "me," but also to feel more a part of the Brady gang. Grunge was in, and the Urban Outfitters that had just opened on Sixth Avenue was selling it. All the girls in the cast either shopped there or looked like they had. Skirts, plaid, and cowboy boots were a hot look in this circle. I was not much of a skirt wearer, so my interpretation of this look was long underwear bottoms that I wore *under* flannel boxer shorts, plus the boots. This would have been an excellent choice if my goal had been to look like a homeless cowhand. I also stopped shaving my legs and underarms, which was actually somewhat fashionable at the time. This was a fairly radical departure for me, as heretofore I'd been a fan of Peter Pan collars. Like a character you grow into by putting on the wardrobe, I loosened up, accessed my inner earth mother, and found some compassion for myself.

I became obsessed with the Indigo Girls and started to write my own music, tunes with titles like "A Blood Red Tear Stains My Face" and "I Gave You the Gun to Shoot Me." I think I was trying to impose some Sturm und Drang on my story, so I wouldn't feel so woefully inadequate in the drama department. Though they were written in earnest, I would use one of the songs years later to get huge laughs in a one-person show.

I started taking yoga and began reading *Goddesses in Every-woman* by Jean Shinoda Bolen. She wrote about the stories of goddesses and how these classic figures exemplify aspects of every female self. I fell in love with her notion of archetypes and that they live in all of us. I used this idea to methodically take apart my own psyche and apply a goddess to each proclivity. My inability to connect intimately with another human being was the goddess Artemis operating in my psyche; she rode solo, was chaste and immune to love. My one-track mind and ability to focus on a goal to the exclusion of all else was my inner Athena. I looked for the goddesses operating in others as well. It was a methodical and organized way to understand something that overwhelmed me. Reductionist, yes, ridiculous, perhaps, but it inspired me and helped me to understand my own self and the world.

It was the exploration of my inner Aphrodite that led me to the 10th Street Baths in the East Village. Wednesday was Ladies Day, and I was enraptured from the first moment. All stone walls and wooden benches, the place made me feel like I'd been transported way back in time to the Isle of Lesbos. Naked ladies of all shapes and sizes lounged about and luxuriated themselves like Greek goddesses. In the steam room I saw one woman comb conditioner into the hair of another. Next to the baths, an impromptu yoga class was doing downward facing dog while giving the rest of us an anatomy lesson. The cold wading pool was filled with the freshly steamed. I left all body shame at the door, and on that first day, I did it all: I steamed, I sauna-ed, I dunked my naked body in the cold water, and I sipped hot tea. At the end of the day I had a massage with a Russian man named Boris who said I could call him Bob. As he rubbed baby oil farther and farther up the inside of my thigh he purred, "I am like doctor, yes?"

I left thoroughly uplifted and full of bliss. I also took home a yeast infection and a cold sore on my lip, but I went back the next week.

I started going to AA meetings at the Gay and Lesbian Community Center on 13th Street in the West Village, not because I was looking for love (in fact, relationships and sex were the furthest things from my mind) but because all the best "circuit" speakers seemed to pop up there. Circuit speakers were sought after and known for their awesome stories of transformation. Mostly, these were drug addicts who had been at death's door and who, through AA and finding a power greater than themselves, had been reborn.

I also met one of my best friends, Laura Coyle, through that Center, though she never was in AA herself. When I started going to AA meetings, I met her girlfriend, Trixie, a triple Leo who basically sucked up all the energy in a room, including the energy that was Laura Coyle. Laura has never been a shrinking violet, but in the glare of Trixie, she was kind of a vague background haze. . . . That is, until one day in yoga class.

I was a devotee of Integral Yoga, which was across the street from the Gay and Lesbian Community Center. After we'd go through all the asanas and breathing exercises, stretching and energizing every muscle in our bodies and exchanging all the stale air in our lungs for fresh, we would chant. This was my absolute favorite part. In a half lotus, I'd rock back and forth and bliss out to the experience of sound resonating in my body. It felt like my soul was being massaged, and I just loved it. On the day that Laura Coyle became something other than a vague presence to me, we had a substitute teacher. When this female instructor I'd never seen before began to lead us in the chant, I couldn't believe what I was hearing. She sounded like Miss Hathaway from *The Beverly Hillbillies*: thin and reedy voice, and absolutely no ear or rhythm. *Why is this happening? Who allowed this?* Appalled, I opened my eyes and looked around the room. *Am I the only one who notices this?* I caught the eye of Laura Coyle, who, unbeknownst to me, was also taking this class. I saw she was having the same experience of yogic horror, and as that recognition passed between us, we started to giggle. I looked away and dropped my head forward so I wouldn't laugh out loud, but of course I had to look up at her again. Laura was doubled over. When she looked up at me, I saw she had tears running down her cheeks and that her shoulders had started to shake, and I lost it. I was lucky I didn't pee through

New best buddies. Me and Laura in the yoga changing room.

the long underwear I was wearing for everything now, including yoga.

And with that, a lifelong friendship was born.

Throughout my life, friends would come and go. Laura stayed. Although in the glare of her girlfriend Trixie she had seemed almost retiring, I would very quickly discover her huge and loving energy. She is the most emotionally available person I've ever met. However, her blasting energy and love of life are not for the faint of heart. Her humor is fast and manic and goofy; she will tweak your nipple after just meeting you. In later years we would watch episodes of *Absolutely Fabulous* together. She is the perfect Edina to my Patsy, and she would go all-out to re-enact moments from the show for me because she knew how much it slayed me.

We were in a crowded Sears one day and it was over one hundred degrees outside. While I was waiting in line to pay she said, "Watch." She walked out the automatic glass doors in full view of everyone in the store, and when she hit the heat outside, à la the "Morocco" episode, she collapsed into a heap on the pavement. Who would do that for a friend?! Laura Coyle, that's who.

We would find something hilarious and play the joke to each other all day long. Like the day we kept seeing empty strollers all over Santa Monica. We walked all over yelling to each other in horror, *"Where are all the babies?!"* The humor would usually be lost on others long before it would die for us as we'd play it over and over. Laura would say, "We just *killed* that!"

Laura is a singer/songwriter. Her voice is incredibly beautiful, and she plays the guitar as if it were an extension of her very soul. She writes fantastic songs, and she holds the stage like few others. She can be singing about the joy of falling in love in one moment, and making you cry the next with a song about loss. Offstage she makes these emotional jumps with nary a transition. She can be cracking up about something in one moment and then crying about the plight of dolphins in the next. She has great compassion and can easily take on the suffering of others. I always say "Now, don't go global on me!"

When I met Laura in New York, I had always been quick to end friendships. I would semiconsciously build a case against them, and at some point it would come to a head and I'd have to say, "I'm outta here." Laura would not let me do this, though I tried in dramatic fashion more than once.

The closest I came to succeeding was in 1998 when we were roommates in Los Angeles. We were hiking the ridge up Runyon Canyon, talking. I had been resenting what I interpreted as her flirtation with a woman I had a crush on. All the way up the ridge, I built a case against her. I needed her to admit it, and apologize, but she would have none of it. I got all worked up, and by the time we hit the top I was yelling and she was crying. She could not admit what she didn't believe she'd done, and I could not let go of what I thought I'd seen. So I said, "That's it! If you won't cop to this, I am through with you."

We walked down the hill and got into the car in silence. I was a wreck, still hurt that she wouldn't tell me what I wanted to hear, but more than that I was afraid I had gone too far with my anger. I had pushed her away, and I found myself terrified that she would actually go. But Laura said, "You know, Jane. I'm not going anywhere." And I started to cry.

It had never occurred to me that a friendship could survive a huge blowout like that. I tended to whip up a gigantic outrage (something at which I excel) so that I could dump my friends before they dumped me. I believed it was "one strike and you're out."

But Laura and I have been friends for twenty years now. I credit the longevity of our friendship to that moment in the car at Runyon Canyon. It was the turning point for me. Trust replaced tests.

. . .

THE REAL LIVE BRADY BUNCH RAN FOR TEN MONTHS in New York, and then in 1992 the Soloways took it to Los Angeles, to the Westwood Playhouse (now the Geffen Playhouse). I went to the Chase Manhattan Bank in New York and withdrew my life's savings—$10,000—and lit out for Hollywood.

We all got apartments in Westwood, at a huge student housing–type building on Le Conte and Gayley, a bit down the street and across the road from the theater. Again, everyone bunked up together except for me. I got a huge one-bedroom that I furnished sparsely from a furniture rental place on Wilshire. It was all very white-lacquered and faux Southwestern. It looked more like a cheap hotel in Phoenix than a home.

Laura and Trixie called me on opening night to say break a leg. They also gave me the great news that they were about to make the cross-country trip via Route 66 to Los Angeles. Trixie was thinking of opening a restaurant in town, and Laura was still in her shadow, following along. "Hiding her light under a bushel," as her mom would say. Though I had only known Laura for a few months, I was thrilled to have my pal on her way to me.

I was nursing a huge, naive crush on Laura at this point, too.

I chastely idealized her and daydreamed about having her sing just for me: any thought of sex or carnal desires would have sullied it. Her music made me swoon as I listened to it on cassette tapes in my car and on a boom box in my cavernous apartment. She wrote such beautiful songs of longing and lost love, and I lost myself in the quiet yearning and almost mournful quality of the words. I *exalted* her. She became an ethereal goddess to me.

Now, if you met Laura Coyle, the last word you would use to describe her is ethereal. She is firmly on the ground. But such was the extent of my projection, and my need for an enchanted love that lived only in the confines of my own imagination. I really don't think I wanted Laura to be my girlfriend, but I did want her to let me fantasize about how perfect our love could be. I chose the wrong girl.

Laura arrived and we started hanging out all the time. She and Trixie moved into an apartment on Speedway, the last street before you hit the Pacific Ocean in Venice Beach. They convinced me to move from my apartment in Westwood to a second-floor ocean-view studio a few buildings down the street from them. It was tiny but clean and open and only eight hundred bucks a month. I was tickled pink that these gals wanted me. I also secretly prayed for the demise of Laura's relationship with Trixie, so that I could have the fantasy of her all to myself.

Laura was on to me. "What's up with you, Jane? Are you in love with me?" "What?!" I would say incredulously. "Think highly of yourself much?" She said, "You're all goo-goo-eyed right now and I want to know what's going on with you." I'd dismiss her, hoping she couldn't see what she was obviously very hip to. Damn if she wasn't trying to kill my crush for me by making me come down to earth and talk about it. Reality always kills a good fantasy. I hated to lose this one, but as the good times continued to roll with Laura and I got to see more and more of who she really was, our true real-life friendship solidified itself. In other words, I gradually stopped projecting on to her who I thought I wanted her to be and fell in love with my friendship with the real Laura.

So much so that when she told me she and Trixie were going back to New York, I was devastated. They had moved me all the way out to Venice Beach, away from the only friends I had (such as they were), only to leave me alone, again.

Right before Laura left, she looked me directly in the eye and said, "Please don't think I'm abandoning you."

She knew me well. I didn't want to be known that well. I wanted her to know the good and funny me, not this dark and tender me. I, of course, denied that I would be affected in the least by her absence and urged her to have a great trip! But I'd never felt as alone as I did in those days after Laura left.

After Laura's exit, Venice Beach revealed itself as an increasingly unfriendly and hostile place. I had to park in a lot a few blocks from my apartment, and I'd walk down Speedway at night, jumping at every noise. I always thought I was going to get raped. My head, which is usually a very busy place, would fill up with gruesome images of what could happen to me.

I couldn't even get joy out of living by the ocean. The vast expanse of blue extending to the horizon made me feel frighteningly insignificant, so I kept my shades closed at all times. If I happened to catch people walking down the beach, I would wonder why they were so happy when I was not.

One night, an earthquake rocked my little apartment just as

I was taking a middle-of-the-night pee. The shower curtain rolled back and forth on the rod and I couldn't stop peeing quickly enough. I took this as an act of nature aimed aggressively and directly at me.

Then in the very early morning hours of July 14—my thirty-second birthday—I awoke to a bloodcurdling scream. I looked out my window to see a guy with a shaved head and covered with tattoos, obviously drunk, brandishing a machete at another guy and cutting him, just slicing him up. There was blood all over the pavement, I could hear sirens coming, and I just thought, *WHAT THE FUCK! IT'S MY BIRTHDAY!*

While this certainly didn't endear me to my beach apartment, it did make for a rather witty share at my AA meeting that day. I got laughs and lots of "Happy Birthday"s out of it. Most people thought I'd been in AA for years because of the way I told stories. I spoke at a lot of meetings and turned down a lot of women who wanted me to be their sponsor. Thinking back on it, I probably could've made some good friends. I just couldn't get past the fear that once they got to know me, they would be disappointed. So I walked around like a circuit speaker, and I acted as if I knew and liked who I was—even though on the inside I was feeling more and more like a fraud and a dark mess.

During the day I was fine because I was busy and had the comfort of routine. Every day started with coffee, then a meeting in the morning, errands, a nummy lunch out at one of my favorite joints in the afternoon, and then the show at night. But by the time I took the terrifying walk from my parking space to my apartment, I was so sad and alone. I went to bed that way, and throughout the night I would wake up darkly depressed.

Once, in the middle of the night, during a time when I was almost paralyzed with grief, I awoke from a deep sleep into a vivid illusion. Lying in bed, I felt warm, loving arms go around me, as if someone were holding me. Though there was no one there, I was suffused with a feeling of pure love and comfort, and I fell back into my deep sleep. I was in the car in the early afternoon of the next day when, with a start, I remembered it. I had the distinct feeling that *I was not alone*. It was such a relief.

Soon after, I met the woman who would help me make my next huge leap. I found her at a women's AA meeting. She was in her late fifties, with a solemn, world-weary demeanor. Though she was quiet most of the time, when she did speak, everyone leaned in to listen. Her compassion was palpable. I never knew exactly what her story was, but I had shared something at a meeting one day that had to do with feeling disconnected from my family. I don't remember exactly what I said, but it was one of those honest, revealing things I regretted saying as soon as it came out of my mouth. After the meeting, she came up to me and said, "I can hear how painful this is for you and how much you love your family, and just know it is never too late." I felt I had been heard and *gotten*. I found out she was a therapist. I went to a few more of these meetings before I asked if I could make an appointment with her.

The time had come for me to do something about feeling so alone. I had slowly but surely been distancing myself from my mom and dad for years. Julie and Bob were barely on my radar. Julie had gotten married and had four kids I barely knew. Though I knew where he worked, I wasn't really sure what Bob did for a living or if he had a girlfriend. Family was supposed to be your rock; mine felt like something I had set sail from a long, long time ago. Why had I cut myself off from them, when I really loved them? It was the gay thing. I still hadn't told them.

I went home every year for Christmas, and we would spend time together doing holiday stuff. But the conversation always stayed on the surface of things, and I talked mostly about my career. What personal details I did share didn't land as I wanted them to. For instance, I told them I was in AA, and they just didn't get it. My mom told me she thought I was just going through a drinking phase in college. Later she told me she thought I joined AA because I wanted attention. It wasn't something I could convince her of. I hadn't only drunk less than most people in AA, I looked like a lightweight next to many members of the extended family. I remember hearing about an uncle on my mom's side who lost a leg due to gangrene from alcohol poisoning. When I suggested that he might have been an alcoholic, as people do not normally lose limbs to moderate drinking, my mom dismissed me with "No, he just liked to have a good time."

I was extremely edgy during those visits. With so many things unsaid, I became very short and critical with everyone. They all felt uncomfortable, too, and I could feel them walking on eggshells around me. They weren't asking, and I wasn't telling.

But we went right on visiting. One time, when they came to visit me in my beach house of sadness, I showed them some recent Brady pictures. My dad saw one photo of a couple of guy friends with their arms around each other. He pinched up his face and pointed to it and said, "What's with those guys? Are they gay together?" I could hear the nail in the coffin of self-disclosure. I was sure I would never tell them I was gay.

So, back to the wise late-middle-aged lady therapist. I told her all about my relationship with my family. She quite simply asked me, "Do you want to lose them?" I said no. So she said to write my parents a letter. "You don't have to send it," she said. "Tell them how you feel about them and why you want them in your life. Tell them why you've distanced yourself from them and what you're afraid they will do if they knew this about you. Then come back next week and read it to me.

"Again, you don't have to send it."

Now, we all know where this is going. Therapists always tell you that you can write the letter, but you don't have to send it. Because no one will ever read it, you pour your heart out in writing it. Then, you anxiously read it to your therapist, hoping to be heard and approved of. At this point the therapist gives you a nudge—all it takes at that point is a nudge—and you put the damn stamp on it. It is a ruse. If you don't want to end up sending the letter, don't write it.

But the thing was, I wanted to fix these relationships. As I wrote the letter, my love for my mom and dad flowed freely. I realized how much I missed them and what fabulous people my parents are. It was absolutely honest. I wrote that I could feel us drifting apart, and that a lot of it had to do with who I was: that I was gay, and that although I hadn't had any real relationships yet, whenever I did it would be with a woman. I told them that I wanted them to know this, so we could be closer.

I finished the letter and I felt good about how I'd expressed myself. I was able to articulate my fears, and my hopes for the future, and the whole thing was just very cathartic. When I read the letter out loud in therapy, I got all choked up and felt like I might hurl. My lady therapist said, "That's lovely."

Like I said, all it takes is a nudge. . . . I said, "I think I'll send it." She said, "Okay."

Then I had to drop it in the mailbox. I had to physically let it go, and I literally shook as it fell from my fingers. I immediately worried about my mother and what she would say to her friends. Would she be ashamed or embarrassed? Then I thought of how confused my dad might be. He wasn't a homophobe, but this was so far from his experience. He didn't understand "gay." *What have I just done?* And then the mailbox clanged shut, and it was gone.

I ran home and called my brother, Bob, at work back in Chicago. "Are you sitting down?" I asked.

"Oh my god," Bob said. "What's going on?"

"I just sent Mom and Dad a letter about something they don't know about me."

"Okay . . . ," Bob said, his voice tight.

". . . I told them I'm gay."

"Ahh!" Bob said, sounding relieved. "That's it? I thought you were sick, like you had AIDS or cancer or something. Don't worry about it. I'll tell them the letter's coming, and to call me when it gets there."

I was so nervous in the two or three days it took for the letter to get there. But when it did, my mom opened it and read it out loud to my dad. When she finished, they looked at each other, and he said, "That's okay, right?" And she said, "Of course it's okay!" Then, as she later told me, she took the letter over to my sister Julie's house and read it to her. Everybody was very sympathetic and understanding and kind of concerned for me—for how I was dealing with it. They all wanted me to know it was okay; everything was all right.

Just like Bob, my mom had been worried I was trying to tell them I had some sort of disease. This was understandable given that the preamble to the letter was something like "I have to share a secret that I've been keeping inside, something very important, but if I don't tell you, you'll never know a vital part of me. . . ." It took me ages in the letter to get around to saying I was gay. So when we talked on the phone next, my mom said, "We were just glad you weren't sick."

. . .

AS IT TURNED OUT, MY MOM AND DAD HAD EACH WON-dered whether I was gay, but they had never talked about it with each other. This surprised me because they talked about everything, especially sex. They had always tried to get us to talk about the birds and bees when we were young, and we would have none of it. We were prudish children. But I guess homosexuality was just out of their area of expertise, so they steered clear of talking about it, even with each other. They hadn't known anyone who was gay (and out). But now they knew me, and they loved me.

They really stepped up after I told them, even in their politics. A Reagan Democrat, my dad did not care for Bill Clinton at all. But in 1992, he voted for him. I was shocked. I asked my mom what had possessed my dad to vote for Bill Clinton. She said because "he was for the gays." (You'll recall that Clinton campaigned on the promise that he would end the ban on homosexuals in the military. Of course, he would go "halfway" and sign Don't Ask Don't Tell into law. Not exactly a gay-friendly policy.)

But my mom, bless her, still had one question that was obviously bugging her.

"What about Ronny Howard?"

7

Angry Lady

I N THE AUTUMN OF 1992, WHEN *THE REAL LIVE Brady Bunch* was about to end its run at the Westwood Playhouse, Steppenwolf Theatre asked me to audition for their winter show, *Inspecting Carol* by Daniel Sullivan, a farcical comedy about a small-time theater company putting on a production of *A Christmas Carol*. I flew back home to Chicago on my own nickel to read for them, and as soon as I got back to LA to finish the *Brady Bunch* run, I got a call that I'd been cast, meaning I would have to leave *The Brady Bunch* a week shy of its final show to start rehearsals in Chicago. I returned my furniture to the rental place, threw out my smelly Brady clothes, and left my red VW Golf with Andy Richter. (Andy would amass over $600 in parking tickets. He finally paid up when he got the job as a writer, and eventual cohost, for Conan O'Brien.)

This time, coming home to Chicago was magical. I moved in with Jill and Faith Soloway's mom, Elaine. She had been divorced from their dad, a Freudian analyst, for a couple of years and was on her own hero's journey. She had spent twenty-plus years of marriage neglecting her own needs and desires and was embarking on the adventure of "finding herself" as an independent adult, just like I was.

She had a cool town house in a newly developed area near Clybourne and Armitage, on the north side. As soon as I hit town, I moved into the basement. The whole thing felt like a metaphor—I had found refuge in a safe, warm, maternal womb kind of place. I was still reading my goddess books, so the symbolism meant a lot to me. I felt protected.

Elaine and I would have coffee and talk every day, after her morning run. She worked for herself, having started a PR company post-divorce. We really connected. I trusted her enough to talk about what was going on in my life, even things I still felt self-conscious about, like being in AA. She supported me and would tell me what an open heart I had. I felt nurtured and that she *got* me. For me, the feeling that someone understood me was so important and felt so good.

Soon, her new boyfriend, Don, started to join us. He was recently divorced as well. Perhaps in rebellious response to her ex's Freudian bent, Elaine loved Don's fascination with Jungian thought. They both were really small and Jewish, and I was this big Aryan person coming to the breakfast table looking for a hug. We would start every morning with Don saying in his gravelly voice, "Tell me about your dreams last night, Janie."

I ate it up. I was in my great period of self-preoccupation, and so I was utterly captivated by my own inner landscape, including my dreams. I kept a microcassette voice recorder at my bedside to capture them upon waking. Don would then analyze them for me over breakfast, and I was a rapt audience. "Don't be afraid of the shadow, Janie," he would say. "It's where the most fertile material lives." This piece of advice would actually be the key to my integrating all this navel-gazing into something productive.

What I came to know was that it was the shadow, the great unclaimed areas of the psyche, that my best work would come out of. If I feel proud of anything I've done in my acting career, it came from the stuff that is hard to look at; stuff that feels sticky and dark. These parts tend to want to stay far from the light of day, as they conjure fear or shame. At the time I was living with Elaine and Don, I was just getting to know my own vulnerable, tender parts. I hadn't yet learned how valuable these places are creatively.

Don was always very loving, always asking questions and taking as much interest in me as I did in myself. He reminded me of Ira Glick and Boris Lorwin, the PR team who put up with me in New York. I love the little Jewish guys, and they love me. Jill and Faith, however, did not cotton to him at all. To them, he was the new-agey pervert *schtupping* their mom.

I started going to AA meetings in the neighborhood, on the first floor of an old Chicago-style three-story walk-up on Shef- field Avenue. The noon meeting always had a bunch of guys on their lunch hour—good old Chicago guys, some of them blue collar, some running their own businesses, all of them sober ten-plus years, which sounded like an eternity to me. This group embraced me and I became one of them. Most of them had been meth addicts and had stories like you wouldn't believe: "Hi, my name is so-and-so, and I'm an alcoholic. I destroyed my family, my kids won't talk to me, and I basically ruined all our lives. I once chained myself to a radiator so I wouldn't take cocaine, but I found a knife and cut away at it. . . ." But the end- ings were all happy, because the guys were here and could laugh about it. These guys had repaired their lives and relationships, so when new people came in off the street still ensconced in their own horrendous stories, they found hope in this room. I didn't realize until much later that many people, including people in that room, went in and out of AA, having periods of sobriety interspersed with periods of addiction. But these guys seemed like they would be okay forever, and this made me feel safe. Between Elaine and Don and my AA guys, I could feel that vise grip around my heart loosening up.

I met a lovely girl named Holly at these meetings. She had been sober for a few years and then stopped going to meetings, only to get her ass kicked again. I met her at her first meeting back in the program, the day after her last walk of shame after having boozed it up good. We saw each other quite a bit at the meetings, and I thought she was so cute. I would stare at her hands—she had kind of a round baby face, but her hands were long and elegant, and I wanted to hold one of them. I didn't dare, of course, because not only did the thought of intimacy make my insides churn, but I was crushing out on a straight girl.

One day when we were talking rather deeply and intimately, I felt like she was going to ask me to be her sponsor, but she asked me out instead. I guess she wasn't *that* straight.

. . .

HOLLY JOINED OUR LITTLE JUNGIAN COFFEE KLATCH. It was Don, Elaine, Holly, and me, all of us pretty much on the same page, journey-wise. Don and Elaine were post-divorce, and Holly and I were freshly sober. We felt like we were all seeing the world with fresh eyes, and that anything was possible. It was heavenly. Caffeine was my new drug, and, overindulgent as usual, I drank way too much of it. I shook all day long and felt very anxious. I had to mete out my intake throughout the day so that I wouldn't jump out of my skin, which meant I was always wanting a little more. This wasn't a bad problem to have, overall, since life otherwise was feeling pretty good. I was dating a cutie pie, living in a womblike basement, working as an actor in a good play, and making money doing radio voice-overs for the Spiegel catalogue.

Things got even better when a call came from out of nowhere that I had an offer for a role in the Harrison Ford film coming to town: *The Fugitive*. It would be directed by Andy Davis, a native Chicagoan himself, who had a bunch of successful action films under his belt. It turned out that a friend of Jill Soloway had seen me in *The Real Live Brady Bunch* and told Andy that he should cast me. I still have no idea what the friend saw in my Carol Brady that would make her think I could play a forensic scientist, but I got the part.

This was a huge deal—my first big Hollywood movie. I played Dr. Kathy Wahlund, a researcher and forensic scientist who helps Richard Kimble prove his innocence. As was so often the case with parts I played, it was originally written for a man. It wasn't a big part, but I would have scenes with Harrison Ford. And I was getting paid eight grand for it, which seemed like a ton of money at the time.

I got a call from a wardrobe person who was coming from San Francisco to do the movie. "This is my idea for your character," she said. "In the script it says you wear a leather jacket, but I think that says 'lesbian.' This part was originally written for a man, and I think they want to make you mannish, and

I'm not going to let them. So I'm gonna put you in something else."

"Whoa, whoa, wait a minute," I said—being an actor in stage shows, I was used to being listened to when it came to character. "I think it's important that the leather jacket is in, because in the script, when I'm revealed, the first shot is of my leather jacket. It says something about my character."

She didn't like this. "The script can be changed and probably will be changed and you don't tell me how to design costumes," she said. "I'm trying to build a character here."

"I think that's my job," I snarked. When we hung up, I was terrified they would fire me.

I got a call from my agent the next day. "You'll wear a burlap sack if they want you to," she said. I scared easily back then, so I gave in.

I showed up for the first fitting and discovered that Wardrobe had bombarded my white lab coat with buttons sporting political messages: "Hate Is Not a Family Value," "Mind Your Own Uterus," etc., slogans that had more to do with the wardrobe person's agenda than with my character's. She had a thing about Hollywood being run by men and all the stories being male-centered. But who doesn't? "You're one of the only women in this hospital, and damn it, I'm gonna make my statement," she declared. I didn't want to fight, but I couldn't stop myself. I said, "Look, I'm a liberal, I support these causes. But you don't just impose this stuff onto a char—"

"Listen, Jane," she interrupted, and proceeded to tell me all the liberal organizations she volunteered for and the ones she gave money to. Then she told me that she had adopted a black child. I could think of no acceptable response but to go along with my character wearing the buttons. Later, a friend said, "You should have told her, 'Well, I have a black inner child.' "

My first day of shooting, I was at the craft services table and I saw in my periphery that Harrison Ford was walking up behind me. I was trying to play it cool, but I was starstruck. And he was walking up on my deaf side, so I wouldn't be able to hear it if he was talking to me. But what if he just wanted a sandwich, then would I look like a goofy fan? I gave up and turned to look at him.

"Jane!" he said, a bit exasperated, like I hadn't heard him the first time. "Are you okay with your wardrobe?" he asked. Obviously, word had gotten to him.

"Oh, yeah," I said, casually. "Everything worked out, thanks for asking." He'd asked me actor-to-actor—kind of like "Is everything square?" like we were in cahoots, rather than critically, like "I hear there's some trouble between you and Wardrobe." Which made me think he was on my side if I needed him.

And that was how I met Harrison Ford. He was always really nice to me, and I really enjoyed working with him. There was tension on the set between him and the director, Andy Davis. Harrison is an inner-directed guy, so if he didn't like something, he'd just kind of fume silently. I was a little afraid of him in those moments, as he could do some powerful silent fuming, but overall, we got along well.

He taught me a few things as well. Once, he took me aside and said, "Jane, this scene is shit. Let's you and me go into my trailer and work it out." It was raining, and he put his arm around me and pulled me under his umbrella as we walked.

His trailer had that dank man-smell to it. He had a bottle of Scotch, and he poured himself a glass and said, "Okay, here's what we're gonna do." And we figured the scene out—the one where we're at the microscope looking at liver samples, and I'm supposed to say something like "It shows a lot of periportal inflammation loaded with eosinophils." As I remember, we simplified it and made it actable, and I couldn't stop thinking, *I'm holding my own with Harrison Ford.*

During another scene, he leaned in and gave me one of the best pieces of acting advice I had received in a while: "If you leave your mouth open, no matter how smart you are, you still look stupid." My mouth closed immediately. (However, for some characters I *choose* to leave my mouth open.)

Of course, my family was thrilled that I was in a movie with a real Hollywood star. During the time we were shooting *The Fugitive,* my uncle Bill died, and when I went to the funeral and walked up to my aunt Betty and said, "I'm so sorry," she looked up at me and said, "What's Harrison Ford like?"

. . .

SUDDENLY IT SEEMED THAT HOLLY HAD BROKEN UP WITH me. She didn't say so, but all of a sudden she was curiously absent. When I heard from someone at the meeting we both went to that she was seeing a guy, I felt like I'd been punched in the gut. I remember thinking, *I can't compete with a guy.* But looking back, I realize that the gender of her new love was irrelevant. It was truly a case of our time being up. We were to be together for a season, as they say. I wasn't in love and neither was she. But still, I took the opportunity to suffer over this perceived rejection, as I had when I had been fired from the Civic Opera House, or when I left the Shakespeare Company and

The Second City. The gig was up and it had to end some way or another, but I always chose the path of *woe is me*. This time, I ran away from my pain by going back to Los Angeles.

Moving also made sense professionally. *The Fugitive* would open that fall of '93, and if I was in LA, I could capitalize on it. I said good-bye to Elaine and Don. Before I left, I had a lunch date with Holly where *I* did the official breaking up. She graciously accepted my need to be the one to call it off, and she wished me well.

I bought a round-trip plane ticket going out to LA on September 1, 1993, and returning to Chicago on October 1. But I never used the return half of that ticket.

I got an apartment on Cheremoya Avenue in Beachwood Canyon, down the street from Jill Soloway and a hop and a skip from most of the Brady contingent. It was a little studio apartment in an old Spanish building with lots of windows and good light. Every day, I woke up to sunshine. I could look out at all the bougainvillea and the hummingbirds darting from flower to flower. The hills and valleys of the canyon had a rugged beauty in which I felt nestled and calm. I was starting to feel LA's charm.

After my many years of transience, I had figured out what to do to make a "home" for myself. I set up my LA life with all of my essential comforts in place. I loved my apartment, as tiny and spare as it was. I had a little coffeemaker and a kind of Mary Tyler Moore setup, with a pony wall between the kitchen and living room. I picked up a dining room table off the side of the road on Beachwood Drive. I got myself a rescue kitten, whom I named after my first true obsession, Greta. I burned sage and said Indian prayers before bed. I still had that voice recorder next to my bed so I could mumble unintelligibly into it post-dream. And I secured myself a bunch of very powerful women's-only AA meetings to go to and attended a meeting every day of the week.

To do AA by the book, you need to have a sponsor. I'm a rule-follower, so I set out to find me one. I feared this process like I feared intimate relationships: it was fraught with the same kind of emotional danger and could easily result in rejection. Even if I escaped snubbing, choosing a new person to be in my life was usually accompanied by a lesson that felt like a sharp stick in the eye.

Soon after returning to LA, I was at one of my women's meetings when I felt a cool breeze with the faint scent of disapproval. When I found its source, I immediately thought I'd found my new sponsor. She was hip, maybe a bit older than me, with spiky hair and a stern countenance, so I sort of sidled up to her, and, though not jumping up and down about it, she agreed to have coffee with me.

Before I had even put cream in my coffee, she said, "I assume you want me to sponsor you." Not much for chitchat, this one. She very methodically laid out her sponsoring style and how she worked with spons-ees, or her "babies" as she called them. Although her use of the word "babies" in reference to full-grown people gave me pause, I kept going forward as though I had yet to see the red flag waving.

"Does this mean you are agreeing to sponsor me?" I asked. I wasn't sure how this worked. "That's your choice, Jane. I am at your service. But before you decide, come to my home group meeting tonight at eight P.M. You can meet all my other babies."

Of course I went to the meeting. I walked into the appointed room at the appointed time and saw my would-be sponsor sitting in a chair, rocking back and forth, bawling her eyes out. A bunch of women, some of whom I assume were her "babies," were kind of holding her in a group embrace and cooing as she moaned and groaned. I didn't know what to do. I just sat down in an empty chair across the room from them, filled with dread.

I searched my mind frantically. *What did I do?* I racked my brain. I was certain that somehow my fifteen minutes of coffee and conversation with this woman earlier in the day had caused her to have the nervous breakdown I was witnessing. I thought I was such a bad person that I could have that kind of huge, instantaneously negative effect on someone. There's a saying in AA about how in the same moment we can be both self-condemning and grandiose: *I'm the biggest piece of shit in the world.* I excelled at this.

The meeting started, and I could barely listen for my self-mortification. I wanted the hour to end so I could ask her what it was I had done. And then, all of a sudden, it hit me—*boing!* This had NOTHING to do with me. I felt a wave of relief, an internal shift like I had just had a chiropractic adjustment. I realized that I had made something that had nothing to do with me into something that was all about me.

I saw that I had been doing this all my life. When I was a kid, my mom was easily annoyed, and I always figured it was me bugging her. After growing up like that, I was forever making myself the cause of other people's pain. It was self-centered and rendered me incapable of compassion for others, because I'm no good to anybody else when it's all about me. And frankly, most things have nothing to do with me. It was very adolescent, really. I got it, suddenly and profoundly.

I later found out that my would-be sponsor had been upset that her boyfriend had cheated on her. I got to know her a bit later, and she was nice enough, but also a bit of a drama queen. They say that when you choose a sponsor, you should *want what they have*. I passed.

In settling into my LA life, I reunited with my Brady Bunch friends and began doing stage sketch shows with them. We rented out theaters and put on shows that inevitably ended with us singing songs in our underwear. I also got an agent. This was no small feat, as one can go years without getting an agent in Los Angeles. If you don't have an agent, getting a job is pretty much impossible. My agency in Chicago had a branch office in LA, so I met with an agent there. During our meeting, his first item of business was to hop up on his desk to show me his Mae West impression. Then he sat me down to lay out his personal rules of the road. I was never to call him—he would call me. He didn't do small talk on the phone, so please don't ask him how his day was going. It went on and on.

This agency would probably be classified as mid- to low-level, which means there were lots people behind desks who had "power" issues. These agents will find ways to impress upon you that they hold the keys to the kingdom you want, and if you don't appreciate them often, they will never call you with a job. Actors want to work. Most of us would sell our souls to the devil to get a crack at a job, and we will hand over our power so fast it would make your head spin. And beggars can't be choosers, so I signed with these people and I endured.

The Fugitive would be coming out soon, and since I had a featured role (if not a big one), these new people took some interest in me. My first audition was for a part on a new and soon-to-be-canceled show called *Joe's Life* starring Peter Onorati. Not at all aware of the irony, my new agent told me that what made this sitcom unique was that the comedy came out of the situation.

My first time out and damn if I didn't book the job. My heart was pounding when I called my mom to tell her the big news. She met my enthusiasm with a sincere, if oddly directed, query: "What will you wear?"

I played a saleslady trying to help Joe of *Joe's Life* find a birthday present for his wife in the women's wear department. Hilarity would ensue.

The prop department asked me what to put on my employee name tag, and I told them Eileen, which was my mom's name. In a tribute to my mom's enormous concern about my wardrobe, her name would literally be what I was wearing. I told my dad, and it was our big secret. But when the show aired, I asked my mom what she thought when she saw the name tag. She said, completely deadpan, "I didn't read it."

. . .

SUFFICE IT TO SAY, THERE WERE NO MACHETE-WIELDING madmen in my life in LA this time around, like there had been back in Venice Beach.

I'd zip up and down Beachwood Canyon in the little red VW Golf that I'd recovered from Andy Richter, relishing being a working actress in sunny Los Angeles. A friend used to say, "You always look like you're going somewhere." And I was. With an LA-based television job under my belt, my agents started to send me out more and more. If I didn't get jobs, I at least got callbacks. My beeper was buzzing like crazy. I was in the game.

Jill, ever the entrepreneur, created a weekly stage sketch show called *The Beachwood Palace Jubilee* at what was then the Tamarind Theatre down the street from where a lot of us were living in Beachwood Canyon. She would offer fifteen or so slots to performers to do their thing. We branched out from our little Chicago circle and started meeting other comedy people in town. Will Ferrell and Chris Kattan did their Roxbury Boys scene for the Jubilee when they were both at The Groundlings, LA's version of The Second City. Molly Shannon was around, as was Ana Gasteyer, until they both left for *Saturday Night Live*.

When Jill went on to do something else, my friend Barry Salzman and I took over the show, and I got my first experience as a producer. Looking dapper in a tuxedo, Barry was our host for the evening of acts as his alter-ego "Adamola Olegabufola," a kind of Catskills MC knockoff. We performed every Monday evening and closed every show with a group musical number from a Broadway hit we had no business doing. None of us were dancers, or singers really, but we committed ourselves to the moves nonetheless. The audience found our awkward but well-intentioned efforts to be hilarious. The night's entire ensemble performed a very earnest yet sexually charged version of "My Favorite Things" from *The Sound of Music*. And in perhaps one of my all-time favorite moments on stage ever, three of us performed and ineptly danced a fully committed "At the Ballet" from *A Chorus Line*.

After a couple of years, I dumped that first TV and film

agent when I received a "Dear Client" form letter informing me that, even though they were not entitled to commissions on residuals, they would now be taking them anyway. I signed with another agent, Chris Sherman at Halpern and Associates. He was my champion. I wanted to work, work, and work some more, so he submitted me for everything he could find. I told him to go for the guy parts, too. He was already on it. He would call casting people and say, "Could you see this character as a woman?" They'd say "Maybe." I'd come in and do my authority thing, and sometimes I'd get hired and they'd get to feel like geniuses because they'd thought outside the box. I loaded up my résumé with TV guest spots playing doctors, teachers, lawyers, detectives, and other authority figures—many of them written as male.

I have to say I don't know why I am so frequently cast in the role of an authority figure, since the core of these characters does not match mine. I don't have that kind of confidence. I *certainly* don't experience the level of delusional cockiness I can portray in a role. But authority is so often projected onto me, in art and life. I first noticed how people listen to me early on in AA, when people seemed to hang on my words. Back then, I felt even less confident, so the difference between how I was seen and my inner reality was ample and unnerving. Sometimes I felt the expectation so intensely that I would start pretending to be overconfident in my day-to-day life. Now that I have earned more than a bit of my own confidence, I still don't really understand why people see me as so absolutely self-assured. I get that I am tall, and that I walk the man-woman line energetically, and that now I have a history of being seen in roles meant for men, who are just granted more authority, so that adds to it. But how this pattern was established, I have no idea. But more and more, I have learned to accept, and even enjoy it.

This bossy "know it all" vibe I gave off became my calling card, and I created a little niche for myself. As far as I could see, no one else was competing with me for it. I began to find different colors within it and was happy to use it. I would be cast as the emergency room physician, conveying grave concern, or the crusading attorney authoritatively fighting for the rights of the downtrodden. For comedy, I could do all sorts of over-the-top, self-important characters. I'd be the guru/therapist offering ridiculous advice as if it were the obvious choice, or the controlling and demeaning television director abusing my minions. I did these variations over and over again. I was working all the time, and really I'd do any character for any job. Chris started to say that I'd work for a buck fifty and a steak, and warned that I should be careful and perhaps a bit more discerning. A fan of food metaphors, he said, "I'm not going to let you trot out your cookies for just any old thing."

He might have had a point. I didn't confine my obsessive need to work to paying gigs, or even free steak. I did things I thought were stupid, for free. I would be in anyone's short film, one-act play, or stage sketch comedy show. I enjoyed doing my thing for its own sake.

A friend would call and say, "I'm going to do a short and you're going to play the boss," and I'd be rolling my eyes, anticipating how disorganized the production was going to be, knowing I'd be bringing my own clothes and doing my own makeup and making up my own lines. . . . But it was always "Okay, I'll do it."

I said yes all the time because I love performing, but also because I didn't want to tempt the acting gods to punish me for being ungrateful. I also wanted people to like me and be grateful to *me*. Quid pro quo, baby. Unlike in the old days, when I sold my soul hawking cubic zirconia while auditioning my own replacements on *America's Shopping Place*, I started getting back what I was putting in. I began to see how important good relationships are in this business. I've always been naturally thorough and well prepared, and by my mid-thirties I had worked out the worst kinks in my personality. I might have even become someone who was nice to have around.

It wasn't about being famous, like it had been when I was a kid. Back in Dolton, when I was writing letters to Hollywood agents, my objective was to be adored, fawned over. I wanted people to scream for me, like I remembered screaming for the Monkees when I saw them in a mall. Had I become famous as a younger person, it might have been a disaster for my insecure self. I would have been swayed by the public's opinion, pro or con, and my sense of self-worth would have been at their mercy. I'd have believed the hype and the trash talk, and probably would have trusted the wrong people. But once I'd reached my thirties, I just wanted to work. I didn't need to hang around for very long, so short-term gigs were fine. Just as with my relationship dalliances, I was happy to get in and get out fast.

And that seemed to be how my romantic relationships were going, when they were happening at all. After all the drama of coming out to myself and then to my family, my sex life lay fairly dormant. I was just starting to be good at friendship. I was really taking my time with the intimacy thing.

I did have a four-month-long relationship with a woman who

felt curiously familiar and deeply psychologically attractive. Growing up with a Swedish-leaning mother, I've always been attracted to the cool breeze in the room, and this icy woman fit the bill. I even accidentally called her "Mom" several times. She was rather emotionally cut off to say the least, which left me plenty of room to project onto her the image of a deeply compassionate and wise soul who would nurture me. Imagine my disappointment when all my need came crashing down on her and she headed for the hills.

My mourning over the loss of this four-month relationship was nearing the two-year mark when a friend sent me to her therapist, Nicki.

Nicki was fabulous: openhearted and sensible and not afraid of my neediness. Yet she was also hilarious and deeply soulful and not in the least bit phony: she had come through the dark into the light via her own battles with addiction and self-worth but still had great reverence for the shadow. Just like Don, my Jungian dream analyzer before her, she saw its great gift. She had a lyrical quality when she spoke about the psyche. Every session was like spending an hour with Auntie Mame, and I couldn't wait for my next appointment. Working with her, my idealization and preciousness about intimacy got slapped down. There was no room for it. When I would start to romanticize about how relationships should be, she would question and dismantle my defenses. She helped me understand what was *really* in my heart. I began to believe in my own goodness, and to disregard my self-contempt. She laughed at my jokes and we both laughed at my foibles. At the end of each hour, she would hug me. One day she said, "Caring for you is my job. The love is extra." She was tailor-made for me. She loved me until I could love myself.

When I was training for the AIDS Ride (a seven-day bike ride from San Francisco to Los Angeles to raise money for the LA Gay and Lesbian Center), I told Nicki about an extremely frustrating encounter I'd had on the bike path in Santa Monica. Cyclists are supposed to pass to the other cyclists' left. It's *understood*. But one Sunday, I was passed on my right, *continually*. As I was retelling the story to Nicki, I became more and more enraged. "It's inconsiderate and it's dangerous!" I fumed. Nicki started to laugh, and then so did I. "You have to write a monologue in this voice," she said. Thus was born "The Angry Lady."

The following week, I read Nicki a rough version of what would become the first character I ever purposefully created from deep within my own shadow. I made productive work of the less attractive parts of my insides.

I visualized performing her like this:

Seething with rage, The Angry Lady could barely speak above a whisper. She wore a redhead wig with tight, angry curls, one of my mom's old Janet Reno suits in a breezy red polka dot, and a store-bought surgical neck brace. To Wagner's "Ride of the Valkyries," a single spotlight followed as she slowly and painfully made her way to a microphone at the center of a bare stage.

I performed it for the first time at a night of solo comedy acts at Highways in Santa Monica. I either knew personally or knew of almost everybody there. Kathy Griffin and Nora Dunn were among those performing that night, and I was humbled and nervous to be among their company. This night was all solo artists who did their own thing, and it was not lost on me that I was entering a whole new rank. The energy was electric, but loose. We walked through the tops and bottoms of our acts for light and sound cues before the show. I had done this hundreds of times in the past, but this time I was going to be alone up there.

I had never written anything before, and there I was in a wig and a silly costume with my Valkyrie music on a cassette tape, about to perform for a theater full of people expecting to laugh. I had no idea if this piece would work, absolutely none. The Angry Lady moved and spoke v-e-r-y s-l-o-w-l-y, so I had to have the audience with me from the start or it would have been a horrendously painful ten minutes. I was scared to death. And my pits stank with fear.

To my relief, it all worked perfectly. They laughed from the first moment and throughout the piece, at all the right times. Taylor Negron, an incredibly funny performer and writer, walked up to me after the show and said, "You're a writer. And you *know* things." I was flying high.

The Angry Lady's first tale of woe was, of course, a recounting of the bike path incident. I had it occurring on Presidents Day because I thought "you ruined my Presidents Day" would be a funny line. Subsequent monologues would always have three elements: a holiday, an injustice, and a humiliation (she would always end up wetting her pants). Even within a world I created, I had to have rules to follow. It's how I roll. I would write two more tales for The Angry Lady, sporting two more injuries (an eye patch, then a splint on her broken middle finger), so I had three total.

It turned out my work with Nicki was more productive than

any acting class I had ever taken. I learned the essential lesson that all the material, everything, I will ever need to create characters who are true and effective is in me already. Nicky would tell me not to back away from the dark stuff, but to "lean into it." I believe that in creating The Angry Lady from within my deepest self, my work became really good.

I was experiencing a greater satisfaction in all aspects of my life. I was also finally cultivating some real friendships. I found that I didn't need quantity, just quality. Though I can "act as if" in big groups, I'm really a one-on-one person.

I was newly signed with Jeff Danis in the voice-over department at ICM. Clients would come into the office to read voice-over copy for radio and television commercials sent by advertising agencies. We would record the auditions in recording booths at Jeff's office. Every day when I went in, the other women in the waiting room ignored me. The guys were welcoming and playful, but the women actually shined me! It was such a silly and insecure thing to do, and in the past I might have found it hurtful, but I was able to find it curious instead. Then one day, I came in later than usual and there was only one woman on the couch, but instead of ignoring me she smiled right at me and said, "Hi! You're new. I'm Jeannie." I told her she was the only woman there who had ever given me the time of day. And then, apropos of nothing, she asked, "Do you like sushi?" I did, very much in fact, so she told me about Crazy Fish on Robertson, where the fish is fresh and the portions are huge. So after my auditions, I headed over to Crazy Fish for lunch, and there was Jeannie at the end of the bar. "Join me," she said. I did.

As I would learn that day, Jeannie is a food enthusiast. Anyone who knows her would agree that that's putting it mildly.

Her eyes have been known to well up with tears when describing a wonderful meal. She had Crohn's disease as a child and spent much of her youth in the hospital, unable to eat, so as an adult, she made up for those lost meals. She would not waste one of them on a subpar experience, so she was forever sending food back. When we first started getting meals together, I was mortified. The good girl in me thought you should not make trouble and should eat what they give you. She said, "Fuck that, I'm paying for it." Before digging into a meal, another friend would always ask Jeannie first, "Can I eat now, or will you be sending yours back?"

Jeannie's priorities in life were simple: relationships and food. Everything else she did was a means to those ends. In a town where everyone is striving to be something or somewhere they are not, she was happy just as she was, where she was. She just wanted to be with the people she loved and have enough money to eat well and travel . . . to places where she could eat well.

Like Laura before her, Jeannie was all about connection. She was so inclusive, and invited me everywhere. She was also the best listener I've ever known. Because she always came from compassion, the direct "no bullshit" way she communicated would never sting me, and I'm a tender person. She felt *with* you. I thought I was empathetic, but she was past me by a mile. I'd be dating someone and I would feel put out by something and want to break it off. Jeannie would be able to deal with my feelings and be compassionate to the person I was about to leave, and in doing so she would help me see how judgmental I was being. But where we really differed was how we dealt with boundaries. Whereas she wouldn't take on other people's pain, I would not only take it on, I was still looking for ways to be responsible for it. She was more interested in finding solutions than in wallowing. I devoured her wisdom and even today will ask myself, *What would Jeannie do?* There are some who might find her brand of care intrusive. It just made me feel loved and yes, *gotten.*

Jeannie became my everyday friend. My need for her wisdom and take on everything going on with me was becoming so important and valuable that . . . I began building a case against her, looking for a way out. When someone meant a lot to me, it became even harder to be direct, and instead I became resentful. I decided I was getting fat because when she would overeat, it made me do the same. I resented that her intestinal issues gave her a metabolism that moved at the speed of light. She also decided where every meal would be and what we would order. I was feeling controlled and I started to rebel—all indirectly, of course. I became snippy and resentful, and at one point I just stopped calling her. The relationship would have to end. After a few weeks, I ran into her at ICM and she got right in my face and said, "What happened to *you?*" I said something about feeling that she controlled what I ate. "I realize that you've pushed me away," she said. "And whatever your reasons, I just want you to know that I'll be here." And she told me that if we ever ate together again, I could choose the place. It was clear that she respected and valued me, and my protests to the contrary seemed very silly all of a sudden. When it came down to it, I missed her. "Let's have lunch," I said.

To be honest, I really didn't know where I wanted to eat. She knew all the good restaurants. Also, I really didn't care about being the one to decide. I'm a great follower; I don't like the pressure of leading. She was so good at leading. So when it came to food, just like everybody else who knows her, I let go and let Jeannie.

While we were overeating together at the restaurant of her choice, she taught me the lesson of "proximity." "You don't have to throw people away," she said. "You just have to decide how close you want them. Not every person in your life needs to be your best friend: some can be friends or just friendly acquaintances."

Proximity. I decided to keep Jeannie close.

A smiling Jeannie pretending not to be planning her next meal.

8

Walk Like a Man

STANDING ON THE EDGE OF A SHEER CLIFF IN MON-
terey, looking down a hundred-foot drop into a raging
ocean crashing against jagged rocks, I inched toward
oblivion as a man with a beard and long, stringy hair screamed
at me in a German accent, "Move closer to da edge! *Closer to
da edge!*"

The reason I wasn't yelling back something rather harsh of
my own was because the guy yelling at me was the big-shot
director of the commercial I was shooting. He was dressed in
sun-spectrum colors—orange, yellow, red—that reflected his
affiliation with a religious sect that I'd heard he'd joined because the sect's guru was helping him keep his terrible temper
in check. At this point, it didn't seem to be working—he seemed
utterly unconcerned that I was so close to plummeting to my
death, and bellowed furiously at me. As he continued to yell at
me to move closer to the edge, *closer to da edge*, I dutifully shuf-
fled as far as I possibly could. I tried not to think about how far
there was to fall and how sharp those rocks seemed as I looked

into the camera swinging at me off a crane and calmly spoke my lines: "I . . . am every woman."

Although shooting it was a rather bracing experience that I wouldn't care to repeat, when it came out, this national commercial for Nexium paid me enough money to buy my first house. It almost killed me, but I loved the house.

There are many ways for actors to make money in Hollywood, and in the late nineties, I was doing most of them—voice-overs, guest spots on TV shows, and commercials. I had played everything from a guitar-strumming small businessperson for American Express to a Buick-driving mom on a camping trip. Commercials can be an easy way to make good money, as I found out promoting Nexium on the edge of that windblown cliff. But the biggest benefits aren't necessarily monetary.

Although it might seem counterintuitive, sometimes acting in a commercial can put you closer to the work you really want to be doing, the work that would satisfy you artistically.

Case in point: I never would have thought that flacking Frosted Flakes could do so much for my career—not even when I went to a callback for a Frosted Flakes commercial and saw Christopher Guest listed as the director on the sign-in sheet.

A couple of years prior, while I was visiting New York, I had gone solo to the Angelika theater to see Christopher Guest's film *Waiting for Guffman* on opening day. I sat next to a couple of gay guys who were apparently on their first date. The one sitting next to me loved the movie as much as I did, and we guffawed and elbowed each other all the whole way through, while the other guy sat there like he was at a wake. I doubt there was a second date.

Later that summer, I rented the video of *Guffman* to show

Laura. She was still living in New York City. Trixie was long gone, and she had just broken up with her latest love. Wanting to spend some quality soul time together, just Laura and me, we met up at her parents' home in Darien, Connecticut, on our way to visit Martha's Vineyard for a week. "You have to watch this movie," I told her. We rewound it over and over, laughing and punching each other. I said to her, "Oh, god—this is what I want to do. This is how I want to work." This was the stuff that tickled my funny bone and touched my heart—it was human and flawed and raw and funny. All the characters were so real, and they all had one thing in common: they were striving to *be someone,* to *count.* I knew that feeling so well.

I would have done anything to be in a movie like it. But what were the chances? I sighed and filed this thought under Preposterous Fantasies.

Fast-forward one year to the audition for the Frosted Flakes commercial. As I was signing in, I said out loud, "What the hell is Christopher Guest doing directing commercials?" Someone standing nearby told me he did them all the time, adding that any commercial you'd seen on television lately that actually made you laugh was probably directed by him.

Somehow, when I met him, I managed to keep my excitement in check and act nonchalant, even though my heart was pounding like a jackhammer. Effusive is not a word I'd use to describe Christopher Guest, and if I'd bounded all over him like an excited puppy, I doubt the feeling would have been reciprocated. He was very polite and charming, and at one point during my audition he kind of snorted through his nose, which I would later learn meant he was amused. After all was said and done, Chris walked me out the door and said, "Good-bye."

I don't remember much else about the casting session, just that some of the *Guffman* cast were there waiting to audition as well—Michael Hitchcock, Deb Theaker, Don Lake. They each had had such stupendously funny moments in *Guffman*, and I longed to be among them. This may have been the first time in my life when my ambition was actually right on target, and not something that fate would eventually pull me away from to show me where my real place was, like when I was cast in The Second City while trying to enter the world of serious theater.

When I got the part, I was ecstatic. I was to play the wife, and the husband would be played by Sean Masterson, a great guy I'd known since my Second City days. We shot the commercial the way Chris shoots his movies—no script, just some plot points we had to hit in each scene to tell the story.

Unlike with any other commercial I've shot, the client, Kellogg's, was present but nowhere to be seen. Chris ran his own ship, and if you wanted to work with him you had to follow his rules. Sean and I did four spots playing a couple that was earnestly stalking Tony the Tiger, waiting outside the company's headquarters, hoping to catch a glimpse of him.

When we broke for lunch, as I was walking with my tray, looking for a seat, Chris stopped me and said, "You know, I do movies."

"Yeah, I know. . . . *Guffman* was—"

"We shoot them like we did today. No script, no rehearsal . . ."

"Okay."

"Maybe we'll get to work together again."

"Yeah, I'd like that." And he was gone.

It was around this time that I was starting to put together a show of my own. Now, when it comes to performing, I'm a group person. I do enjoy the spotlight, but only for moments at a time, and I would prefer to have others in it with me. It's one thing when you're sharing performance anxiety with a group, and another when you're out there all by your lonesome.

I think my mom's disdain for show-offs, braggarts, and know-it-alls loomed large in me and had always put the kibosh on any desire I might have had to produce *The Jane Lynch Show*. Of course, I was cast all the time as a person whose central attribute was delusional cockiness, and for those women, doing a one-woman show would have been perfectly natural, if not inevitable. But for me, being out there by myself was a daunting prospect. Perhaps through playing those parts, my inner show-off, braggart, and know-it-all got all the exercise it needed.

Now that I had begun creating characters and writing my own material, I was forced to confront this fear of going it alone. It was like I was yelling at myself to go *"closer to da edge."* I had to steel myself and calm some fears in order to feel entitled to take up the audience's time. After performing The Angry Lady that night at Highways in 1997 and writing the two pieces for her, I tried my hand at writing for other characters that had been kicking around in my head. One summer day in 1998, I took everything I had written over to my friend Marla's house.

Marla had run the recording booth at my voice-over agents' office. She was one of the most interesting and funny people I knew, so I picked her to be the one to whom I would read what I had written. This is something I never liked to do because when I write, I intend the words to be performed on a stage, in costume, with music, etc. (If I was performing this book, I promise it would be much funnier.) I needed someone who could imagine those things while I read, and Marla was my choice.

We sat out on the back porch of her West Hollywood home, and I read every one of my monologues out loud to her as she listened and smoked.

It only took about thirty minutes to read them all, which startled me because it had taken about six months of hard work to write them. When I was done, Marla put out her cigarette and paused just a moment before asking, "The Angry Lady. How old is she?"

"Doesn't matter," I said sharply. It was a stupid question, completely irrelevant, and I suddenly regretted choosing Marla for this mission.

"Okay, okay," she said, backing up, and then, after that aborted start, she proceeded to shape the entire show before my very eyes. She gave it not only a flow, but also an emotional through line. As she spoke, I was hit with the inspiration for a general theme I hadn't previously seen. This show would make fun of that which I used to take dead seriously, trolling the murky waters of feminine self-discovery. Each of my characters would have her own hero's journey of having gone through hell and come out of it with a firm understanding of her inner goddess. The passionate navel-gazing that had occupied more than a few of my years would become my playground.

It would be called *Oh Sister, My Sister!: Deeply Feminine Tales of the Deep Feminine*. Sandra Ragsdale, a character I had been doing in sketch for years, would be our host for the evening. She was a former TV *Dateline News* investigative reporter who had been fired for hypocrisy and crappy work. She had a nervous breakdown and was now reinventing herself by recasting it as a nervous break-*through*. She had been reborn as a new-age guru and self-styled "entitled child of God." She saw it as her duty to chronicle other women's journeys, telling the stories of women who had overcome, as she had. Really she was bitter and not that smart, and desperate to get back on TV. She had just written a book called *Listen to Me I'm Talking to You*.

In her quest to document the stories, Sandra would take us to meet The Angry Lady as well as others, including Judith, a radical lesbian folksinger, with a different "life partner" every time she appeared. Brokenhearted, betrayed, and to great laughs, Judith would be the one who sang *I Gave You the Gun to Shoot Me*, the song I had written in dead earnest back in early sobriety. We would also meet the South Side Lady.

In homage to my mom and my beloved aunt Marge, the South Side Lady was the first character I ever created who was free of cynicism. She was recently widowed and went out on a date with a widower she'd known in high school. She came home and found that the Blessed Virgin had fallen off her favorite pendant at some point during the evening. She felt that this was a sign that she hadn't sufficiently mourned her late husband and the Blessed Virgin was letting her know in no uncertain terms. No, she didn't just fall off. She got disgusted and left. The South Side Lady was also an opportunity to use some of the phrases I grew up with, like "There's no one here but the gas and that's escaping" and "I'm so hungry I could eat a horse and chase the rider." I would switch it up sometimes and use the more grisly "I'm so hungry my stomach thinks my throat's been cut."

Following Marla's specifications exactly, I put the show together quickly, typing it up on my first computer, an old Mac desktop that Sue, my brother's new wife, had given me. I was blown away by how easy it made writing. I had never taken my mom's advice and learned to type, but I was speedy at the hunt-and-peck. The minute I finished the script, I went to Kinko's and made a bunch of copies. I really did not want to go it completely alone, so I asked a handful of friends to act supporting roles and produce it with me. Then I rented eight Wednesday nights at the Tamarind Theatre in Hollywood. I moved so fast I didn't have time to think and let the fear stop me. I put my head down like a bull and barreled forward.

Both Soloway sisters jumped in and helped me out. Jill directed and put her brilliantly funny mark on the script. She also made the stage bill so hysterical that the audience was laughing even before the lights went down. Faith let me use her nonsensical power ballad "If Wishes Were Rainbows, So Am I" for Sandra Ragsdale to sing in closing the show. Everything they added was worth its weight in gold to me.

As I was waiting to pick up those hilarious programs at Kinko's on the day of opening night, I noticed a pungent smell. I assumed it was the chemicals from the copiers until I realized that the smell was faintly familiar, and it was coming from me. I reeked of fear.

That first performance was sold out, and it flew by fast and furious. I felt at the top of my game and in my power, going from scene to scene, character to character. The audience was with us the entire time. I'd sent out lots of invitations, but I hadn't wanted to know who was coming, so I never checked the RSVPs. When I went out to the lobby after what felt like the triumph of my lifetime, I was floored by the number of familiar

Something out of nothing.

faces I saw. I was absolutely elated and felt like I was in a dream. I was beside myself with joy. I remember that it was the exact feeling I'd had watching my parents perform at *Port o' Call* way back at St. Jude's.

The reviews were all good. The *LA Times* said: "Talk about taking no prisoners, Jane Lynch's deeply feminine tales of the deep feminine add up to a merciless satire of feminist hypocrisies," and the *LA Weekly* said: "Writer/performer Jane Lynch and songwriters Jill and Faith Soloway explode the common myth about humorless feminists in their stylish send-up, *Oh Sister, My Sister.*"

The show pretty much sold out every one of those Wednesday nights and was named a pick of the week by the *LA Weekly* for the entire run. This brought me to a new place of confidence and belief in myself: I had created and put on my own

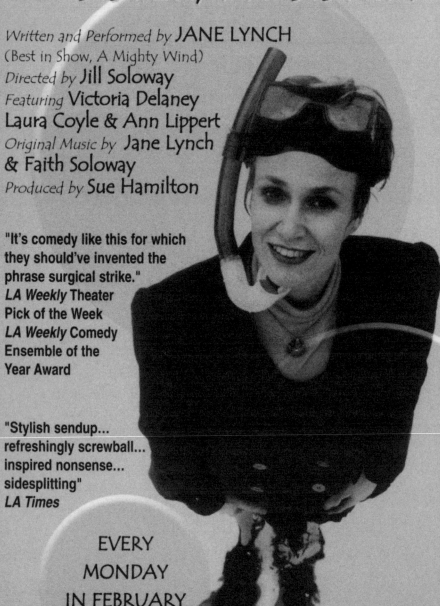

The L.A. Gay & Lesbian Center's
Lily Tomlin/Jane Wagner Cultural Arts Program
presents

OH SISTER, MY SISTER!

Written and Performed by JANE LYNCH
(Best in Show, A Mighty Wind)
Directed by Jill Soloway
Featuring Victoria Delaney
Laura Coyle & Ann Lippert
Original Music by Jane Lynch
& Faith Soloway
Produced by Sue Hamilton

"It's comedy like this for which
they should've invented the
phrase surgical strike."
LA Weekly Theater
Pick of the Week
LA Weekly Comedy
Ensemble of the
Year Award

"Stylish sendup...
refreshingly screwball...
inspired nonsense...
sidesplitting"
LA Times

EVERY
MONDAY
IN FEBRUARY

show. What had been just an idea in my head was now an entity that existed in the world. I had been so reluctant to lead, always preferring the safety of following someone else, but this time, I had somehow summoned up the courage to ask others to join *me*. And they had: my all-gal team had given me their all, for fun and for free and from the goodness of their hearts. I was so proud of them. So imagine how horrible I felt when they found out that despite their generosity, I had deceived one of them. I had fallen in love with my friend/producer's girlfriend—and acted on it.

During the lead-up to the affair, I'd put my conscious mind on hold, except to tell myself that this love I was feeling was "bigger than all of us" and that the rules of right or wrong did not apply. The thought *you've been such a good girl for such a long time and you deserve to be bad* had crossed my mind occasionally as well.

When I told my therapist Nicki about the affair, I tried to put a new-agey spin on it. I used the words "soul" and "destiny" a lot. I was doing that thing that people who are being smarmy and having affairs do: I was elevating my motives to rationalize ignoring the rules of human decency. Nicki put a stop to my nonsense. "You betrayed a friend," she said.

As someone who'd always been obsessed with doing the "right" thing, I'd always prided myself on following the rules, so once I finally allowed the truth of what I'd done to set in, I indulged in some pretty grandiose self-flagellation. I was extreme in my mea culpa, though it was mostly in my head. I

OPPOSITE: *Remounted after the sex scandal.*
(Note: Laura Coyle is in this one.)

tried to make amends, but most of my good friends who knew bits and pieces of the story stopped talking to me. There was no forgiveness coming in my direction, and I had no ability to forgive myself, so I became consumed with my own guilt and spiraled into depression. I didn't even end up with the girl. Our "transcendent love" petered out in the drama as she and her girlfriend broke up. I ended up skulking out of my apartment in the middle of the night because it was across the street from where they'd lived together. I moved back to lonely Venice.

When we won the *LA Weekly* Award for our production of *Oh Sister, My Sister!*, none of us were there to accept. I was relieved to be out of town shooting a commercial the night of the award show, but I was so sad we weren't celebrating this all together. So my good pal Laura, now living with me in Los Angeles, accepted on our behalf—but not without tripping up the stairs to the stage on her Herman Munster platform shoes.

Laura was also my voice of sanity during that time. "Oh my god, so you made a mistake. Let it go!" she'd say, catching me in mid–shame spiral. "You have to *forgive* yourself at some point." She'd also try to buck me up by not letting me hog all the blame: "It takes two to tango, baby." Her efforts provided temporary reprieves, but I was pretty committed to suffering over my suffering.

Shortly after Laura brought back my winning plaque from *Oh Sister, My Sister!*, I was given a terrific distraction—another chance encounter with Christopher Guest.

One morning, after I had been to a chiropractor/allergist who claimed he could cure my milk allergy, I wanted to test it on a cup of coffee with cream. I went to the Newsroom in Beverly Hills, as I was sure my usual haunt, Urth Caffe, would be too busy. Halfway through my coffee-with-cream test, I looked up and saw Chris Guest getting a muffin to go. We caught eyes and he smiled at me. He's usually rather poker-faced, so when he smiles it is like the sun coming out. He motioned me over.

"I'm doing a movie," he said, "and though I probably would have eventually remembered you, I hadn't yet."

"Oh, okay."

"Can you come to my office this afternoon? I have an idea."

"Yes, sure. I can do that," I said, as close to nonchalant as I could be.

Not a bad morning: I passed my milk allergy test and I was invited to talk with the director of my dreams about his upcoming project. But, of course, I wasn't content to simply bask in the glow of what just happened, I had to torture myself with the thought *What if I had gone to Urth Caffe instead?*

That afternoon, I went to Chris's office at Castle Rock, Rob Reiner's production company. First, he asked if I knew who Jennifer Coolidge was. I sure did, and I was a fan. I'd seen her on stage at The Groundlings. More recently, I knew her from a show called *She TV*, an all-female comedy teeming with fresh, new girl talent and writers—so of course, it failed almost immediately. Then he told me that he'd recently been to a dog park with his mutts, and a couple who happened to be dog breeders had looked down on his dogs as inferior. This interaction spurred the idea for a movie about purebred dog owners that would lead up to an event like the Westminster Dog Show.

Just as in *Waiting for Guffman*, this movie would feature characters in an obscure niche of the world with its own rules, hierarchies, and goals. All of the characters would be striving for success within the movie's own culture. It had been Broadway for the Blaine Community Players in *Guffman*, and it was a win at the Mayflower Dog Show for these show dog people. There would be no script or rehearsal, just an outline written by Chris and Eugene Levy.

Chris told me that he had cast Catherine O'Hara as the lesbian partner for Jennifer Coolidge's character but was thinking of moving her to be matched up with Eugene. So, he explained, if he were to do so, he could partner me with Jennifer. He asked if I would be interested in the role.

Cool as a cucumber, I said, "Yes, I would."

Chris is a man of few words, so the meeting was rather short. However, there was an almost paternal warmth to him. I had that glowy feeling you get when you're in the presence of someone who digs you. I probably smiled like a goof. As I was leaving, he said, "I'll give you a call later today, around five."

Easy breezy, I had pulled off the meeting, and stayed calm. Except that I don't remember the ride back to my place in Venice Beach at all, so I know my adrenaline was pumping.

My friend Shaun was staying with me in between his poker tourneys and Chi Gong retreats. He had been a trainer at my gym, and we became friends. He is charming, and I admired how good he was with the ladies. He had a wise guru vibe and would act as my sometimes spiritual advisor. He clocked my nervous energy when I came through the door that day. He instructed me to take a walk on the beach just before 5 P.M. and let Chris leave me a message. "Center yourself in your own power," he said.

This was back in the days when I did not trust myself and figured anyone knew better than me. So at 4:50 P.M. I left the house and took the stupid walk.

My mind was in a panic mode the whole time. Why was I out here? I couldn't have cared less about the sun setting in the east or the west or wherever the hell it sets. After fifteen minutes, I practically ran home.

When I walked in, Shaun greeted me with "Christopher Guest called! I told him I was such a fan, but he was kind of cold to me." He had probably sent me on that walk so he could take the call. Now he looked very hurt that his talk with Chris didn't go as planned, so I suggested he take a walk on the beach to center himself in his own power.

I called Chris back, and he said, "What are you doing in November? Do you want to come to Vancouver to shoot this movie?"

"Yes! Yes!" I effused. I would be cool no more.

Then he corrected himself and said he meant October, not November, and was that still good? Without hesitation, I told him it was. He paused for a second, maybe thinking I needed to check my calendar, to make sure I didn't have any other life-changing movie opportunities already scheduled for October.

Before heading up to Vancouver, I got together with Jennifer Coolidge. We knew of each other but hadn't spent any time together, so we went out for steak at Hal's in Venice. She struck me as unique and funny, and as nervous as I was about joining the unofficial Christopher Guest Players. We started our research into the dog show world by going to a Great Dane show outside of LA, and we really started to hit it off. By the time we were in Vancouver shooting, we were becoming good friends.

In no way would this be an ordinary movie experience. As Chris had said, there were no scripts. Instead, he and Eugene gave us each a wonderful and funny character description and backstory. It would be our job as actors to fill those in and flesh them out. The preparation for this task was much more labor-intensive than any other preparation I'd ever done, because if you don't know *everything* about your character, you don't have the freedom to improvise. You really have to have immersed yourself in the person and answered all the "who, what, and wherefores."

Only on a Christopher Guest movie will the set designer ask you what you think your house looks like, or the prop people ask you for your list. Here, the wardrobe person goes shopping *with* you for clothes. You would never be forced to wear a "Hate Is Not a Family Value" button. I'd never been given so much power as an actor. It was a truly unique and dreamy way to work.

Jennifer played Sherri Ann, the owner of a championship poodle named Rhapsody in White (aka Butch) and married to a rich, old codger who bankrolled the enterprise. My character was Christy Cummings, a top-notch trainer hired to see Butch to a third national championship at the Mayflower Dog Show. Along the way, audiences learn that Sherri and Christy are lovers.

Miraculously, it didn't cross my mind at all that my first big role would be playing a lesbian and that it could possibly "out" me. Not bad for a former closet dweller!

The day before I started working, I visited the set to watch Michael McKean and John Michael Higgins. They were playing a gay couple that adored their Shih Tzus, and this was the scene where they reenacted the classic-film Shih Tzu calendar shoot. Their characters loved old movies and had created a calendar by posing their Shih Tzus as the characters from scenes in classic movies. Today they were shooting *Gone With the Wind*, with the dogs dressed as Rhett and Scarlett. I really wanted to

Power couple. Jennifer Coolidge and me.

"But I like what she did with my hair." Me and Jennifer.

see how things worked on Chris's unique set before it was my
turn. Each take was hilarious and inspired, and when I wasn't
laughing, I was wildly intimidated.

There was a tray of sushi nearby, so I grabbed a tuna roll and
popped it into my mouth. Suddenly, a guy was running toward
me going, "Whoa, whoa, whoa!" Turns out, it was prop sushi

for the scene. One would have thought I was some hick tourist wandering blindly through the movie set rather than an actual, professional actor.

I looked around sheepishly, hoping to god that Chris hadn't seen me chow down on prop food. I think he had, but he acted like he hadn't.

From there, Jennifer and I went to meet the makeup people. As we were absorbing everything and trying to get our bearings, we overheard Eugene Levy and Catherine O'Hara have the following conversation with each other as they sat side by side, looking into the makeup mirror.

"What are you gonna do?" asked Eugene.

"I don't know—what are you gonna do? Have you thought of anything?" Catherine replied.

"I have two left feet and funny teeth. That's all I know. So what are you gonna do?"

"I guess I'm a hussy and I'm gonna try and do that funny thing with my knee. But other than that, I really don't know."

Jennifer and I looked at each other. If they didn't know what *they* were gonna do, what the hell were *we* gonna do?

Eugene and Catherine went out and nailed it, of course. They were pros and had done their preparation. The anxiety about failing they expressed while emoting into the makeup mirror is almost a part of the process for comedy people, I think. We have skills that are hard to measure, and most of us fear being found out for not having any idea what we are doing. We have all fallen flat at some point, and being overconfident is the kiss of death. Maybe this terror keeps us open and vulnerable. I was glad to learn that I was not alone in my fear of making it up as you go along. And I'd made a good choice—early on in my preparation, I decided that my character would be full of anxiety. Luckily for me, I had plenty coursing through my body.

The next day, our first day of shooting, Jennifer and I would be doing the last scene in the movie, set in the offices of our magazine, *American Bitch*. It was weird to shoot the last scene first and to show up for work not having a script with lines or any idea how the day would go.

All I remember from that day is that first take. When I felt tapped out and had nothing more to say and felt the scene was over, I continued to hear the "whirr" of the camera, which meant we were still rolling. I didn't hear "cut" either. We had to keep going, so we did. We were both pretty sure that nothing we did that day could be used in a movie, but I would come to realize that as long as we stayed honest and in the moment, all would be fine. Chris was in charge of putting the whole thing together in the editing room. That's where he worked his magic.

Chris rarely laughs. He rarely gives "direction." He keeps his eye on the story and can let the camera roll for what feels like forever. Incredibly prepared, he works fast and does few takes. The fresh Canadian crew was always shocked by how speedily we moved. In terms of designers, editors, and producers, Chris always works with the same people, over and over. Of actors, I've heard him say that he casts who he casts because he trusts that they know what they are doing, so why bother telling them? As an actor, if you want positive reinforcement or strokes, you must go elsewhere. It was a good thing that I hadn't met him any earlier in my "development."

The net result of *Oh Sister, My Sister!* was not a job or someone handing me a career. What it did was make me much more confident, so that I would be fine without Christopher Guest coming over to me after every take and telling me how fabulous I was.

I still recognized my desire for positive reinforcement, of course, but instead of letting it affect me, I made it my character's struggle. Christy is always trying to prove herself, with an eye out for how well she's pulling it off. She's hoping no one sees the cracks in her armor. In a moment that didn't make the final edit, I had Christy say something about how she hoped everyone in her hometown of Romulus, New York, saw what a winner she was and wished they hadn't been so mean to her. That came right from my *own* soul, out of the shadow and into a movie.

I began to see that there were no "wrong" choices for a character, so long as you were rooted in who the character was and in that moment. The work was to stay within the perspective of the character and, rather than try to be clever, to be honest. Which I think is pretty good acting advice across the board.

When not working, Jennifer and I took walks through Stanley Park in the constant October rain. We were in the same hotel, but for some reason she got porn in her room for free. As we walked, she'd narrate the story of the porn she'd watched the night before. I remember being doubled over, gasping for breath as she reenacted some insane position on a park bench. But she viewed it almost scientifically, mechanically. I came to find out while in Vancouver that Jennifer is not only wildly and singularly hilarious, she's also an incredibly deep thinker and has moments of such intense consideration that time just seems to stop for her. We had a lot of good food and many great talks, and whenever we went out, we almost always had to retrace our steps in the rain because she'd left her wallet somewhere. She was pretty much unfazed by such things. Details are not her strong suit, but I am all about them, so we were a great team. I fell in love with her just a tiny bit.

We were together all the time while filming, often just the two of us. If it weren't for watching dailies with the other cast members in a ballroom at the Sutton Hotel, where we were all staying, Jennifer and I might have felt we were in a movie all by ourselves. It was a heady experience, and I loved every moment of being in Vancouver and being part of such a distinctively talented group of people.

The last day of shooting, Jennifer gave me a ceramic Great Dane she'd bought at that dog show back in LA. It was male,

The premiere of Best in Show *at the Toronto Film Festival.*

and for some reason the dog's penis was circumcised; i.e., it had a visible head. Though she was not usually big on details, this was one she loved.

When I moved from that apartment in Venice, the penis broke off. I still have the dog, just without its manhood.

Best in Show premiered at the 2000 Toronto Film Festival, and Jeannie was my date. We flew with the cast in the Warner Bros. jet, and I walked a red carpet for the first time in my life. We settled into the theater and the lights went down. Watching myself was just awful. I thought I wasn't funny and that I had played it too subtly. I knew what I was trying to do, but it didn't show up on the screen and I was devastated. I felt that everything I *thought* I had done had gotten lost. After the film was over, I was in a state of shock and said to Jeannie, "I was so flat!" She looked at me like I was insane. Sitting there, still in our seats as the theater emptied, Jeannie verbally replayed my performance back for me, complete with nuance. Relieved, I kept saying, "Oh, you got that? You got that?" I had to see it a few more times before I was finally able to see that it was all there, and just enjoy the movie.

9

Canyon Lady

RIGHT AFTER I SHOT *BEST IN SHOW*, AS I WAS sitting on a tumbling dryer at Bubble Beach Laundry in Santa Monica, I had a sudden thought. *I can't be forty and still be doing my laundry at a laundromat.* I was thirty-nine, and no matter how I tried to deny it, I was an adult now, with a bank account and a career. It really was no longer necessary for me to schlep down to the corner and drop quarters into an industrial-size washing machine.

I've always felt young, though not in a breezy, devil-may-care kind of way. I was just immature. This was probably because I spent so much of my younger life drinking, and being drunk makes learning to be a grown-up kind of hard. Even well into adulthood, I had very little confidence in my ability to do grown-up things, and often found myself hoping someone else would swoop down and save me, or at least show me the way. Without my dad calling to remind me to change the oil in my car, I would never have remembered to do it. My friends acted as parents to me as well; I couldn't break up with someone without Jeannie's permission. I acted as if my agents were authority figures that I needed to obey; they decided which jobs or auditions I took. Then, when I realized that some of these people were actually younger than I was, it began to dawn on me that perhaps it was time to grow up.

I had maintained very few obligations and had been slow to do the things adults generally do in order to build an adult life. I always rented apartments and did nothing much to make them my own, never painting a wall or owning a stick of furniture that I didn't garbage-pick or buy off the street. I'd never lived with anyone I was dating, and most of my relationships never lasted longer than a toothbrush. Marriage had never crossed my mind, and because I was such a child myself, I'd certainly never entertained the thought of having one.

My first foray into taking care of something other than myself had come several years prior, when Nicki had wisely suggested I get a cat, my beloved Greta. Revealing the extreme nature of my relationship fears, I pleaded, "But what if it dies?" She replied casually, "You'll get another one."

I had settled happily into my role as nurturer of the fur-covered creature, and at this point I had *two* cats, Greta and Riley, and had just gotten a puppy. (Right after I'd come back from Vancouver, I'd fallen for the doggie in the window and named her Olivia after Olivia Newton-John, a huge high school celebrity crush.) I hadn't moved on to people yet, but I couldn't have loved my animals more. I poured all my previously unexpressed adoration into them. And boy, did I have a lot of it. (Georgie Girl, my Wheaten Terrier, would join us in a few years.)

My friend Jeannie and I shared our enormous love for our animals and created a special language, spoken in a high-

Greta (top) and Riley (above).

pitched voice, just for them: *"Dis gurl what is berry booty-ful,"* we'd mewl. Each animal had his or her own song: *"Greta Maritsky you are very cute, If you were not you'd get das boot."* We once improvised an entire opera for Jeannie's dog, Molly. I'm certain we were utterly intolerable to anyone who happened to hear us.

With all these critters in my care, I decided it was time to woman up and buy a home. I went to an open house in Laurel

Olivia (in flight) and Georgie (seated).

Canyon one Sunday in the pouring rain, and although I was unimpressed with the A-frame I'd set out to see, I had parked in front of another place that also happened to be holding an open house. *What the heck,* I thought, and made my way up the cobblestone path. I peered in through the wide living room window and saw a fire burning in the fireplace, creating a warm, inviting glow made even more enticing by the rain. I walked around the deck to the back and looked in through the bedroom window and saw a black cat on the bed, sound asleep, and I pictured Greta and Riley curled up there. I walked back around to the front door and finally walked inside. My knees went weak, and I blurted out, "I love this house" to the Realtor sitting at the dining room table. My father would have killed me for neutralizing all my bargaining power, but the Realtor was pleased and said, "Well, then you should buy it." So I did, and with my animal kingdom in tow, I moved in.

Smack dab in the middle of the hustle and bustle of Los Angeles, Laurel Canyon is a beautiful and verdant oasis teeming with nature and wildlife. The hills of the canyon rise up, creating nooks spotted with houses in which you are likely to find musicians and old hippies. In spite of my fear that coyotes would devour them, Greta and Riley insisted on being outdoor cats. Though not a believer in God, I prayed a little every time I heard them go out the cat door.

I had been listening to Joni Mitchell's "The Ladies of the Canyon" in my car when fate had led me to park in front of my new house, so I had become a Joni Mitchell fanatic and a regular canyon lady myself: *"Cats and babies 'round her feet / And all are fat and none are thin."* Now that I was living in Laurel Canyon, the lore of its inhabitants of the late sixties and early seventies became fascinating to me. I felt so lucky to be living in the neighborhood where Mama Cass had brought Crosby, Stills, and Nash together, where Carole King had written *Tapestry*, and where Joni and Graham Nash had fallen in love. Some of my neighbors had lived in the area for decades and had fabulous stories. During the time when all these interesting things had been happening in the Canyon, I had been growing up totally immersed in generic pop culture (I knew every episode of *Bewitched* but knew nothing about the Vietnam War), so when I moved to Laurel Canyon, I was discovering it all for the first time.

Cozily ensconced in my house with my animals and my very own washing machine, just a few months shy of my fortieth birthday, I finally felt like a grown-up.

I decided to celebrate my newfound adulthood by throwing myself a birthday party. I hadn't had one since I was a kid, and it felt like it was time again to start celebrating getting older. It didn't hurt that I shared my birthday with Bastille Day. I invited all my nearest and dearest friends, and started a birthday/Bastille Day party tradition that continues to this day. Although it had only eight hundred square feet and two small bedrooms, my house was a perfect party house, with a deck off the kitchen for great indoor-outdoor flow. The only thing I knew how to cook was salmon with teriyaki sauce, so I made that on the new Kenmore gas grill I'd bought right after moving in. I also cooked up some burgers and bought bottles of ketchup and mustard for the very first time in my life.

When I ordered my birthday cake that first year, the woman at the bakery asked if I wanted anything written on it and I said, "Yes. 'Happy Birthday, Jane.'"

"Great," she said. "And what's *your* name?"

"Uh . . . Jane."

"Oh, that's okay," she rushed to say. "Lots of people order their own birthday cake."

I had a house and a menagerie of animals and friends; I had condiments and appliances, but I still didn't have someone special to order my birthday cake for me.

But rather than wallow, I threw myself into homeownership and became a painting junkie. I wanted the rooms in my house to be perfect in hue and tone. This was very frustrating, though, as I had absolutely no talent for choosing colors. At first, my choices were much too vivid and my poor little house looked like a demented nursery school. Then I went through just about every shade of taupe available. I painted all the walls and all the trim in my house over and over and over again. I was obsessed. I couldn't sleep if I hated the color I had just painted a room, and I could be found at the twenty-four-hour Home Depot in the middle of the night, looking at swatches. Jeannie was sure I had lost square footage due to the many coats of paint I'd applied.

I had never decorated before and I had absolutely no knack for it, either. Although I appreciated a well-put-together room, I had no idea how to make one. I could shop, though, so I bought all sorts of furniture. I mixed country chic, shabby chic, Craftsman, cheap Spanish, and early American. None of it worked together, and I kept getting rid of things that didn't match and buying new things that also didn't match. No matter what I did, it always looked jumbled and chaotic, and more like a tag sale than a home.

My little dog Olivia complicated my efforts to decorate when she decided the couch was her toilet. She was clever about it, and peed between the back of the couch and the seat cushions,

Olivia in a diaper.

apparently trying to hide her work. In the course of three years, I purchased three different couches and tried all the different odor removers on the market, to no avail. So I went online and bought the dog a diaper.

I had also reached the point where I could no longer tolerate chaos and clutter. Growing up, I had been a slob who never made her bed, and now I couldn't think straight if a piece of paper was out of place. To this day, I have things in neat piles. I may not know where anything is, but at least there's the appearance of order.

I also had a TV for the first time in my adult life, with a full-on cable package. I watched in shock as Al Gore lost Florida, making George Bush president and turning me into a political junkie. I watched MSNBC at all hours and was a *Hardball* fanatic. Chris Matthews became my best TV friend; he helped me understand what was going on and that made me feel safe. Like Chris, I was always looking for the honest man or woman, regardless of their politics. I mean, I preferred it if my politics lined up with another person's, but in all truthfulness, what was more important to me was knowing the truth of what someone really thought, and not the party line.

It was to my home that all my friends came early on the morning of September 11, 2001, to watch the coverage of the horrible attacks. Everyone stayed all day, and we ordered dinner in because no one wanted to leave. We felt so vulnerable. It was like after the earthquake in 1993: it seemed as if the world could end. We were all in shock and leaning on each other. For the next handful of years, I was religiously devoted to MSNBC. I had felt so unsafe after the attack, but the events that followed, with Bush and Cheney's wars, just made it worse. I didn't trust George Bush and was shocked that someone whom I perceived to be not all that smart could be elected president. I was afraid of what he would do next and feared that he was lying to us all. I needed to be informed to feel safe. I loved putting my feet up in my living room, sitting in front of MSNBC, and soaking in information like heat from a fire.

I now had a home; I had a family, albeit a furry one. I had very strong long-term friendships. I was deeply interested in the political events of my world. I really was an adult. I felt like I was able to handle my own trials and tribulations, without waiting for someone to swoop in and take care of things for me. I was still shopping for furniture, but I was starting to feel settled on the inside.

I also stopped going to Alcoholics Anonymous. I had been going to AA meetings steadily for more than eight years, and I was starting to drift away. I didn't have any urge to drink, and hadn't in what seemed like forever. I was getting my succor from my friends. I left my identification as an alcoholic behind and went about being just myself.

The following January, I passed an important test when I woke up on my tenth AA anniversary in Park City, Utah, with a horrible flu. I was at the Sundance Film Festival with Jeannie and some other friends, enjoying some moviegoing and the winter weather. I didn't have a film in the festival; it was just a beautiful place to hang out and see new independent films. Between screenings, Jeannie skied and I hung out in coffee shops. I loved the vibe of that festival, and because this was in 2002, I had a good chance of getting in to see any movie I wanted.

When I came down with the flu, I just wanted to check out and sleep. Nyquil popped into my consciousness. *Dare I? On my AA anniversary?*

I did, and I fell fast asleep. When I took that shot of Nyquil, I took a huge step toward trusting myself. I knew that I could take it for its intended purpose and trust that when I woke up, I wouldn't make a mad dash for a six of Miller Lite. I woke up feeling rested, less flu-ish, and with no desire to get loaded.

I also readily dispensed with the fear of that unspoken AA notion that if you stop going to meetings, you will surely drink again. I felt I could have my sobriety and take my medicine, too. I have great gratitude toward AA, but my association with it had simply reached its conclusion. Part of me was still unsettled, but I coped through more adaptive methods, like latte consumption and clutter prevention.

. . .

SPEAKING OF COFFEE, I WAS ENJOYING MY "FIRST TOday, badly needed" one morning in the bathtub, when Chris Guest called to tell me we were doing another movie.

"You play the guitar, right?" he said, as if he assumed I did.

"Well, I can play two chords."

"Great. Learn another one." I think it was Bob Dylan who said all you need is three chords and the truth.

The movie was to be called *A Mighty Wind*. It would follow three folk-singing groups of the late sixties and early seventies as we prepared for a tribute concert to honor the recently deceased manager we had shared. The story had us all meeting in New York City's Town Hall to celebrate the music that had shot us "straight to the middle of the charts." We would be "back together for the very first time." The cast was almost identical to that of *Best in Show*, and I was delighted beyond words to be making a musical movie with them.

Chris wanted us not only to sing but to actually play our instruments, and not just random twanging like I'd done at the sixth-grade talent show, but well enough to do a concert tour after the movie came out. So we rehearsed the music for weeks ahead of shooting. Parker Posey learned how to play the mandolin. I actually added several new chords to my repertoire and worked to improve my almost complete lack of rhythm. John Michael Higgins (who we all just called Michael) played a tiny classical guitar that was always falling out of tune. He was also not very good at playing it. At the end of rehearsing a song, he'd play its last chord loudly and with a flourish so we could all hear how wretched it sounded.

In the film, Michael and I were matched up as husband and wife, Laurie and Terry Bohner (pronounced, yes, *boner*). We were members of the folk-singing group the New Main Street Singers, loosely based on the New Christy Minstrels. Michael was our bandleader not only in the movie but also in real life. His guitar playing may not have been very good, but he was a

Me, Parker Posey, and John Michael Higgins.

OPPOSITE: *My inner MILF.*

wonderful director and arranger. Back when we were shooting the dog show scenes in *Best in Show,* Michael had taught us songs with arrestingly beautiful vocal harmonies. We'd gathered to sing at any opportunity during those shoot days, and the music we made together was so beautiful it literally brought tears to our eyes. I knew he'd be superb after the gorgeous sound he'd gotten out of us in between takes of *Best in Show,* and he was. He arranged all of the New Main Street Singers' tunes and even wrote one himself. Michael is a musical savant. He knows every song any vocal group has ever performed and could teach you every part in the arrangement. He has a record collection that fills up an entire room of his house.

In the New Main Street Singers, Michael gave me the high soprano part, which was a real stretch for me, but like everyone else in this group, I worked my butt off and rose to the occasion. For someone like me, who had grown up singing and whose soul was massaged by it, the whole experience was joy, joy, joy. Just like with Jennifer Coolidge before him, my time with Michael felt enchanted, and I fell in love with him just a little bit.

Before shooting *Best in Show,* Jennifer and I had talked a lot about our characters, thinking about all kinds of possibilities for their relationship. Probably because we were so busy focusing on the music, Michael and I barely even had a brief powwow before we started shooting *A Mighty Wind,* so I didn't know what he was going to do and he didn't know what I was going to do. We both heard each other's story for the first time with the cameras rolling.

Being unable to control one's laughter while shooting is not only unprofessional, it ruins the take. Over the years, I've learned some pretty fail-proof techniques for keeping myself from laughing, including biting the inside of my cheek and saying the Hail Mary to myself. I had to do some heavy praying and cheek-biting when Michael began to speak about the "mostly musical in nature" abuse he'd suffered as a child.

For my part, I had decided that Laurie Bohner was a woman with no shame about her porno past. I purposely gave her a womanly sexual confidence because I had no idea what that felt like. I put chicken cutlets in my bra, emphasized my round ass, and sprayed on a tan. Although I couldn't *wait* to shed this getup at the end of the day, it actually got me more in touch with my womanly self. Though I didn't keep using the chicken cutlets, I did continue showing more cleavage after we were done shooting.

In between the shooting of *A Mighty Wind* and its premiere, my dad was diagnosed with lung cancer. It was small cell carcinoma, the kind that's usually too far along by the time it's discovered to do anything about.

My dad was the type of guy who went to the doctor for a cold. He wasn't a hypochondriac, but he was mindful of his health. Like most of his generation, he had smoked when he was a young man and was given a ration of cigarettes while in the service. But he had quit more than thirty years prior, so the diagnosis was a kick in the pants.

He went through a couple of rounds of chemotherapy, but we had all been told that it probably wouldn't do much to stop the cancer. It just made him very weak. My dad had always been the head of the household, the good husband and provider, and I had seen him vulnerable only a few times in my life. But now my mom was fully in charge. He even let her drive. Julie stepped up to help during this time as well, going to their house at all hours to deal with one crisis after another. And I flew back home every couple of weeks to be with them.

While I was there one week, my mom came down with a severe kidney infection and was on fire with fever. She had to be in a separate room because we couldn't risk my dad catching anything, and I remember the doctor telling me I had to get my mother's temperature down by putting wet washcloths under her armpits. She was almost delirious and was resisting me, and oh god it was awful.

Meanwhile, my dad was worried and scared, and turned this into a fixation on some insurance papers that he couldn't find.

My dad as a U.S. soldier in World War II,
guarding the Iranian oil fields.

He kept asking about them, so I told him I would find them, and that all he had to do was focus on feeling better. He said he was relieved, so I searched the house for the insurance papers while trying to take care of him and my mom. I ran up and down the stairs to tend to both of my parents.

At this point it really hit me that I was no longer a kid. The people who had taken care of me now needed me to take care of them.

When her fever finally broke, Mom walked to the stairs to yell down to my dad, who was set up on the first floor, that she loved him.

My dad had gone to twelve years of Catholic school and Mass every Sunday of his life, yet I don't think he ever really thought about his own death. He did what he was supposed to do and kept faithfully moving through life. Now that he was facing his mortality, although he had been such a good man, he seemed frightened of what was to come. I wished he could be at peace.

We took him to hospice in early June and tried to focus on keeping him comfortable. He had been at home for a while, but he was experiencing delirium and needed round-the-clock care. I know my mom had an awful time accepting that she couldn't take care of him anymore.

My old friend Chris's parents, Mike and Joan, had been hospice volunteers for years and had learned a few things about helping people pass away. They told me that people have a hard time letting go if there are matters in life that remain unresolved, or if their loved ones are present in the room. After my dad had been in hospice for about a week, my mom finally found those insurance papers he had been so worried about.

She whispered this in his ear and went down to the gift shop to buy something that had caught her eye earlier. Always the shopper, my mother. When she came back, the nurse told her that my dad was "actively dying." I think he picked his time, and let himself die.

Aunt Marge, my dad's sister, had just arrived as well. She had gotten a feeling that she needed to get to the hospice and had just hopped in a cab.

I was in LA, driving, on June 11, 2003, when my mom called and said, "Honey, he's gone."

A hospice worker gave my mother the candle they'd lit in the chapel for my father, and a few days later when she was at home, she made herself a drink and lit the candle. She toasted the candle with "first today, badly needed." My mom is a pragmatic, unsentimental type, so when she told me the candle emitted a prism of light directly aimed at her, a light that followed her as she walked around it, I believed her. When she said it was Dad sending his love to her, I believed that, too.

This was the first time I had lost someone close to me. The grief came in waves, and has never completely gone away. It still catches me today. I remember the most intense feeling of loss was the sadness I felt for my mother about a year later, at my cousin Maureen's wedding, when the band played one of Mom and Dad's favorite songs, "Can I Have This Dance for the Rest of My Life?" They had some kind of love, my parents.

A Mighty Wind had opened in April, just before my dad died. Though he was pretty sick already, he and my mother had gone to see it. He was thrilled with the music and proud of me. I'm so glad he got to see it.

After we buried my dad, I came back to LA and immediately

went to work on a short called *Little Black Boot*, a retelling of
the Cinderella story. I played the wicked stepmother, the first of
three times I would play that character, in three different movies.

It felt very strange to just go on like that, and I had to talk
myself out of feeling guilty.

That fall, the album for *A Mighty Wind* was released and we
went on tour. We traveled in an actual tour bus and played to
sold-out houses in Philadelphia, New York, Washington, DC,
Vancouver, Seattle, San Francisco, and Los Angeles.

It was a joy to be part of this talented group of good people, a
panacea for my heart and soul. We all loved to sing and we all
loved to laugh, and I no longer felt on the outside of everything.
I was a part of something I loved, and I felt like I deserved to
be there.

I had work already scheduled for after the tour. I was mostly
getting offers with no audition required, and I was partly relieved not to have to do it anymore, but I also sort of missed
auditioning. Unless you are half-assed, you have to prepare for
an audition as you would a performance. For me, that meant
being entirely off book (i.e., knowing all the lines), because I've
found it's almost impossible to do well if I'm half off and half
on. I enjoyed that preparation, but I also liked the feeling of
walking into a room in which no one knows you from Adam,
and making everyone sit up and wonder where you came from.
But still, the pressure of auditioning could be pretty heavy, so I
was fine letting it go.

Let it go I did, until Judd Apatow called me and asked me to
audition for his movie. I was very happy to get to audition one
more time. Not surprisingly, I would be auditioning for a part
originally written for a man.

I'd known Steve Carell since the Second City days; we had been in different touring companies at the same time. When he was getting ready to cast *The 40-Year-Old Virgin* (which he'd written and would be starring in, with Judd directing), Steve's wife, Nancy Walls (a fine actress in her own right), told him he had too many men in his movie. "At least read Jane for the store manager," she said. Bless her for that. So there I was in the waiting area, along with a bunch of guys, all of us auditioning for the store manager of SmartTech.

Steve and I improvised together, and in the scene we created I offered to relieve him of his virginity. When they offered me the role, my new agents advised me to turn it down, because they thought the script was ridiculous (it was) and because I would only be paid scale, which at that time was about $1500 a week. These agents were not going to allow me to work for a buck-fifty and a steak. I listened to them, and for the first time in my life, I turned down (legitimate) work. "If they really want you," my agents said, "they'll come back with a better offer."

The script really wasn't good, but it didn't really matter. It was basically an outline with some suggested dialogue that would be a blueprint from which we would improvise. That's how *Anchorman* had been made, and these were the same producers.

They did come back with a little more money, but my agents said it was still an insult. I held my breath as I turned it down again. But I really wanted it.

Then Steve called me, and said, "Jane, we wrote your audition into the script, verbatim. You have to do this movie." That's all it took.

I called Gabrielle, my point agent at this new agency, and

blurted, "I have to do this movie!!! They *want* me! They *need* me!!! I can't play this game anymore! Please accept their offer!" She accepted for me the next day.

I was called in to work every day that we shot at the fake SmartTech store. The set was built in a warehouse on La Cienega near the freeway. Judd wanted us all there every day because we were making a lot of this movie up as we went along, and he needed us to be handy in case he wanted to throw us into a scene. I felt like I was sitting on the bench and hoping to get called into the game. It was not at all like my experience on the JV basketball team in high school when I prayed "please don't put me in, please don't put me in!"

It was while sitting around waiting to play that I started to put dialogue from my high school Spanish textbook to music. The next day, I'd finished my "Guatemalan Love Song," and I told Steve before we shot the scene that I would be singing to him and not to be alarmed. The song set the pedestrian words of the dialogue to a sweet romantic melody. My character sang the song to Steve as she recalled her own sweet deflowering at the tender age of fourteen by a middle-aged gardener. "*Cuando arreglan mi quarto, no encuentro nada*" translates as "Whenever I clean my room, I can't find anything." Steve's expression was a perfect blend of dumbfounded horror and awe. "*Donde vas con tanta prisa? Al partido de futbol.*" "Where are you going with such haste? To a football game." I blew Steve a kiss, and sauntered away.

As with the Guest films, none of us knew which scenes we shot would end up staying in *The 40-Year-Old Virgin*. We shot so much film; when we hit the million-feet-of-film mark, there was a champagne toast. That's a whole lot of film, and it can't all be in the final movie. I try not to have any investment in whether something is in or out of these films, as I have no control over it. But I couldn't help hoping my little ditty would make the cut.

At the cast and crew screening, Judd came up to me and said, "I think you'll be happy to know there's a Guatemalan love song in this movie. Who's your favorite director?"

The 40-Year-Old Virgin was a hit, and suddenly Judd Apatow was the hottest guy in Hollywood. His next film was *Talladega Nights*, with Will Ferrell playing a famous NASCAR driver, Ricky Bobby. Instead of just offering me a role in that movie, damn it if my favorite director didn't want me to audition again.

Supreme confidence. Steve Carell and me in The 40-Year-Old Virgin.

Honestly, it was probably because Judd was producing this film rather than directing it. Adam McKay, Will Ferrell's producing partner, was directing, and he didn't know me.

On my forty-fifth birthday, I walked into the same room of the same studio as I had for *The 40-Year-Old Virgin* audition. I was up to play Ricky Bobby's sensible mother, and Jack McBrayer, who had a small part in the movie, improvised with me as Ricky Bobby for the audition. Jack had been at The Second City in Chicago as well, but several years after my time. I hadn't met him, but I knew of him. He was adorable and funny and just so quick on his feet. Jack is also a good Georgia boy. He rolled out the "ma'am"s, which on that day served to make me feel every one of my forty-five years. (He's a big honkin' star now on *30 Rock*, as Kenneth the Page, and I couldn't be happier for him.)

I was hired to play Lucy Bobby, Ricky's mother. As on *The 40-Year-Old Virgin,* the script was a work-in-progress and we'd be improvising most of the dialogue. I immediately borrowed a book from Jeannie of expressions and sayings from the Deep South. I loaded myself up with a bunch of them so they'd be on the tip of my tongue. I chuckled through practicing "Well, that just dills my pickle" . . . "She looked rode hard and hung up wet" . . . "I'm gonna paint your back door red." My law-and-order granny was taking shape.

When we started filming, the story line following the rise and fall of Ricky was set, but scenes would be added or cut as we went along. One day, Will came up with a scene he wanted to add in the part of the story where Ricky Bobby is depressed because he's no longer racing and he's moping around Lucy Bobby's house. Will wanted Lucy to confront Ricky about giving up and not trying to do something with his life. Ricky would then very earnestly attempt to impress his mom (me) with his newfound talent of passing gas in complete sentences like "I love you" and "Merry Christmas." I had to say the Hail Mary to myself several times, as it was one of the best fart skits I have had the pleasure of being in. Sadly, it is not in the final cut of the movie, but you can find it among the DVD extras.

We shot the movie in Charlotte, North Carolina, and just as when I'd lived in New York, I made things hard on myself by moving constantly. I could have just moved into the same hotel with the rest of the cast, but I wanted to bring Olivia, to keep me company and because I loved her so. The only hotel that allowed dogs was a shady place on the other side of town. I moved

Will Ferrell with my sister, Julie, and her kids—John, Ellen, and Megan.

in, but despite having Olivia with me, I was lonely. After less than a week, I moved into an apartment downtown where the wardrobe designer I'd befriended was living and where they allowed dogs. But she was so damn busy and I was not, so I rarely saw her, and I was still lonely and still far away from the cast. Finally, I snuck Olivia into an apartment that forbade dogs *next* to the hotel where the cast was staying. I got to hang out with Leslie Bibb, John Reilly, my old pal Andy Richter (whose part was cut from the movie), and of course, Jack.

I finally allowed myself to be a part of the group after hopping around, and to my great surprise and satisfaction, I found I actually preferred my own company; I *liked* hanging out with me. I had a lot of free time, as I had to be in Charlotte for over two months but wasn't shooting that many scenes. I took most of my days off solo, walking around the huge mall near my apartment, carrying Olivia in a shoulder bag, spending all my per diem. I was having a ball.

My apartment was huge, with two large bedrooms. It reminded me of the cavernous apartment I'd rented in Westwood while I was doing *The Real Live Brady Bunch*. But this time it wouldn't stay empty for long. My mother and my sister's family would be coming out to visit, to watch us shoot the race sequences, and I offered a room to anyone who didn't want to stay in the hotel. My mom and my niece Megan (Julie's now twenty-one-year-old daughter, whom I adored) took me up on it and bunked at my place. We all had a great time, but when they left I was just as happy to get back to my solitary and entirely joyful puttering.

I loved creating a temporary home in Charlotte. I had my routines, my friends when I wanted them, and most important, my puppy dog. I had no other worries or cares: I'd left those behind in Los Angeles. When I arrived, I'd brought only Olivia and one huge suitcase. By the time I left, I had accumulated six boxes full of stuff: clothes I had purchased while mall shopping, as well as the home comforts I'd acquired, including sheets, a featherbed, candles, and even throw pillows.

It seemed I had a new compulsion to add to coffee and paper straightening: I was purchasing with abandon. But like my drinking before, it was never bad enough to take me down. I could afford what I was buying, but I could tell the behavior was controlling me, rather than the other way around. I had a low threshold for discomfort, so while it didn't destroy my life, it did nag at me. As fate would have it, and in the form of what seemed like a happy accident, one of the new friends I met in Charlotte was a financial advisor at a local securities company. Marcia, a no-nonsense, straight-talking Southerner, would take me on as a client and become extremely instrumental in getting me to mind my finances and become conscious about my compulsive spending.

A week before we wrapped *Talladega Nights*, I flew back to LA to shoot my three days for Chris Guest's new movie, *For Your Consideration*. We shot at Culver Studios, the old MGM, and I shivered with delight knowing Greta Garbo had shot every movie of hers I'd seen on this very lot.

I was teamed up with Fred Willard, this time as TV co-anchors of an entertainment show called *Hollywood Now*. Fred is a national treasure. He has more trivia, statistics, and useless information in his head than anyone I've ever known, and he knows just how to jumble it all up. Using this, he can hold forth

Me and Fred Willard on the set of Hollywood Now.

on any number of topics, sounding fully confident while confusing all the facts.

For this movie, the pressure was almost completely off me, as most of my scenes were not only scripted but displayed for me on a teleprompter. From having watched entertainment shows for many years, I'd noticed that the female hosts stand at a sort of a forty-five-degree angle from the waist down, with shoulders squared to the camera, giving the impression of having a tiny waist, long legs, and a small ass. If you hold that pose and speak A LITTLE LOUDER THAN NECESSARY, you're golden. So that was my plan.

Fred had another plan, completely unknown to me. The first scene we shot, the only scene Fred and I had to improvise, we were to interview the cast of *Home for Purim*, the movie within our movie. For the first take, Chris had told Fred not to allow me to finish a sentence or get a word in edgewise.

Fred asked him, "Shouldn't we tell Jane?"

Chris said, "No."

So while Fred was talking over me and cutting me off, I was getting more and more annoyed and thinking *I wonder if Fred is going to let me talk in this movie.* After that first take, Catherine O'Hara pulled me aside and said, "You've just been Willard-ed."

But of course, it wasn't Fred's fault, it was Chris's—he wanted me to be genuinely frustrated, and it worked. Fred is not only a genius but a real gentleman, so he rushed up to me right away to fess up. He hated the thought that I would think he'd done such a thing on purpose. By the end of *For Your Consideration*, Fred Willard and I were pals.

IO

Jobber

BY THE TIME I HIT MY MID-FORTIES, I HAD DONE guest spots on countless television series. I really enjoyed many of these gigs: I'd be on the set for a day, do my thing, and then be off to the next one. But they were kind of like one-night stands: in and out, no strings attached. I approached the TV pilot season every year with the hope that I'd land something that might give me a steady paycheck and a place to call home for a while. But my lot seemed to be that of the grateful hired gun. But then one show came along that I wanted to be a part of so much that I actively made a play for it.

The L Word was more than just a hit Showtime series: it was a television revolution for lesbians. For the first time, a lesbian couple (Bette and Tina) were the central characters in a serial drama. Not only that, the show was cast with phenomenally talented—and attractive—actors. Shortly after I'd lost a day to a marathon DVD viewing session of the first season, I went to a panel where the show's creator, Ilene Chaiken, was appearing with Jennifer Beals, Mia Kirshner, and a few of the other actors. I didn't want to be obvious or to set myself up for rejection, but I *really* wanted to be on that show and I wanted to let Ilene know.

The place was packed with lesbians, and after the panelists finished, half the audience crowded around to meet them. I managed to find Ilene, and shook her hand and said, "I *love* the show." She asked me if I would consider doing it, and I answered, "In a New York minute." It felt like an offer, and I sure hoped it would happen.

I was elated, and I became fixated on imagining how she was going to fit me into the series and what kind of character I would play. Before the script arrived, Ilene called and told me I would be playing Joyce Wischnia, a feminist lesbian lawyer hired by Tina (Laurel Holloman). Ilene explained to me her (more than a little bit idealistic) notion of who Joyce Wischnia was. Yes, yes, she was cocky and full of herself, and yes, she did try to seduce a pregnant client in her first episode, but Ilene saw her as a trailblazer, and a fighter, not just for lesbian rights, but also for human rights. Joyce wanted to be the big daddy and take care of people, to be their savior. A perfect life partner for Joyce Wischnia wouldn't be a wife so much as an assistant.

What thrilled me the most (and titillated me almost shamefully) was that Ilene wanted Joyce to dress like a fifty-year-old male lawyer at a successful firm. This meant that I would get to wear tailor-made suits accessorized with cuff links, pocket squares, and tie clips.

The first time I put on the outfit, it took me back to those childhood days when I would lock my parents' bedroom door and put on a suit and tie from my dad's closet. I half-expected someone to burst into my trailer and cry out in shock, "Jane?

What are you doing?" Despite feeling a tiny bit embarrassed by how much I loved dressing in male drag, I was absolutely thrilled to get to do it. And this time, all the clothes would be made especially for me so I wouldn't look like a girl wearing her father's clothing.

As I looked at myself in the mirror, all decked out, it occurred to me that I'd never really understood or had much empathy for men or women who felt trapped in their bodies to the degree that they wanted to switch sexual genders. I realized, standing there in front of the mirror, feeling *good* in this suit and tie, that I lacked this empathy because I had never accepted and loved the part of myself that felt more than a little bit male. I nodded appreciatively to my inner fella there in the mirror, and once again I felt broadened as a person by a role I was playing.

Despite all the TV and movie roles I had done, I'd never kissed anyone on screen. That changed in *The L Word*, where the unofficial rule was that everybody gets to kiss somebody. In my first three episodes, a pregnant Tina hires Joyce to be her lawyer during her separation from her partner, Bette (Jennifer Beals). Joyce, being Joyce, tries not only to assist the lovely Tina in her legal battle but also to seduce her. In full-on smarmy seduction mode, wearing a smoking jacket and having just shoved a piece of tuna sushi down my throat, Joyce leans in for a kiss with the words, "Don't worry. I've been with a pregnant woman before." She forces a kiss on Tina, who pushes her away.

You always hear actors say that love scenes are not at all exciting, but are instead really uncomfortable and embarrassing, and I'm here to tell you it's true: there is nothing sexy about shooting them, even though they may end up looking pretty hot on the screen. But somehow, despite this, in my last take of this scene, my natural make-out instincts had kicked in a little. I felt I had to find Laurel Holloman to apologize.

"I'm sorry, I seem to have slipped in a little tongue there at the end," I said.

She looked up from the magazine she was reading. "Oh, that's all right," she said, returning to her reading. For her, it was just another day at the office on *The L Word*.

In the early days of my run with the show, I worked mostly with Laurel and Jennifer. Acting in a scene with Jennifer Beals is like driving a Porsche; you don't grasp the extent of its power until you hit the gas. At different times, Joyce Wischnia represented each of them in their legal actions against each other, which made real-world legal ethics people crazy (I was forever telling lesbian lawyers who cornered me at parties, "I don't write the stuff") but made for great drama.

Instead of a "one and gone" spot, I had a recurring role on this show. I'd do two or three episodes a season, and I couldn't wait to get the scripts in my PO box. I'd open them up right away and read all of them standing there in the post office.

I jumped up and down and whooped audibly on the day I read that Joyce was to get together with Phyllis, played by none other than gorgeous television icon Cybill Shepherd.

I had worked with Cybill briefly before, in a guest spot on her sitcom, *Cybill*. Although she had no memory of me from that time, we hit it off during our filming of *The L Word*.

In our first real love scene, we were lying in bed, postcoital, her head on my chest. Hidden by the covers was the fact that we were wearing boxer shorts and pieces of tape over our nipples.

This kept the camera and crew from seeing any of our lady bits. The young stars of *The L Word* showed nipples and butts all the time, but no one wanted to see us middle-aged broads naked.

Cybill had played love scenes in the past, but had never kissed a woman, either in front of the camera or in real life, so in this instance I was the veteran. I could tell she wanted me to lead the way, and so I prepared to summon up my inner Joyce Wischnia: I could not let myself be frozen in fear by the thought *I am about to make out with Cybill Shepherd*. But I needn't have worried.

She snuggled into my armpit, and I made a joke about how well we'd shaved our underarms for each other. When it came time for the kissing, in her spirited attempt to get past the discomfort, Cybill wound up taking the lead and dove in with enthusiasm, cutting me off with kisses before I could finish any of my lines. I appreciated her commitment, but I did need to get my lines out, so we eventually had to map out the scene, planning each kiss.

My stints shooting the *The L Word* in Vancouver were usually for only a day or two between other guest spots and commercials back in LA. I loved being in Vancouver again and tried to make the most of my time there, walking through Stanley Park, biking the seawall, and eating great food before returning to California. But although it was a pleasant little trip to make periodically, after a while I found myself becoming envious of the women who were regulars on the show, who had a gig with a steady paycheck, who knew where they'd be from week to week.

I was having a great time and loved being that one recurring character, but overall I was starting to tire of the hectic pace of my career, mostly going from one set to another with different faces and different rules; I felt I was an eternal guest rather than someone who had a "work home." It was still more of a "wham bam" feeling than one of being a central part of something.

I had really started wishing for the same thing in my love life, too, but although I was in my forties, I was still having the same issues with women that I'd always had. Every year or so, I'd play out the same cycle: I'd fall hard for someone, projecting onto her all kinds of fabulous traits she didn't actually have, and declare my love. After we'd been involved for a short time, I'd find myself horribly disappointed when I realized I had created an image that didn't really match the person, and so I'd break up with her. I didn't know how to fall in love with an actual person, but boy could I create a great one in my imagination.

I really did want to break this pattern, but no amount of processing, journaling, or inner child nurturing seemed to help. I had good strong friendships; why couldn't I translate that ability into a love partnership? Why was I still ordering my own birthday cake? I was a smart girl, but I had no clue what I was doing wrong.

Along about the time that I was seriously starting to wonder if there was something wrong with me in the romance department, I was offered a part that would make me look a little further into this particular shadow of my self. The part was in a new TV comedy called *Lovespring International*, and I was to play a character who had no relationship skills. The joke was that my character was to be the head of an exclusive match-making service, like those you see advertised in airline magazines, that provided ridiculously bad service for thousands of dollars a pop.

At first I had no interest in the project and was going to pass on the audition. Like other work I had done, it was to be improvised from an outline of a script, and my experience had shown me that in the wrong hands, improvised shows could be truly awful. I didn't have much information, but I did know it sounded half-assed, the pay was not good, and it would be on the Lifetime network, a channel I'd always thought of as a home for schlocky dramas about abused women and reruns of eighties sitcoms. Other than Eric McCormack of *Will and Grace* fame, I didn't recognize any of the producer/writer names. Frankly, I was no longer that hard up for work.

But they persisted, and called to say they would just like to have a meeting and I wouldn't have to audition because they knew I'd "knock it out of the park anyway." I was still a sucker for flattery—I hadn't completely changed my stripes—so I relented. Eric was engaging and charming and took charge of the meeting, while the other producers, including the director Guy Shalem, sat quietly in the background. They showed me the fifteen-minute pilot they'd already shot as a rough example of what they were going for in the show. The first face that popped up on the screen was that of Sam Pancake, an old colleague from a show I'd done when I first came to LA called *Baby Jesus and His Holiday Pixies*. Sam is sharp and quick, and a real Southern gentleman, who had escaped from West Virginia to come and live in Hollywood with the other homosexuals.

Although I found the pilot kind of sloppy and all over the place, it looked like it could be fun, so when the part was offered to me, I said yes. I was delighted to be hooking back up with Sam and had been looking for a place to hang my hat. Now I'd found one.

I got to name my character, and I chose Victoria Ratchford because I thought it sounded patrician and almost violent at the same time. I would be the hard-edged business owner with a very large soft spot for her incompetent staff of relationship counselors. Though she threatens to fire them on a daily basis, she loves them and can't live without them. She also knows her business is a sinking ship, as the online dating sites, the match.coms of the world, are starting to take over.

No one on staff at *Lovespring International*, including Victoria Ratchford herself, had any business dabbling in other people's love lives. Sam created the relationship counselor Burke Kristopher, a severely closeted gay man married to a frumpy woman frequently mistaken for his mother. Wendi McLendon-Covey played another counselor, Lydia Mayhew, who had dated the same married man for twenty years. Jennifer Elise Cox was our daffy and deadpan receptionist, Tiffany Riley; and Jack Plotnick was Steve Morris, the agency psychologist and a war veteran suffering from PTSD. Finally, Mystro Clark was the videographer with Hollywood ambitions.

Our first day of work was a "rehearsal day," which sounded to me like a complete waste of time and, sadly, was. If you're going to do an improv show, just set up the cameras and shoot. My old inner diva emerged and I was rather intolerant of the entire process; we did long, directionless improvs in which it seemed like everyone was just trying to top one another with funny lines. We did the kind of "acting exercises" that I had hated even back when I was in school. I was rolling my eyes like crazy and being more than a little bratty. The biggest problem, though, was that we had two directors, Guy Shalem and Jack Plotnick. Guy was laid back and didn't say much, and Jack was high energy and talked too much and was also an actor in the cast. They gave conflicting direction and I was fit to be tied. I pleaded to Sam, "Please tell me it's not going to be like this."

It wouldn't be. With Sam and me leading the charge, the powers that be agreed that there would only be one director and it would be Guy, who had also created the series. Jack graciously stepped back, returning full-time to acting his part.

The set and production offices were housed on one floor of an office building in Topanga Canyon. The show was shot guerrilla-style, with two handheld digital cameras. After we had stumbled our way through the first episode, I had lost all faith in Guy Shalem as a director. The soft-spoken and retiring young man from the rehearsal day was gone, and in his place was this thirty-two-year-old Israeli upstart who would shout senseless direction while never looking up from behind his handheld monitor.

In the middle of a scene where I was telling the receptionist about my vacation, he yelled, "Tell her she's terrible at her job!"

I looked over to Guy in disbelief and shouted back, "Why would I do that? What has she done to justify my demeaning her like that?"

"Fire her!" he yelled.

I was dumbfounded. It almost felt like he was speaking to us as if we were chess pieces, not actors. When he had that monitor in hand he seemed to be in a zone where we as people did not exist. In between takes, he returned to being the sweet and shy Guy I had met the first day, but I ignored him and gave him no love.

When you're improvising, you let it all hang out, you're not editing yourself; it's a very vulnerable place to be and you count on your director/editor to keep an eye not only on the story but on you as an actor so you don't look like a fool. I didn't trust Guy, and the exposure risk made me cranky. The fact that he would be the one editing the show only served to make me regret having agreed to be in it.

Though I felt like I started to find my stride during the second episode, I was still very skeptical about Guy's abilities and I did nothing to hide that wariness; I was now giving him the stink-eye with every piece of direction he gave me.

Even though I was a bitch with him, he was still nice to me. During a break one day, he smiled cheerily and motioned me into the editing room: "Hey, Jane. I finished cutting the first episode and I want you to watch it." He left me alone with the remote, and I watched the first episode of *Lovespring International*. He came back in all cocky and "Do you trust me now?" I was not just relieved, I was elated. "I love it. I would have never thought you'd . . . I can't believe . . ." Words escaped me. From the opening credits all the way through to the end, I was just delighted. It was a show I would enjoy watching.

Looking at Guy's edits, I could tell he wasn't afraid to let a scene breathe. Unlike the typical sitcom, in which every moment lands with a thud and a guffaw, *Lovespring International* flowed more like a British comedy, with ample room for the sly and subtle along with the big laughs. I had been afraid the more understated moments would be lost, but Guy had caught them. In terms of my appraisal of Guy as an editor, a director, and a person, the page had turned. I started to understand the wisdom of his style: he was trying to shake us up, so we'd do something different and out of the ordinary. It worked and made for some outlandishly funny moments.

Over time, I developed an implicit trust in Guy and I couldn't wait to get to work every day. I felt that I had asked the universe for a regular gig, and with it I had also gotten a lesson. By sticking around in one place, I was able to see past my initial impressions and assumptions about someone, and to see as well the limitations of my judgment about how he did things. I was also fortunate that Guy forgave my bitchiness and we became friends.

Lovespring itself did not have such a happy outcome. The show not only had trouble getting the ratings we needed to stay on the air, but we actually angered the Lifetime network's loyal

Me and Guy.

viewers: *Lovespring* had replaced one of the several daily reruns of *The Golden Girls* when we took the (apparently coveted) 11 P.M. slot on Mondays. The network not only received vehement complaints, but angry middle-aged housewives took to the message boards to insult the hair and figures of our female cast members, myself included. After thirteen delightful episodes, the plug was pulled on *Lovespring International,* and I went back to being a jobber.

. . .

LOOKING BACK, I CAN SEE THAT MY GUEST-SPOT GIGS evolved over time. When I first started getting them, back in the nineties, I would be in one episode of a show and play characters who were written to be forgotten the minute they left the screen. By the time I was doing *The L Word*, I was being offered characters who would appear in multiple episodes and would be an important part of the plotline. These roles would give me more of a sense of belonging within the cast of the show, or would at least give me more of a chance to grow as an actor and person. Some of them were also very enjoyable, for a variety of reasons.

One of the most entertaining started while I was doing a single guest spot for a forgotten series. I was guest starring with a fellow actor I had seen around town but didn't really know. As actors are wont to do, we immediately told each other our life stories in between takes. His was an absolute doozy.

When he had been living in San Francisco as a young, deeply closeted gay man, he had wanted help with his inability to have sex with women. He didn't actually have a problem, of course, because he was gay, and gay men aren't supposed to want to have sex with women. But he hadn't figured that out yet, so he went to a female sexual surrogate, a therapist who actually has sex with clients to help them overcome fears of intimacy. I had never heard of this, but apparently it's legal in some states; you can actually get a license for it.

As the therapist makes love with you, she talks to you every step of the way, explaining what she is going to do, asking you how it feels and if you like it. (His story completely turned me on, and I began wondering if there was a porno movie out there with this plot.) These methods, however, would not work for someone like my friend, whose issue had been that he didn't want to be gay. When his sex therapist informed him that the following week's lesson would be cunnilingus, he quit.

Oddly enough, about a year later I got cast on *Boston Legal* to play . . . wait for it . . . a sexual surrogate therapist.

My character, Joanna Monroe, was the former sex therapist of Alan Shore (played by James Spader). She was called back into action because Alan's friend, who had Asperger's syndrome, had fallen in love with his blow-up sex doll and needed her help. Her license had expired because, who'd have thunk it, her husband wanted her out of the sex game, but nevertheless, she agreed to help.

I couldn't wait. I had the story I'd found fascinating the year before to use as background research, and although I was kind of embarrassed because the script called for me to drop my robe and stand virtually naked in a room full of cast and crew who were strangers to me, I was excited to try my hand at being intimate with a clinical bent.

I ended up having fun with the whole run. Joanna Monroe

would eventually be busted for prostitution while in bed with the client, and Alan Shore would successfully defend her. I recurred in this role for three more episodes, at the end of which Joanna (with Alan as her lawyer) would prevent her now ex-husband from taking her daughter away from her. (He had this funny thing about his kid's mother being in the sex trade.)

Despite the fast pace of the shooting on this show, James Spader and I had some really lovely talks, and I found him to be extremely smart and deeply thoughtful. Though I never saw him be anything but courteous to everyone on that set, I could sense that he was not a man who suffered fools. Almost as if explaining what I was thinking, he offered this: "A long time ago I asked myself, do I want to be right or do I want to be kind? I opted for kind." This little piece of wisdom reverberated through my occasionally bitchy self.

I saw James perform a four-page closing argument in one flawless take. He always had reams of dialogue and he was always off book and word perfect. You had to be when you worked for David Kelley. Though I never actually laid eyes on him, David Kelley's words were known to be meticulously crafted, and were to be spoken *as written*. Even though I have a lot of improvisation under my belt, I don't mind in the least speaking someone else's words. It's almost a relief. I'm a pretty quick study and enjoy the certainty of knowing exactly what I'm going to say.

But nonetheless, one day on the set, for the life of me, I could not remember my lines. In the scene, Joanna Monroe was testifying in an effort to keep her daughter, when I was suddenly afflicted with a terrible case of actor fog. It was the moment of my close-up, a shot that included an intricate camera move initiated by a line in my monologue, but because I kept blowing the lines, the camera kept having to go all the way back to the beginning position (which was an ordeal) and we would have to start all over. Now, in my defense, I can say the speech was wordy and full of run-on sentences, though I am sure it was written that way intentionally. I kept blowing it, take after take after take, on and on for what felt like hours. The crew must have been frustrated and the cast bored. (Lainie Kazan was playing the judge, and every time I looked up at her I was more thrown off, because she was sound asleep.) And then in the midst of it all, we had to stop shooting, because it was my birthday and someone had brought a cake.

I felt like an amateur. The marvelous actress Pamela Adlon, who was playing my husband's attorney, will always have my love and undying gratitude for her comforting words, actor-to-actor: "Jane, it happens to all of us. We all go brain dead. Today it's your turn."

It was my turn. Happy Birthday!

. . .

WHEN I GOT THE CALL TO AUDITION FOR THE ROLE OF the psychiatrist on *Two and a Half Men*, I was excited for about a minute before realizing I couldn't make it on the day they wanted me to read. Chuck Lorre cast me anyway. I learned firsthand a very valuable lesson: the more unavailable you are, the more they want you.

It was the second year of the series, and as Dr. Linda Freeman I was, at first, the psychiatrist for Jake, the kid played by Angus T. Jones. Before the end of that season, Dr. Freeman would have therapy sessions with both Alan, played by Jon Cryer, and Charlie (Sheen). Eventually, she was sitting down with just Charlie.

This role was layered with irony: as our characters went through the motions, both the doctor and the patient knew full well that any hope for therapeutic change on Charlie's part was futile. In his constant pursuit of gratification, the character Charlie would return to therapy whenever he ran into a barrier he couldn't skirt. I, as the therapist, enjoyed dryly busting his chops.

I absolutely loved locking eyes with him and playing these incredibly well-crafted scenes. If we could get through those several-page scenes all in one take, which we managed to do much of the time, it felt like a great accomplishment. Although a few of my appearances were pretaped, most were performed in front of the live audience, which always added a punch of adrenaline.

I would be invited back to the show three, sometimes four, times every year, and I was always thrilled to get the call. The writing was just outstanding and it was a very happy set, and Charlie Sheen was also such a pro. Our scenes could sometimes be up to eight pages long, and I'd work my butt off to learn the lines. Meanwhile, Charlie had not only our scene to learn but the entire rest of the show; he was always in almost every scene, with the show taped in front of a live audience. Twenty-some shows a season for so many years: he was a machine. He was also a kindhearted gentleman who was loved by the cast and crew. He further won me over by texting words of praise to me whenever he happened to catch me in a guest spot or movie.

Though I still longed for my own regular gig, I thoroughly enjoyed returning to see friends.

Friends were also great because they kindly remembered me when they were looking to cast projects they were working on. When I had worked with Paul Rudd on *The 40-Year-Old Virgin*, he told me about some projects he was hoping to produce. One was a TV series about caterers in Hollywood; the other was a movie about energy drink salesmen. We both had wanted to work together again, and he had said he'd be in touch. Then one day, I got the call.

Paul was developing the catering TV series with the creative team behind *Veronica Mars*: Rob Thomas, Dan Etheridge, and John Enbom. I had done a guest spot on that show and I had really enjoyed working with them. For this series, each show would be set at a different catering gig around Los Angeles and would focus on the personalities and relationships of the waiters. Instead of pitching the idea around to get a pilot deal, as is customary in Hollywood, they'd decided to shoot it on their own nickel and shop that around. In June of 2007, we all got together at Rob's house in the Hollywood Hills and shot the first episode of *Party Down*. Because they were paying for it themselves, the pilot was shot on a shoestring budget. Between shots we all hung out in Rob's bedroom getting to know each other and laughing a lot. I've found that doing something for fun and almost for free (we each got $100 for the day) can bring out the best in people. Plus, there's nothing like undressing in front of folks you just met to inspire humility and togetherness.

The day was great fun for me, as I was hooked up with a whole new bunch of fabulously funny actors I'd never worked with before, including Ryan Hansen (*Veronica Mars*), Ken Marino (*Wet Hot American Summer*), and Andrea Savage (*Dog Bites Man*). Paul had intended to play the part of Henry, a frustrated actor who quits the acting game and becomes a cater-waiter, but his movie career was suddenly on fire, with one project lined up after the other, so he had to replace himself. He brought in his extremely handsome and self-effacing friend Adam Scott. We were also very lucky to have the entire *Veronica Mars* crew working on our humble low-budget pilot, so the shoot went swimmingly and the pilot ended up looking great.

The guys in charge told me I could do anything I wanted with my character. Her name was Constance Carmell, she was a forty-nine-year-old actress whose ship had sailed and who had therefore become a cater-waiter. Rather than doing my stock-in-trade of smirking arrogantly and waxing superior, I made Constance into a sweet and passive soul who lived in a delusion of grandeur about her acting days gone by. Remembering Harrison Ford's warning that leaving your mouth open made you look stupid, I let Constance's mouth hang open a fair bit of the time. It was such a relief to play someone who wasn't trying to dominate or impress. I loved everything about this project, and unlike many other projects I had done, I let myself want this one to succeed.

But after more than a year with no word of a deal, I woefully assumed *Party Down* was dead. I chalked it up to a very good time had with a bunch of fun people.

Paul Rudd came through again a couple of months later, when I saw him at the premiere of *Superbad* and he asked me what I was doing in the next few months. I said, "If I you want me to do your movie, then I will be doing your movie in the next few months."

Little Big Men, as it was known at that point, was the story of two screwup sales reps for an energy drink called Minotaur.

Four members of the unofficial comedy ensemble community: Kerri Kenney, Ken Marino, A. D. Miles, and me in Role Models.

After they destroy the company's Minotaur SUV (a van adorned with bull horns) and some public property, the guys are given the choice of serving hard jail time or doing community service through a Big Brother–type program called Sturdy Wings. Of course they choose community service (who wouldn't?). This choice puts them at the mercy of my character, Gail Sweeny, who runs the program. Paul wrote the script with his friends and collaborators, David Wain (who would be directing) and Ken Marino, who had slayed me on *Party Down* with his character Ron Donald.

The movie would come to be called *Role Models*, and the two main guys were played to perfection by Paul Rudd and Seann William Scott. I played another version of my completely deluded, cocky characters, with Gail Sweeny boasting of heroically conquering addictions to booze, drugs, pills, and "bad thoughts." Gail claimed she used to have cocaine for breakfast, lunch, and dinner, but now she was "addicted to helping." As a survivor, she believed that this descent into hell and subsequent return uniquely qualified her to mentor children.

Warning them of my aversion to B.S.:
Seann William Scott, Paul Rudd, and me.

Playing this part, I was lucky to get to perform some of the most deliciously ridiculous lines ever written. Taking an instant dislike to Seann's Wheeler and Paul's Danny, Gail pointedly informs them, "I'm not here to service you, I'm here to service these young boys."

To this day, at least once a month a fella somewhere between adolescence and early manhood will sidle up to me and ask, "What did you have for breakfast?" It took me a while to realize they just wanted to hear me sneer "cocaine."

We started filming in Venice Beach in September of 2007. As evidence of the power of "it's who you know" in getting asked to be in comedy ensemble movies, this movie was peopled with actors from David's movie *Wet Hot American Summer*, his improv group The State, and folks from Judd Apatow films that Paul had been in. The cast included an incredible lineup of funny people: Elizabeth Banks, A. D. Miles, Joe Lo Truglio, Kerri Kenney, Ken Marino, Bobb'e J. Thompson, Christopher Mintz-Plasse, Ken Jeong, and Joe Walsh. I knew some of them from before but was meeting many others for the first time. But because we were all part of this larger "ensemble comedy" community, we were almost immediately comfortable with one another. I love that, and it also helped that in ensemble comedy projects, selfishness just doesn't fly. Whether you're a big star (Paul, Seann) or a jobber like everybody else, everyone takes turns in the spotlight, supporting one another and understanding that the best joke always wins.

At the end of the shoot, the main characters dressed up as KISS and drove the Minotaur SUV they had destroyed earlier in the movie to fight the Battle Royal for LAIRE, a medieval war reenactment game played in a nature park. The entire cast came together to film these scenes, and the hundreds of extras partaking in the battle were actual medieval role-play enthusiasts playing their own characters, complete with costumes and weapons. The day shooting this was off-the-charts fun.

It's usually pretty easy for me to end a project and just walk away, because I'm so used to doing it. But leaving behind the cast and crew of *Role Models* was very difficult; I really loved these people and had had the time of my life. I was so grateful to have been a part of such an awesome group.

The Dangers of Flattery

A	S I WAS WAITING TO SEE IF THE UNIVERSE WOULD
answer my request for a steady meal ticket, I was not
unappreciative of the short-term cherries I was being
fed. A particularly juicy and delicious one came from Nora
Ephron. I'd been a fan ever since I saw and loved her movie
Heartburn in 1986.

I first met Nora at a screening of *A Mighty Wind* at the Directors Guild in 2003. This was not a formal introduction; rather,
I was on my way into the ladies' room as she was coming out. I
was not only a huge fan of her movies, I'd become a fan of her
blogging on The Huffington Post, so I almost lost my breath
when, instead of passing me, she reached out to take my hand.
I think I said, "I love you." She said something about *A Mighty
Wind* and my part, and I'm pretty sure it was positive because
she left me with "Maybe we'll work together someday."

About three years later, when I was invited to a brunch in my
Laurel Canyon neighborhood, I was thrilled to see Nora Ephron
there. It was a lovely all-girl affair, and Nora was particularly
sharp, witty, and interesting. I felt like I was holding my own

until we started talking about the upcoming presidential election and I said something about Hillary Clinton having a "Pisces moon," outing myself as an armchair astrologer. Even as it was coming out of my mouth, I regretted it. Out of the corner of my eye, I could see Nora, the unsentimental pragmatic New Yorker, wince, and I felt like an idiot.

This obviously did not turn her completely off to me, because in late 2007, when I was visiting Laura Coyle (who had moved to Connecticut to be with her parents), my agent Gabrielle called and said, "Can you get into Manhattan to have breakfast with Nora Ephron?"

The next morning, Laura and I hopped on the train into the city. Not even something as magnificent as my heading to brunch with Nora Ephron could keep us from our riotous silliness: the whole way down, we watched and rewatched a YouTube video in which Leslie Uggams completely forgets the words to "June Is Busting Out All Over." We just killed it.

When we got off the train at Grand Central, we split up and I took the long walk uptown to Nora's favorite breakfast place, a little deli joint called E.A.T. on Madison Avenue between 80th and 81st Streets. She raved about the food and then ate only a few bites of her eggs. (This must be how she can be a foodie and stay so thin.) Almost casually, she told me she was writing a movie about Julia Child. She told me the story of how Meryl Streep had launched into her imitation of Julia while they were both leaving the theater after a play, and Nora had insisted she play her in the movie.

Nora then started to describe the role of Julia Child's sister, Dorothy. Though Dorothy would be in only a few scenes, she and Julia had a close and loving relationship, and depiction of this relationship was essential to an accurate portrayal of Julia. Then Nora said, "You're the tallest actress I know," and asked if I might be interested in playing this small but essential role. The question was presented as if I could possibly be insulted by being asked to play Meryl Streep's sister in a Nora Ephron movie. To sweeten the pot, she added, "You'll get a trip to Paris out of it." (The fact that the scenes I was supposed to shoot in Paris ended up being shot in Hoboken, New Jersey, did not make me regret accepting her offer one bit.)

In May of 2008, I started shooting *Julie & Julia*. Nora had written a screenplay based on two memoirs—one by Julie Powell and one written by Julia Child and her nephew Alex Prud'homme—and would be directing. The story intertwined two stories: that of Julia Child's journey to writing and publishing her cookbook *Mastering the Art of French Cooking* and that of Julie Powell (played by Amy Adams) in her attempt, decades later, to whip up the tome's 524 recipes in 365 days. By the time I arrived in New York City to begin work on the movie, the story of Powell's time in Queens in the early 2000s was in the can, and the filming of Julia Child's story in Paris during the 1950s was commencing.

I was excited and nervous. I would be working with the upper echelon of New York's dramatic art world, including the woman everyone, including me, calls the "best actress alive." I checked into the Empire Hotel near Lincoln Center and immediately had a wardrobe fitting for my authentic 1950s garb with Ann Roth, the Oscar-winning designer. She, like almost everyone I would meet henceforth on this project, was brusque and to the point. Not exactly cold, but definitely of New York. The LA small talk and superficial yet comforting intimacy were nowhere to be found, and I had to be a big girl and soothe myself.

I went to the set on my second day because Nora wanted me to see Meryl Streep at work and look at some dailies so I could tailor my performance to hers. The sister relationship depicted in the film was very important to Nora; she was very close to her own three sisters and wanted to do justice to Julia and Dorothy's bond.

When I arrived on the set at Silvercup Studios, they were shooting the scene in which Julia's husband, Paul Child (Stanley Tucci), is forced to leave the apartment because he is overwhelmed by the fumes caused by his wife's chopping of dozens of onions. Meryl's embodiment of Julia Child was uncanny and uncompromising. The voice was dead-on, and the open heart and charm of Julia Child were alive again in her performance. I had expected nothing less of Meryl and was hoping that the strong choices I had made for the vocal and physical aspects of Dorothy would ring as true. But I had no way to know until I started shooting; I would either be fabulous or ridiculously over-the-top. I knew that staying rooted in the exuberance of Dorothy McWilliams, in spite of my fears, would be key.

Julia and Dorothy were said to be peas in a pod when it came to their lively, eccentric natures. Six foot two and six foot four inches, respectively, they would have been very tall women by today's standards. In 1950s Paris, they would have been enormous. One can only imagine how the reserved and relatively petite Parisians would have responded to such huge, foreign, emotive women. Julia was said to have won them over with her charm, genuine curiosity, and love of Parisian culture.

Nora introduced me to Meryl Streep and Stanley Tucci in

between camera setups. Though a quick meeting, they were both lovely and polite. Meryl was wearing specially made platform shoes to make her tower over Stanley, but even with the special shoes, I was still much taller than her. We had a laugh about how I'd probably have to shoot barefoot in our scenes to get our heights right. Just as when I had first sat down with Nora, I struggled internally to convince myself that I belonged in this company. In any other cohort, on any other set, I'm pretty confident of my abilities and my value to a project. But this time, I was nervous. The caliber of the group had me reeling a bit, yet it also invigorated me. I relished the challenge ahead.

I was indeed barefoot when I shot my first scene as Dorothy to Meryl Streep's Julia. It was the scene in which we were helping each other get ready for the big party Julia was throwing to introduce Dorothy to her Paris friends. We primped a bit in front of a full-length mirror and then stepped back, scrutinizing our reflections until Julia declared, "Good enough," and the sisters laughed. We would reshoot this scene later on, with me in a different dress and the moment more quiet, with less chatting. Nora wanted to get this scene just right; it was important to her that the audience understand the deep affection these sisters had and the comfort they gave each other, as well as their shared sense of humor. Having my own Julie for a sister with whom I shared a family sense of humor, I had something to draw on.

My first speaking scene was shot in a Brooklyn restaurant posing as the Parisian café where Dorothy has her first delicious taste of Brie cheese. After the first take, in which I was able to successfully transform my own nervous energy into Dorothy's exuberance for the Brie, Nora leaned over to me, pleased as punch, and whispered, "I'm just delighted with what you're doing, Jane!" I was relieved and thrilled.

It's difficult not to use clichés when talking about Meryl Streep's talent. I had been absolutely captivated by the depth, passion, and masterful restraint of her work back in the early part of her career, and I continue to watch with delight as she writes her own script for her post-middle-age life and work. Sitting close to her, I had to try not to stare; her features are so arrestingly beautiful, and in spite of myself, I could not take my eyes off her. Her presence, even while sitting and waiting, is alive and bright. That's genuine star quality. I understood what Mike Nichols meant when he famously said in a *Vanity Fair* article that she looked like someone who "just swallowed a lightbulb."

It's also very interesting (and very odd) to meet someone in one moment and then in the next launch into portraying an intimate relationship with her, one where the two characters adore each other and are free with their physical affection. In each of the few scenes I had with Meryl, this is what we did. As we shot, we were sisters, but I did not really know Meryl, and in between takes she was rather reserved. I didn't take this personally, but instead saw it as her shielding herself so she could focus on the job at hand and not be distracted. I respected what I perceived as her need for space, and kept my raves about *Sophie's Choice* and all the stupid small talk that ran through my head to myself.

Then one day, after we had finished shooting a scene and were headed back to our trailers, we were waiting for the traffic light to change so we could cross the street. As we started to move forward, Meryl took a half step closer to me and slipped her arm in mine, and we crossed the street together, arm in arm. I smiled inside and out and was so glad I hadn't pushed myself on her and instead had allowed her to come to me. I also wished that someone had a camera.

At the Los Angeles premiere of *Julie & Julia* in July of 2009, my mother, my sister, Julie, and my nineteen-year-old niece (and aspiring actress) Ellen came out from La Grange, Illinois, to be my dates. While I was on the red carpet doing an interview with *Access Hollywood*, I heard a loud cheer go up from the fans behind the barricades. Meryl Streep had arrived. In the time it took me to look her way, my late-to-the-punchline, slow-synapse-firing eighty-one-year-old mother made a beeline straight toward her, moving faster than I had ever seen her move in my life. She grabbed both hands of a shocked Meryl Streep and croaked loudly, "I'm Jane Lynch's mother!" By the time I got there to peel my mom away, Meryl was graciously complimenting her on "having such a lovely daughter." The photographers started snapping pictures of Meryl and me together, and if you look closely you can see my mother, starstruck and agape, in the background. You can also see her mad dash to Meryl online, right behind me as I'm giving an interview to *Access Hollywood*.

. . .

WHEN I RETURNED FROM NEW YORK IN THE SPRING of 2008 after shooting *Julie & Julia*, Gabrielle sent me the script for a TV pilot audition. It was a sitcom about a man who was recently sober and trying to adapt to his new life. I was going to read for the woman who was his AA sponsor. I didn't laugh once reading the script and barely finished it, so I passed on

Mom (top left), Meryl Streep, and me.

auditioning. When they came and asked that we just meet, no audition, I thought, *Well, that's flattering!* I went to the meeting, and they were all very nice and, most important, seemed to really want me, so I quickly accepted the role when they offered it. I signed on, and my agreement meant that if this project was green-lighted, I was obligated to be in it for up to five seasons.

On the drive home from the meeting, trying to rationalize what I'd just impulsively done, I reasoned thus: although I wasn't thrilled with the show, I didn't hate it. There were good people behind it. If it was picked up, I would have the steady employment I was looking for. At the very least, it was a good paycheck. And did I mention they really wanted me? I had made snap decisions based on less (see *Lovespring International*) and nothing horrible had happened.

We shot the pilot in a week that felt like a month. We all feigned excited anticipation and mutual congratulation, but we all knew it wasn't very good. As is the case with all pilots, the next step was to wait and see if the network would pick it up. I walked away underwhelmed and went on with my life.

In the following October, I got a call from Gabrielle that Ryan Murphy was doing a TV pilot about a high school glee club. They'd just added a character, a cheerleading coach, who would be the group's nemesis, and Ryan wanted me to play her. I had worked with Ryan several years prior, on his show *Popular*, and he was now coming off the huge success of *Nip/Tuck*. I loved everything he did. He's sharp and smart and fascinated by people, especially their quirks and absurdities. Where *Nip/Tuck* was dark, odd, and cynical, *Glee* was to be upbeat, hopeful, and innocent. When Kevin Riley, the head of Fox TV, suggested that Ryan's script needed a villain whose mission would be to destroy the glee club, I've heard it said that Ryan proclaimed, "Her name will be Sue Sylvester, and she will be played by Jane Lynch." He handed off the job of creating this menacing cheerleading coach to the thirty-two-year-old writer/actor Ian Brennan.

It was Ian who had originally pitched *Glee* to Ryan, but as a very dark movie about high school. Ryan decided it would work better on television as a series, and decided to shoot the pilot. Ian was brought on board, along with Ryan and his producing partner Brad Falchuk, as writer/executive producer. Ian dove deep and made contact with his own inner mean-girl, and threw in a large helping of the diva side of Ryan Murphy. They came up with Sue Sylvester, coach of the McKinley High School

Cheerios!, who was hell-bent on destroying the McKinley High School glee club, New Directions. Sue Sylvester would be the darkness in this otherwise cheery and innocent world. But unlike Hannibal Lecter or Freddie Krueger, she wouldn't be dangerous, but instead would be laughable in her ambitious, contentious, and persistent nature. The first words used to describe her in the script were: "Sue Sylvester may or may not have posed for *Penthouse*. She may or may not be on horse estrogen." I wanted in. As wrong and uninspiring as that last pilot had felt, *Glee* felt right and inevitable.

Unfortunately for me, I was contractually committed to that wrong and uninspiring pilot. I tortured myself with *Did I just blow my chance to star in a Ryan Murphy TV pilot? Is this punishment for my impulsive nature and susceptibility to flattery?* Luckily, Ryan and company allowed me to do the pilot as a guest star and not a series regular, taking the chance that the other yucky pilot would not be picked up, and if *Glee* went to series, I would be available. I tried not to worry myself with the what-ifs and to just be grateful that I got to be in the pilot. Trusting that all would be well and as it was meant to be required a supreme act of will on my part.

In October of 2009, we shot the *Glee* pilot at Cabrillo High School in Long Beach. Ryan Murphy is very specific about everything and always knows very definitively what he wants. He also shares my mother's obsession with clothing. Sue Sylvester would wear only tracksuits. They could come in any variety of color combinations, but tracksuits would be her uniform, her armor; Sue Sylvester was a warrior.

The first scene I shot was in the teachers' lounge when Sue

OPPOSITE: *Sue Sylvester armed for battle.*

Sylvester presents a gift of lattes to her fellow teachers. This was a device to enable my character to ruefully emphasize that the coffee budget had been cut to pay for something the Cheerios! needed. Ryan worked on the script as we shot. From the moment he instructed me to say I like my coffee *scalding*, the tone was set; there would be no moderation for this cheerleading coach.

What I love about Ryan is that he is always looking to find the line that marks the boundary of civility, beyond which one should go no further. Then he crosses that line. Ryan had no difficulty showing me who Sue was to be, and he could completely bring to life Sue's outlandish haughtiness and arrogance. I embraced the lawlessness. With this newfound tone of extremity still wafting about my person, I fairly strutted through the hallway back to my trailer. Catching my reflection in the glass of a trophy case, I gave myself a snarl. I was enjoying myself immensely and felt as if my whole life had been meant to lead me here, to this show, this character, and this moment.

The actors playing the *Glee* kids were all TV unknowns, and for some of them this was the first acting job of their life. I met them on the day they performed "Don't Stop Believin'," and I was blown away. Not because of the production values; there was nothing flashy or showy about it. What got me was the ache and hunger of that song matched up with their sweet and hopeful yearning to belong. They were the underdogs of William McKinley High and took slushies to the face for wanting to sing in the glee club.

There was something so moving about a group of kids coming together to express their hopes and fears by raising their voices in song. It was vulnerable and it was raw. It was that same desire to express our feelings and be in the midst of like-minded others that drew Chris and me to the choir room at Thornridge High School. It seemed to speak to the disowned and discarded parts within us all. I knew that this show could find an audience. I wasn't sure if it would be a big audience, but I was pretty sure it would be a devoted one. I had no idea, however, that they'd be called Gleeks.

I walked away from that pilot shoot of *Glee* hoping and praying that the deal with the other pilot would fall apart. Nothing is ever a *sure thing* in Hollywood, but I would've bet the farm that *Glee* would be picked up and on TV in short order. And when that happened, I didn't know how I would be able to stand not playing Sue Sylvester on it. I shuddered to think of it and sometimes had to consciously switch channels in my mind to avoid doing so.

While I was waiting to see what was going to happen to these two competing deals, I still needed something to do with myself. I was shooting commercials, doing more guest spots and recording voice-overs, when Providence brought me an unexpected bounty. In December of 2009, I was pleasantly surprised to hear that the Starz network had ordered ten episodes of *Party Down*. It had been a year and a half since we'd done the pilot, and I had already mourned what I had assumed to be the loss of the show.

I was thrilled to have it resurrected with a promise of ten weeks of work. Of course, there were some changes. We lost Andrea Savage due to pregnancy but gained Lizzy Caplan (*Mean Girls*) as the wannabe comedian and love interest to Henry (Adam Scott). We also added Martin Starr (*Freaks and Geeks*) as the aspiring science fiction writer. With our somewhat altered cast assembled and our black bow ties replaced with pink ones, we reshot the pilot, launching us into the first season of *Party Down*.

On the first day of work, I walked onto the set of the private home we were shooting in and saw Fred Savage sitting at the kitchen island. I went up to him and said, "Do you remember me?" Before he had come out to Los Angeles to star in *The Wonder Years*, he played the kid who swapped identities with Judge Reinhold in a movie shot in our hometown of Chicago

Ken Marino, Ryan Hansen, Adam Scott,
Martin Starr, Lizzy Caplan, and me

called *Vice Versa*. I was about twenty-seven back then, and I'd had a small part in it. Fred had been about ten. "Of course I remember you!" he said. When I asked him, "What the heck are *you* doing here?" he looked at me strangely and said, "I'm directing the episode." I don't tend to read call sheets and was surprised to say the least to see him there. When did he get old enough to be in charge? He directed every other episode, and Brian Gordon (*Curb Your Enthusiasm*) helmed the others. They were both great fun and moved fast and furious, as we had only four days to shoot each show.

Like *Lovespring International*, *Party Down* was a low-budget and high-octane shoot. This was just the way I liked it: very little time in between setups and a great group of actors. As a cast, we actually adored one another. Lizzy was a cigarette smoker, and by the second or third episode we were all puffing away together in the early morning freezing cold outside our trailers. We'd hang out on base camp laughing, goofing around, and having great talks. Our writer Jon Enbom captured each of our characters' voices so well in his scripts that we pretty much stuck to his words. The exception was Martin Starr, who is constitutionally incapable of speaking anything written for him. He made up everything that came out of his mouth to great effect, and it was different for every take. I loved the one-on-one relationships we started to build between the characters within the catering company. My Constance Carmell had great empathy for the foibles of Ken Marino's Ron Donald, and both characters were equally clueless. No one made me laugh harder and more often than Ken, and it got so that I couldn't even look at him without having to say an internal Hail Mary.

Though she had never been much more than an extra in her

acting career, Constance had many stories to tell of her mostly imagined halcyon days. The most willing ear became that of Kyle Bradway (played by the adorable Ryan Hansen), a young blond actor whose trade was what Paul Rudd called the "handsome business." Not only did Constance narcissistically see Kyle as a younger male version of herself, she regarded him as her protégé. Kyle was just as thick and deluded as she, and I can't tell you how much I enjoyed pontificating to him about the "actor's life."

The fact that I was contracted to the other dreaded pilot and that they could rightfully pull me off the set of *Party Down* at any time was always in the back of my mind. That *Glee* could shorten my time on *Party Down* were *it* picked up didn't weigh as heavily on me. Having to lose my catering job to join the glee club would be another one of those luxury problems and, in truth, a win-win.

A twelve-episode pickup for *Glee* was announced midway through shooting *Party Down*, and they offered to have me continue to play Sue Sylvester as a guest star for as long as I could before, and if, the other pilot called me away.

The eighth episode of *Party Down* would be my last, and the cast threw me a surprise going-away party that included a lap dance by a real stripper. She smelled like McDonald's and was about as comfortable writhing on my lap as I was having her there. It had been Ken Marino's idea; he loved watching me suffer and couldn't get enough of it, whooping it up, screaming, "Yeah! That's what I'm talkin' about!" There's nothing sexy about getting a lap dance in front of your coworkers, and I'm pretty sure I wouldn't enjoy it in private either. I was embarrassed and felt really sorry for the girl. Everyone, including the crew, watched uncomfortably, until Ryan Hansen came to my rescue and whispered in my ear, "You don't have to do this," and led me away.

Later that night on the deck of my canyon home I wrote this e-mail to the cast:

> I am basking in the afterglow of a wonderful finale after a perfect eight weeks. I'm home nursing a near-beer and the shame from the lap dance is almost gone. My mind swims with memories and laughs created by all of you wonderful, talented, wild and weird people. I had a blast, to put it simply. I don't think I've ever laughed so heartily or felt such deep affection for my co-workers.
>
> I picture us all dining at Pace in the canyon, at an outside table laughing and smoking. We're enjoying good food, good drink and you're all impressed with how the staff kisses my ass because I go there all the time. Let's commit to do this soon. If not a Monday in the next few weeks, let's nail something down after *Party Down* wraps.
>
> I'm a lucky gal. My joy and bliss was so complete after this evening that I fully expected to be killed in a car crash on the way home.
>
> Enjoy each other and remember how special and unique is our band of merry players!
>
> xxoojane

And with that bittersweet parting, on to *Glee* I would go! While shooting the third episode, I got a call from Gabrielle, my beloved, and generally even-keeled, agent. She was screaming, "They released you! They released you!" The producers of the bad pilot had bailed on the project, the deal had fallen apart, and I was now able to be a regular cast member of *Glee*.

I brought a pillow and a blow-dryer to my trailer the very next day, because I was home.

"Perfect"

T HE *GLEE* PILOT PREMIERED ON FOX ON MAY 20, 2009, in the time slot right after *American Idol*. The Nielsen ratings didn't live up to the advance hype, but it didn't much matter; we were in a whole new era in which success was gauged by a different set of metrics. Instead of just counting the number of households tuning in, the network executives were looking at what the 18–34 demographic had to say about the show via the Web, including Twitter, Facebook, MySpace, Hulu, Fox.com, iTunes, entertainment websites, and blogs. By that measure, the *Glee* pilot was an undisputed hit. The kids' rendition of "Don't Stop Believin'" was the number one download on iTunes the following day and a *Billboard* top five hit that week. The pilot episode (the only one that had been aired) became a viral phenomenon on the Internet, and over the summer, the absence of *Glee* from the airwaves seemed to just make hearts grow fonder. One critic throbbed, "I think I'm in love and I can't wait until August." In fact, these newly minted Gleeks would have to wait until September to get more of the McKinley High School glee club and its nemesis, Sue Sylvester.

The reviews for the *Glee* pilot episode were just fabulous. The reviews for me personally were almost over-the-top in their use of superlatives. For a girl who had wanted nothing more than to be seen as special for her entire life, my internal response was surprisingly muted. As I pondered my reaction, it occurred to me that I might have actually *matured* a bit over the years. Had this level of adoration been heaped upon me in my younger, more insecure days, I would undoubtedly have disappeared into the hype, believing it all. This would have been disastrous, because inevitably the excitement dies down, and once that happened I would have been left without a firm ground of self-esteem to stand on, chasing praise, endlessly. Luckily, at the tender age of forty-eight, I was neither dependent on the attention for validation nor was I unmoved by it. I could enjoy it for what it was and put it in the context of the stronger sense of self I had developed.

Nevertheless, the effect on my life was big. I immediately became more recognizable on the street and in restaurants and grocery stores. Almost everywhere I went, people seemed compelled to stop me to tell me how much they loved *Glee* and why. There was an almost religious fervor to the encounters; these people needed me to appreciate how much the show lifted them. "No, you don't understand! I *LOVE* this show" was a common refrain. A fifty-year-old guy friend of mine, cynical as they come, was moved to tell me that he cried when the kids starting to sing "Don't Stop Believin'." The appreciation wasn't always for the feel-good qualities of the show, either: parents and teachers often came up to me telling me they *wished* they could talk to their kids the way Sue Sylvester did.

The audience did not seem to be confined to any one demographic. All kinds of people—young, old, married, single, black, and white—were digging the show. The broad appeal was largely due to the fact that *Glee*'s lovable cast of high school losers came in every size, shape, and color. Everyone watching could find someone to root for. They were played by a fabulous group of mostly newcomers. The jock was played by Cory Monteith, the handsome Canadian. The head cheerleader was played by the lovely Dianna Agron. The dark and mysterious Mark Salling was the bad-boy punk character. The African-American diva was played by the astoundingly talented Amber Riley. Chris Colfer, with his beautiful baby face, was cast as the gay kid. Of course, some of the kids in the cast had been singing and dancing for years. Darling and dimpled Jenna Ushkowitz, who played the adopted Asian, had been performing on Broadway since she was ten. Lea Michele, having starred in *Les Miz* at age eight, was a Broadway veteran as well when she was cast as Rachel, the overambitious star in the making. Kevin McHale had been drawn to performing since he was a youngster and had been in a boy band for a couple of years before he was cast as the kid in the wheelchair. This group, along with the fabulously talented and sexy Matt Morrison, who played Will Schuester, was drawing fans from all walks of life.

Back at Paramount Studios, we had been in the midst of shooting our first handful of episodes when the first one ran. We had been working on the show since February and had been in a bubble of sorts, since nothing had been on the air yet. When the pilot aired, we were all blown away by the reaction. It felt so unreal. Could our little show really be a *phenomenon*?

Right after the airing of the pilot, we went on a mini-hiatus for about a month before returning in mid-June to complete the network's order for thirteen episodes. Meanwhile, my life was about to undergo another big change.

During my break, my good friend (and *The L Word* creator) Ilene Chaiken was being honored at the National Center for Lesbian Rights gala in San Francisco. She was being given the Voice and Visibility award and asked me to present it to her. NCLR is the leading legal advocacy group for gay and lesbian families, and Ilene is a passionate supporter. In fact, she had created my character on *The L Word*, Joyce Wischnia, as a hero of the movement. I loved NCLR as well, and I found Kate Kendall, the brilliant and tireless leader, to be an inspiration. I felt privileged to be supporting this organization and especially to be the one to give Ilene this well-deserved honor.

After landing in San Francisco, I checked into the hotel where the event was to be held. The festivities would be under way shortly, starting with a photo session for the award winners and presenters, and I needed a coffee to rev me up. I found the closest Starbucks and then returned with my soy latte to the vast, multiwinged hotel lobby and promptly got lost trying to get back to my room. I wandered around, frustrated, looking for the correct bank of elevators. Unbeknownst to me my wife-to-be was lost as well, looking for the photo session I would join after a quick trip to my room. When she saw me as I strode across the lobby, she would later tell me that she felt pulled to follow me, and told herself that this was a good idea because I might know where I was going. This rationalization faltered when after a few steps she realized I was headed elsewhere, but, she later confessed, she continued to check me out and liked what she saw.

Once in my room, I brushed the coffee breath from my teeth,

put on my fancy duds, and headed to the photo session a few floors down. When I arrived, one of the handlers said the Justice Award winner in from Sarasota, Florida, would like to take a picture with me and asked if that was okay. Expecting to meet your run-of-the-mill *The L Word* fan, I said, "Sure."

When I was escorted over to where Lara Embry was being photographed, I saw that she was anything but run-of-the-mill. Instead she was gorgeous, even more so when she smiled at me. I immediately began to pray that she was gay. While we were posing for the photographer, she jokingly said something about her best friend telling her she should ask me to sign her breast. My heart went *boom*, and I got all hyped up. In a split second, my mind wanted to know *Who is this "friend"?* and *Does she really want me to sign her breast?* and *I hope she doesn't mean to fix me up with this friend because I want HER.* I mustered up a cocky flirtatiousness that didn't at all suit me and retorted, "I'll sign anything you want." Off my game yet all atwitter, I allowed the photographer to put us in some schlocky poses that on any other day I would have nixed. But I was literally in an altered state, so I happily stood back to back with Lara, arms folded, and yucked it up for the camera.

As we dutifully followed directions, I checked her out. Lara was a bright light, all shiny and glowy, and had the most beautiful smile; I noted the perfection of her teeth. She was wearing a tight-fitting black cocktail dress that hugged her incredible body like a glove. She had "curves on her curves" as my mom used to say, and her arms looked strikingly toned. The soft, dark brown curls of her hair contrasted with her beautiful porcelain white skin. I was immediately smitten.

With the moment coming to a close, I brazenly said to her,

"You know, in ten years, we can show our kids a photo of the moment we met." I was all the way in, and yes, I had only known her a minute.

As we went our separate ways toward the ballroom for the event, I watched her from afar interacting with the handlers and well-wishers. Her elegance and grace came along with a certain cool reserve that I found intensely compelling and attractive. I guessed correctly that people tended to come to *her*. The fact that she had approached me, and with such warmth, filled my heart with joy.

I also noticed with dread that she was accompanied by a woman who I feared might be her girlfriend. I sized the chick up and concluded smugly, *I could break that up.* I still wasn't sure she was even gay, and I hoped to god I wasn't falling for the one girl in the room who didn't play for my team. After a quick investigation, I found out that the woman with her, Kate, was an old friend from their days together at Smith College (a liberal lezzie school, so that answered the gay question) and that Lara was unattached. I was very relieved and glad I wouldn't have to destroy another's happiness to go after mine with Lara Embry.

At the dinner, although we were seated at different tables, we were facing directly across from each other. I couldn't take my eyes off of her. Remembering what I had been figuring out about my tendency to lump huge, outlandish projections onto people, I wisely restrained myself from crying out, "I love you!" right then and there. It was hard, though. I caught her eye several times, and to my shock, she held my gaze.

OPPOSITE: *Photographic evidence of the moment I met Lara Embry.*

She was receiving the Justice Award for fighting (and ultimately winning) an appeal establishing that out-of-state gay and lesbian adoptions had to be recognized in Florida. I learned the story as she was being introduced by Shannon Minter, the NCLR legal director. While in a relationship for ten years, Lara's partner had given birth to their first child, and Lara gave birth to their second. The women had cross-adopted the girls in Washington State, where they had been living and where it is legal for gay people to adopt children as a second parent. The two little girls were being raised as sisters. After they moved to Florida, Lara and her partner eventually broke up, but they continued co-parenting for several years, until her ex-partner suddenly and unilaterally cut off Lara's contact with their older daughter, who was then seven years old, and walked away from the five-year-old girl Lara had given birth to. Even though the adoption that had taken place in Washington State was perfectly legal, an incompetent judge ruled that it was not binding in Florida because of that state's disgraceful anti-gay adoption policy. All of a sudden, Lara was no longer considered to be a parent to her older daughter.

Lara had contacted NCLR and they had successfully represented her in appealing that ruling. It was a rout, with NCLR cleaning the floor with the legal team from the Liberty Counsel, Jerry Falwell's nonprofit legal organization for the defense of "Christian religious liberty . . . and the traditional family." The ruling meant that Florida had to follow the Constitution and recognize gay and lesbian adoptions from other states. It was a victory that meant that gay and lesbian families could rest assured that the children they legally adopted could not be taken away from them because of the parents' sexual orientation.

You could hear a pin drop as Lara accepted her award and talked about her story to a captivated ballroom at the NCLR gala. Her poise and self-possession were awe-inspiring, especially since, although she had a legal victory to celebrate, Lara was still being kept from her daughter, and the sisters were still separated. The legal process that followed the appeal was long and arduous, and reunification would not occur until after a custody evaluation and subsequent mediation more than a year later.

Because of her strong and steady nature, Lara's plight did not trigger my "rescue" impulse, as it might have otherwise. She was a *substantial* person, with great integrity, and that was clearly no projection on my part. I was, however, in danger of falling into hero-worship and idealization, but Lara would not be amenable to taking this on, as I would find out later that night. . . .

Lara's best friend (and soon-to-be maid of honor at our wedding), Trish, was the one who had told Lara to get me to sign her boob. In between the time Lara saw me in the lobby and this photo session, she figured out that I was the actress Trish wanted her to meet. Trish was a *Two and a Half Men* fanatic, and when Lara had told her I would be at the event, her first response had been a very jealous "You suck." So I have her to thank for putting me on Lara's radar. Trish had been trying to get Lara to watch my portrayal as Charlie's therapist for a long time, telling her she would love me. Though Lara had never caught the show, Trish was *convinced* we would have a lot in common: I played a therapist and she *was* a therapist; I was a lesbian, and she was a lesbian, too. It was perfect! *She* was perfect! And that night as we were making out in her hotel room, I told her so.

"You're perfect!" I exclaimed.

"No, I'm not," she said in a very measured tone. "You're turned on and I happen to be the woman who is on top of you."

Oh my god, I thought, *even more perfect!*

In between kisses during *the* best make-out session I've ever had, we talked and talked. She had just turned forty and had a therapy practice in Sarasota. She'd gotten her bachelor's from Smith College, master's in philosophy from Columbia, and a PhD in psychology from the University of Washington. I don't think I had ever kissed anyone so educated. She was originally from Alabama, and her parents were both doctors, Mom a radiologist and Dad a forensic pathologist. (I'd *played* a forensic scientist in *The Fugitive*, so I sort of knew what that was.) She had a brother who was doing his residency in radiology and he was married, with a little boy. She had acquired those terrific guns from rowing, which she had done since her Smith crew team days. She loved her kids fiercely; her birth daughter, Haden, was seven and, as she put it, a "pip." (When I met the child the next day, I would find that to be an understatement.) She showed me a school photo of her freckle-faced older daughter, by then nine years old and at that time in neither Lara's nor Haden's life.

As I listened and Lara offered me bits of her life story, the piece of her past that seemed to weigh the heaviest on her was the devastating loss of her older sister in a car crash when they were in their early teens. That her two daughters had lost each other was unbearable; it was clear that she would do everything in her power to reunite these sisters.

I was so taken with her peaceful countenance and self-assurance, in part because it contrasted so much with me. I am a whippersnapper, full of anxious energy and all go-go-go. Her steady tempo calmed me, and helped me keep guard over my enthusiasm, because after one evening with someone, even someone this wonderful, I had no business deciding I'd found my soul mate. And yet that was what I was feeling.

At around 3 A.M., Lara needed to take her leave. Haden had slept over at a cousin's home nearby so Lara could attend the event, and Lara didn't want her to wake up in the middle of the night and not know where her mom was. This warmed my already warm heart. My insides jumped up and down when she agreed that I should return to her hotel room in the morning with coffee for us. I also wished I had brought one more outfit to wear.

I went back to my hotel room and barely slept, watching the clock, waiting for the moment when I could get up and get the coffee and see her again. Could she possibly be as wonderful as I felt she was? I did not want to repeat my tendency to create, sometimes out of whole cloth, an entire person based on nothing other than my projections, resulting in my being shocked (*shocked*, I tell you!) when she turned out to be someone completely different.

Dressed in the clothes she'd seen me wearing in the lobby the day before, I went to Starbucks and got us soy lattes. After I got back to the hotel, I realized I had completely forgotten to get anything for the kid: no hot chocolate, no treats. I was not at all used to considering the needs of children, and this wouldn't be the last time I would forget to feed the child.

Haden was in the shower when I arrived, which gave me a moment to look at Lara in the light of the morning. My feelings for her had not eroded in the least during the night. I was still completely goo-goo-eyed.

Then I met the freshly showered Haden. Seven years old, with long, curly brown hair just like her mom's, she wore glasses with transition lenses that were starting to go dark in the bright sunlight pouring into the hotel room. My dad had worn transition lenses, as had many old people I'd known, but I'd never seen them on a child. She danced around, kicking up her legs for us to examine the pants she was wearing, wondering aloud if they qualified as capris or gauchos. I suggested they were gauchos because they had very wide legs. She considered this a bit and then agreed. Suddenly we heard a loud noise from down on the street below and a man yelling furiously. Haden raised her eyebrows and said, "*Someone's* having a bad day."

I've never found kids very interesting; I'm a dog person. But this kid was charming and she was *ironic*. I thought that maybe I could deal with a kid if it's *this* kid. Again, I had to be careful to keep my feet on the ground, e.g., not suggest they move across the country to live with me just yet. Before they left, the kid sat in my lap for a photo.

They were flying back home to Sarasota later that day, so I said good-bye. As I was leaving the hotel room, Lara took me in her arms and held me; it felt so wonderful and right. As I walked to the door, I sang, "*When will I see you again?*"

She smiled. "I hope soon."

We would talk even sooner. While I was in the airport later that day waiting for my plane back to LA, we talked on the phone for about two hours. We were having the "relationship interview," the conversation where you learn as much as you can about each other, usually served up in sound bites. We lined up in all the important areas: she loved coffee and the *New York Times* columnist Frank Rich; her few good friends were long-

term and of good quality. I remember I had just passed through
security when she brought up the subject of my past relationships. My heart started to pound and I felt all the blood rush to
my face. I did not look good on paper; I was nearing fifty, and
with a couple of exceptions, most of my relationships had lasted

Photographic evidence of the moment I met Haden Ryan Embry.

two months, max. As I had in the past felt embarrassed talking about my relatively unremarkable drinking history, I was ashamed of my pitiful dating life and seeming inability to connect—I sounded like such an underachiever. But she did not gasp in shock or send me on my way. She simply listened with what felt like no judgment and then shared her answer to that same question: she had been with her ex-partner for almost ten years, but she said that it probably should have been over much sooner. I thought to myself: *So her relationship history isn't anything to write home about either.* As I breathed a sigh of relief, we hung up so I could board the plane back to LA. Once on board, I got on my BlackBerry to look into flights to Sarasota.

I was so elated to find there was a direct flight to Tampa from LAX; I don't change planes. Tampa was only an hour drive from her home in Sarasota. I checked the schedule and called Lara right there on the runway. "I can come to Sarasota next weekend. Are you around?" She had a very good friend coming into town that weekend and was so sorry, but she wouldn't be available. I was afraid that the shock of my relationship history had sunk in and she was blowing me off, until she asked, "How about the week after that?" I would be back to work on *Glee*, so no could do. We hung up saying we would talk again when I landed.

Just before the plane took off and I was about to turn off my phone, she called me back. "My friend is fine with your coming into town the same time she's here, so book that flight for next weekend." This was Lisa, her best friend from high school who was like a sister to her. Wanting Lara to find love, Lisa even offered to watch Haden so we could have some time together.

This was music to my one hearing ear. My heart was full and pounded all the way back to LA.

My hopeful mind reeled along with my heart: *Could this wonderful, amazing, beautiful woman be "the one"?*

Whereupon my practical mind interjected: *There's no such thing as "the one," Jane.*

And my hopeful mind snapped at my practical mind, *Why do you have to be such a killjoy?*

When the appointed day and time arrived for me to board the plane to visit Lara in Sarasota, I was on the phone with her. I said, "I just want to say how brave we both are right now. Me for getting on a plane to fly across the country to visit someone I just met, and you for inviting someone you just met to fly across the country." She agreed. I flew on the direct red-eye flight into Tampa, arriving at about five-thirty in the morning. Already almost ninety degrees and about 80 percent humidity, the hostility of the air almost knocked me to the pavement, a la Patsy and Edina in the "Morocco" *Absolutely Fabulous* episode. I hoped to god she didn't want to live in Florida forever.

No rental car company would give me a car, because I had only brought a debit card and they required a regular credit card, so I took a cab to Sarasota that cost me around $200. I declined to tell Lara about this, as I didn't want to look like an idiot right away. I was staying in Turtle Beach, about a fifteen-minute drive from Lara's home. She had cleared her Friday of appointments save one first thing in the morning and would arrive at around 10 A.M. As it was early in the morning and the front office of the small resort where I was staying was not open yet, a key to my little cabin on the bay had been left for me, taped to the screen door. I walked in after my all-night flight, thrilled but exhausted. When my head hit the pillow of the huge bed that took up the entire room, I fell into a deep sleep and had a very vivid dream that Lara, followed by what I imagined was her Mexican cleaning lady and her Mexican cleaning lady's family all carrying suitcases, had filed into my hotel room. I made the mistake of texting this dream to Lara before I could think about it, and she texted back, "Worried I might have too much baggage?" I learned another important lesson: never tell a therapist a dream unless you want it analyzed and your covers pulled.

I was coming into Lara's life during a very trying time for her. She had a lot on her plate; she was raising one child by herself, fighting to regain joint custody of the other, all the while needing to be available and sane enough to deal with other people's problems in her very busy therapy practice. I had a job on a TV show that had the potential to become a phenomenon and felt myself to be on the brink of a career explosion. Perhaps that dream was my subconscious trying to knock on my door of awareness: *Do you want to get involved in all this? Do you really want to take this on?*

I had no answer just yet; all I wanted was for her to get to my cabin, already. She arrived mid-morning, all dreamy-looking and self-assured and bearing soy lattes. I met her at the door with a kiss, after which we rarely left my place for the rest of the weekend. We took full advantage of Lara's friend Lisa, happily having Haden play with her daughter, Amelia.

In and out of sleep on our first night together, I had another very vivid dream. In it, a trio of lisping musicians dressed as clowns was performing an oompah band rendition of "At Last."

This time, I didn't need a psychologist to tell me that I was falling deeply in love with Lara.

She really was up to her ears in her own life, with a long road ahead of her full of legal twists and turns as she fought for her daughters. I would watch as she underwent this ordeal, amazed at the way she always remained calm and steady and focused. Even on the rare occasions when she became frustrated or angry, I never saw her freak out or lose her temper.

What I found most delightful was how much she loved Haden. It moved me to the core, how absolutely enchanted she was with her daughter. She beautifully mirrored Haden's bright light back to her. She adored her child beyond measure, and my heart ached for the daughter who wasn't around to know Lara's brand of love. Lara was her best person with Haden.

In the months to come, Lara's concerns, hopes, and dreams would become my own. And mine would become hers. This, I was discovering, was what relationships were about.

I returned to Los Angeles a woman in love. I hit the ground running, going right back to Paramount Studios to shoot the remaining episodes of our first season of *Glee*.

The night before we started shooting, Fox TV execs Dana Walden and Gary Newman took the cast and executive producers out to dinner. We sat down to steaks in a private room at BLT Steak, and Dana made a toast to the success of the pilot and expressed the high hopes we all had for *Glee* as a TV series. She basically said to all of us, "Your life as it now stands is over." I'd heard this sentiment before at other cast dinners for pilots past, but this time it caused me to pause and ponder. I didn't know anyone in the cast very well, and it was a very strange and delightful thing to look around the room and

think, *I may well be going on a lovely journey with these people.*
This also may have been the last time that Cory, Lea, and all
the *Glee* kids would leave a restaurant without being hounded
by TMZ or paparazzi.

We got word from Fox International that the *Glee* pilot had
also been a huge hit in Australia; on the night it aired, one of every two televisions in Australia had been tuned to *Glee.* So in
September of 2009, the execs sent the entire cast down under to
Melbourne and Sydney to promote the show. By this time Lara
and I had made a handful of trips to see each other, and it
couldn't have been going better. I was having a real, live grown-
up relationship with a wonderful woman. As I kissed her good-
bye right before I would be flying to Australia, I was hit with a
wave of panic. *What if I'm killed in a plane crash and Lara and I
never get to have a life together?* I said it, and she told me that she'd
had the same thought. I had something so special to live for: Lara
and little Haden. We were becoming a family. I reluctantly flew
off to Australia with the rest of the cast and breathed a sigh of
relief when on each leg of the trip the plane landed safely.

While we were in Sydney, Fox announced that we were getting an order for what's called the "back nine" episodes. Only
the pilot had aired so far, but Fox was confident enough in the
success of the show that it wanted us to film an entire season,
twenty-two total, including the pilot.

As an actor, I had never known job security, so having just
been contracted to work through May of the following year
couldn't have pleased me more. I'd spent many years going
from job to job never knowing what would be next, and I
heaved a huge sigh of relief to have a place to hang my hat for at
least a while. Although I was doing quite well in my efforts to

root myself firmly "in the moment" as far as my relationships with Lara and Haden were concerned, I was nonetheless very heartened to know that I would have a nice bit of money coming in were we to become a family.

As I have described before, in relationships I had a tendency to jump in right away and then take it all back when I came to my senses. This time I was trying very hard to avoid this pattern. I was quite conscious of keeping my mouth shut and resisting my desire to start promising things to her. This turned out to be a very wise choice, because there's nothing speedy about Lara.

I was learning that Lara moved slowly, carefully, and with great deliberation. We were out-and-out polar opposites in this regard. I moved crazy fast and then cleaned up any mess afterward. She wouldn't make her flight reservations until she had fully analyzed the calendar and then sat on it for a while to be sure, whereas I was always making and then canceling them. She was like that about relationships, too, it seemed.

I was also fascinated with how she didn't dwell on setbacks, great or small, or feel the need to apologize for who she was. It amplified my feeling that I was always bemoaning some slight, or feeling sorry about something. She was extraordinarily patient with me and charmed by my desire to be efficient and do the right thing. And she was grateful for the way I got things done in a timely manner, even if I had to go back and correct a mistake or two from moving too fast. "I hope you still find this cute in a year or two," I'd say to her. As I raced around the house and my life like a chicken with its head cut off, she'd just smile at me, allowing me to be me and loving me for it. I was seen and I was gotten.

I also spent the first months of our relationship in wonder at her ability to let things go and to very carefully choose the battles she would fight, especially with respect to the custody drama. When I asked her about how she was able to do this, her response was "I have more patience than they have anger."

One great benefit of *Glee*'s success was that I now had a hiatus. It wouldn't be until January that we started shooting again, so I had months in which I could visit Lara frequently in between other bits of work. When I was in Sarasota, ensconced in her life completely, with no fish of my own to fry, I began to explore a whole new part of myself heretofore unexpressed; I became "wifely." Lara would work all day, seeing patients, whereas I had my daily list of errands. I would drive the station wagon to Whole Foods, then head to the dry cleaners, and then zip over to the hardware store to pick up lightbulbs. I loved taking care of my girls.

I also got to develop a real relationship with Haden and to learn just how special she is. I went to lunch with her in the schoolyard most days, bringing food for us to share. On October 2, her eighth birthday, I brought her a McDonald's apple pie. She took a bite, closed her eyes, and said, "Now *that* tastes like October." I always forgot to bring a ball to play with, so we would play catch with wood chips from the yard. I'd pick up Haden after school, and we would do her homework together. She was smart as a whip and she'd blow through it fast. Then we'd have a snack and settle in for a few Tivo-ed episodes of *iCarly* until Mom came home. The show was so clever, and Haden and I would laugh out loud, watching funny moments over and over again, and then repeating the lines to each other, laughing some more. We'd just *kill* it.

One afternoon, I was watching a particularly surreal and dreamlike sequence in the movie *Nine* with Daniel Day-Lewis when Haden joined me. She watched for a bit then paused the TV and, looking at me with great consternation, said, "Okay. Walk me through it." I *loved* this kid.

One morning when I was back in LA, Lara called to tell me that when she had been walking Haden into school that morning, Haden had been deep in thought, and Lara had asked her what she was thinking about. Haden had said, "Look-alikes. I've been thinking about look-alikes."

"Oh, yeah? How's that?" Lara asked.

"Well," Haden said, "I look like you. I mean I am smaller, but I look just like you."

Lara had started to say something to Haden about genetics, when Haden cut to the chase. "Yeah, yeah, I look like you, but I'm funny like *Jane*."

When Lara told me this, my heart melted; she'd *claimed* me.

Allowing me to get to know Haden and be a part of her life was also something special; I knew Lara wasn't going to allow just any girlfriend to bond with her child unless she meant business.

. . .

BACK WHEN I HAD BEEN SHOOTING *JULIE & JULIA*, Nora Ephron, being the foodie she is, told me that any significant moment in her life is always accompanied by the memory of what she ate. I told her that my mother, being the clotheshorse she is, remembered what she wore. Nora gasped, "You must do our play!"

Nora and her sister Delia had put together an all-woman staged reading called *Love, Loss, and What I Wore*, based on a book of the same name by Ilene Beckerman. Performing at the Westside Theater in New York City, the Ephron sisters put together a delightful and sometimes moving series of stories where each turning point in a woman's life becomes associated with an article of clothing. The reading would have a revolving cast, the lineup changing each month. They invited me to be in the second group, which would begin performing in October of 2009. During my *Glee* hiatus, I spent a month in New York, renting my friend Kara Swisher's mother's apartment on 57th Street near Park Avenue.

It was just an idyllic situation, and I couldn't have fantasized it any better: New York in the fall, doing a play where I got to sit down the entire time. I had no lines to learn as it was literally a reading, with a notebook in front of each actor, and we were performing for extremely delighted audiences. Add to that a fabulous cast of women I'd never met before, including the profoundly wonderful Tyne Daly (who upon meeting me said, "I don't know your work but I understand you're a credit to your profession"), and I was pinching myself to see if I was dreaming. For this brief time I got to live the life of a theater actor doing a play off-Broadway.

Lara came up to visit for the weekend, and we had a wonderful time pretending to live in the city. Her parents had gone down to Florida to take care of Haden, in yet another complicated travel arrangement. After Lara got home, we had a long talk on the phone in which Lara's practical, planning side was fully engaged. Lara suggested that we get married and she and Haden move out to LA. It wasn't a very romantic conversation;

it was more of a logistical one. We both acknowledged that we wanted to be together, and having a long-term long-distance relationship was not plausible given the demands of our lives. We also missed each other too much. I was at the start of a potential five-year contract with *Glee* that would keep me in Los Angeles ten months of each year. Her career as a psychologist was more mobile, so they should be the ones to move. It would be better for Haden to start in a new school at the beginning of the school year, so the move should take place over the summer. Lara would also need a while to close her practice, and that process should start soon if she was going to be able to move during the following summer. And Lara didn't want to pick up and move her entire life without being married, so we should do that in the spring. I agreed with all of it and agreed quickly.

Then I freaked out. Everything became very real and I tossed and turned all that night. *This is happening too fast. We are now involving a child. Will Lara be able to create a life for herself outside of our relationship in Los Angeles? What if it doesn't work and we break up? We've only known each other for a handful of months!* When Lara awoke the next morning, she found these questions and concerns on her phone from me via text message.

I was just falling asleep when my phone buzzed at around 5 A.M. with her response. She was nervous, too, and sympathized with me. "If we do this and then break up," she said, "I will be sad but I will go on." I was relieved and unburdened. I now could enjoy and celebrate as we started planning. And that's all I needed, and I loved her even more for her honesty and bravery.

I was all in now, committed to her and my new family, excited to meet and embrace her older daughter, thrilled to officially become Haden's parent. But I balked at the word "marriage."

Domestic partnership in California is almost as strong as marriage, so why not just go that route? But Lara wanted to get "married" and nothing less; we had a child, and her older daughter would most likely be a part of our life, too. Lara wanted commitment, and she saw that as being contained in the word "marriage."

I looked at my resistance to the word and discovered a latent childhood belief that "marriage" was for straight people, and that gays were not entitled to it. Maybe it was because she is younger than I am, or maybe it was her education, but Lara felt that marriage was a perfectly natural word to use. I loved her sense of entitlement, and I used her conviction to help me vanquish my old belief, and I came to agree that there was no reason we shouldn't be married.

My next level of resistance was my fear of telling my mother. She had completely embraced both my sexual orientation and me, but I hadn't been in many relationships, let alone one that would lead to marriage, so this would be brand-new territory for my mom. I was pretty sure that she had no idea gay couples could get married in some states, and indeed, when I called her to tell her Lara and I were getting married, she paused for a moment and then asked in pure bewilderment, "How?"

But Mom survived the news, so I was able to move on to the great fun of making marriage plans with the woman I loved. First off, we had to pick a state where gay marriage was legal. Massachusetts won because Lara had gone to Smith College and she loved Northampton. We also decided it would be a very small wedding, with four friends each, and that we would save the family celebrations for parties we would have in each of our hometowns. Our families were already planning on meeting up in New York while I was doing the play, so we quickly scheduled an engagement brunch at a restaurant in the Village.

Her educated and fabulously Southern family mixed beautifully with my funny and sweet Chicago-bred Irish Catholic family. Everyone was just tickled that Lara and I had found each other, and even more tickled that we were getting married. Lara's dad was an odd breed of Southern liberal, committed to justice for all and firmly in support of gay marriage. Her mom loved nothing more than a good wedding party. My extended family has always been very kid-focused, and they were delighted that I would be having the chance to be a parent. Haden was just a bit younger than my brother Bob's son Erik, who was thrilled to have a new cousin his age. Julie's four kids were now terrific and witty young adults who claimed Haden as their own. Lara's brother was there as well, with his three-year-old son, Alabama, and his pregnant wife, Pam. Pam's sister Elizabeth brought her newborn daughter, Ophelia, who was passed around and made everyone smile with her cooing. The brunch was filled with a sense of joyous beginnings and the warmth of family.

Lucky for us, Lara's sister-in-law is also an amazing jeweler. During our stay in New York, we went to the shop she shares with Elizabeth in Soho, called Doyle and Doyle. She helped us select the elegant platinum bands we gave each other when we proposed to each other properly. Lara gave me mine when we were in Alabama, walking by the tree-lined lake of Indian Springs School, her high school campus. I gave her hers when we traveled to Chicago. I took her to Table 52, my favorite romantic restaurant, and proposed. I was so pleased that I already knew the answer. We were getting married.

. . .

ON MAY 31, EXACTLY ONE YEAR TO THE DAY AFTER WE
had met, we got married.

Lara's four friends and my four friends, and a few of their
guests, gathered on the patio of a beautiful old courthouse
building turned restaurant called the Blue Heron, in Sunder-
land, Massachusetts. The restaurant was closed for the day to
have our simple, but beautiful, wedding. To preserve the intimacy of the event, most of our guests did double duty. Laura
Coyle sang, and began the ceremony with a gorgeous rendition
of the k.d. lang song "Beautifully Combined." Jeannie performed the ceremony, having been ordained online by the Universal Life Church (just click on *Ordain Me Now!*). She officiated
the ceremony with reverence, joy, and good humor, mixing in

The wedding party.

My family: Lara, Haden, and Jane.

bits of different traditions that signified the commitment we were making. Jeannie's husband, David, a drummer, put to-gether a four-piece ensemble of wonderful jazz musicians who played through the night. Guy, the director I'd grown to love on *Lovespring International*, was our official wedding photographer. Lara's best friend, Trish, read a poem. Lara's oldest friends, Lisa and Heather, were in attendance, too, and supplied the tears of joy. Her brother, Joe, and his wife, Pam, brought their son and new baby girl. I said my vows to Lara, and Lara said her vows to me. Then, I said my vows to Haden, promising to cherish her as my daughter for the rest of our lives. By the power vested in Jeannie, we were now a family. Right on cue, Laura began to sing her surprise gift to us, a very meaningful, clown-free, and lispless but still joyful version of "At Last." Then we all sat down together to a delicious meal at a huge long table and danced into the night.

13

Feast

D O YOU KNOW THAT FEELING, WHEN YOU FINALLY arrive somewhere after a long trip, of being able to relax and *breathe*? Like you are free to focus on where you *are* rather than on how to get where you *want to be*? This is how I feel much of the time these days. Now, I am not presuming to say that I am done growing as a person, just that the things I have been pursuing for so long are now mine. And amazingly enough, they all fell into place at pretty much the same time.

This doesn't mean that I'm not still constantly surprised by the delicious treats life sends my way. Indeed, these happy accidents seem to be coming at a faster clip than ever now. This is especially true of the parade of good fortune I have had while working on *Glee*.

When I returned to work in LA after my off-Broadway stint, an engaged lady, after those first twelve episodes aired, the show had exploded in popularity, and everyone was soaking it in. There was no time for me to bask, though, because I learned almost immediately that I was due for my first musical number of the show, and that it would be nothing less than a remake of the video for Madonna's hit song "Vogue."

This was big. Madonna had provided the soundtrack for the 1990s, and we were going to devote an entire episode to her music. This song in particular had been an overwhelming hit in the clubs, renewing and expanding a dance craze called "Voguing." I mostly kept to my bar stool in those days, but I remember the kids on the dance floor framing their faces with their hands as they contorted themselves into various model-like poses. The original video, directed by David Fincher, is a strikingly gorgeous tribute to the Golden Age of Hollywood. We were going to reshoot the video, basically frame by frame, with Sue Sylvester as Madonna.

The premise would be that Kurt, the gay fashionista played by Chris Colfer, and Mercedes, the diva played by Amber Riley, decide that Sue needs a makeover, so they kindly offer their skills to help Sue explore a variety of possible looks. In a moment of compromised confidence, Sue accepts, resulting in the "Vogue" video remake. (She ultimately comes to her senses, after poking a student's eye out with one of her Gaultier-inspired black conical boobs, and returns to wearing nothing but tracksuits.)

Just before the Christmas break, I had my first rehearsal with our awesome and completely overworked choreographer Zach Woodlee and his kick-ass assistant Brooke Lipton. Although we wouldn't be shooting the video until late January, they wanted to help me get a leg up (if you will) on the dancing. This was wise of them. Let's just say that I am not known for my abilities as a dancer; I only dance when forced to, and left to my own devices I do the same basic move repeatedly, one that looks entirely appropriate at a hoedown. Learning Madonna's fancy moves was going to be challenging, to say the least. One particularly formidable sequence—a sort of running-in-place pantomime with very precise, almost military arm gestures—loomed with the potential to be my own personal Waterloo. I did not take naturally to this dance, and the first rehearsal left me in a bit of a panic.

When we broke for the holidays, I went to Sarasota to be with the girls, and from there we embarked on a "family tour." First we flew to Alabama to be with Lara's family, then to Chicago to be with mine. Then we headed to LA to hang out a bit before Lara and Haden flew back to Sarasota.

I taught Haden the dance sequence one day during her school lunch break before we left for Alabama. Of course, the kid picked it up instantly, and after that was basically teaching *me*. We practiced together the entire Christmas tour, dancing in airports, on the plane (with just our feet, mind you), in my mom's TV room, and anywhere else we happened to pause and catch each other's eyes. And yes, we also performed the dance for the guests at our wedding (but that was long after we shot the video).

Even with all of this practicing under the excellent tutelage of Haden, I was still very iffy with the moves when I returned to *Glee* first thing in the New Year. Luckily, because this video was Ryan's baby and he was absolutely obsessed with making it perfect, the shoot had been pushed to the middle of February. It had been in preproduction for months, much longer than any other *Glee* musical number before (and probably since).

I could do the basic motions with my arms and legs, but there was absolutely no rhythm involved and it certainly didn't look anything like dancing. In my last rehearsal with Zach and

Brooke a few days before we were to shoot the video, it seemed, embarrassingly, like I hadn't practiced at all. They taught the steps to Chris and Amber just in case Ryan wanted to add their characters to that sequence (he didn't), and to my chagrin, they picked it up right then and there, no problem. I was in a panic and feared embarrassing myself in front of everyone, and disappointing Ryan, as I struggled through the moves. Finally, the day before the shoot, miracle of miracles, somehow the dance seemed to make it out of my head and into my body. By god, I was dancing!

Our costume designer Lou Eyrich worked with Ali Rahimi, the fabulous designer who had gained my affection by making me look good a few weeks earlier for the Golden Globes, to reproduce Madonna's wardrobe for me. We even found some of the prop pieces, columns and such, from the original video to use in our remake. Chris Baffa, our director of photography, meticulously replicated the lighting for the black-and-white shoot. Ryan had two monitors set up for himself side by side: one played the original "Vogue" video while the other showed him what we were shooting. I was also able to watch a sequence of the original before we shot our version of it. Stacey K. Black meticulously styled each wig, and Kelley Mitchell replicated the classical Hollywood movie makeup. All decked out in my Madonna "Vogue"-wear, with Chris, Amber, and four stunning male dancers in white tuxedos and slicked-back hair, we set about to re-create the "Vogue" video à la *Glee*.

The challenging dance sequence was near the top of the shot list, and I was grateful for that; I wanted to get it over with so I didn't have to angst about it. But in the final rehearsal right before shooting, I fell behind immediately. (The beat was going so *fast*! I didn't remember it being so *fast*!) I asked Brooke to count it out for me as we shot—*one and two and three and four and*— and because I had to be able to hear it over the playback, she had to pretty much scream it. The amazingly gorgeous and

Me as Sue Sylvester as Madonna.

lithe black man I was dancing with (who of course had learned the steps only the day before) was all fluid arms and legs. But somehow, instead of being intimidated by his acuity, I allowed him to inspire me.

Fancying myself to be as good a dancer as he for that one brief shining moment, I rose to the occasion, and that first take *rocked*. It all fell apart for me on the second attempt, but that was okay; I only needed to do it right once. I'm so proud of that damn sequence.

The rest of the shoot was a breeze. Ryan added some vintage Sue moments along the way that deviated from Madonna's video. He had Sue slap away the makeup artist in one shot and replaced "*Bette Davis, we love you*" with "*Will Schuester, I hate you*." But the rest of the video was true to the original and, in my humble opinion, was flawless.

At the end of the long but wonderfully satisfying day, Ryan called out to me, "Jane, thank you for making my gay dream come true."

Many dreams, gay and otherwise, had come true just before Christmas when *Glee* was nominated for several Golden Globe Awards. I was nominated for best supporting actress. I always thought I'd be on cloud nine if I got an acting award nomination, but instead, I was somewhat unnerved by it. I almost purposefully slept through the announcement, which is broadcast at 5 A.M. Pacific Time, as I didn't want to want it too much. I woke up a couple hours later to seven messages, three of them from my agent Gabrielle.

Gabrielle is almost always calm. She delivers the news "you got the job" or "you didn't get the job" in exactly the same tone of voice. To be my agent she has the perfect mix of temperament; she is tenacious, loyal, and so completely averse to drama that at times I've thought she didn't care. But I know she does, as she studies the industry like no one I know, watching hours and hours of television and going to countless movie screenings to keep ahead. Gabrielle takes care of everything for me that a manager and publicist would and goes out of her way to accompany me to key events. The voice on my machine was like nothing I had heard from her before; it was urgent and giggly. By her third message she was just screaming "wake up, wake up, why are you sleeping" into the phone. When I called her back that morning, I felt her excitement so fully that I wanted to have it as well.

Nevertheless, I found myself struggling a bit with those age-old feelings of unworthiness. When I tried to muster a feeling of "deserving" the nomination, I could still feel the effect of my mother's aversion to show-offs and braggarts. At forty-nine years old! Man, that stuff hangs on.

The morning of the nominations, we were all called to the set for a press event. When asked about my reaction to the nomination, I said all the right things, acting as if I was joyous and grateful. I didn't let on that I feared looking conceited, or that being nominated would invite closer scrutiny that would lead to someone "finding out" that I really wasn't all that talented. Eventually I was able to soothe myself; I was very proud of my work on *Glee*, and there was no reason for me to feel so self-conscious. So after the initial wash of feeling, I found my balance and arrived at a place of equanimity. Others seemed more excited than I was about it, but I felt good about my nomination. My central fear was that I would never find a dress to fit me.

Gabrielle arranged to have me meet with Ali Rahimi to talk about possibly making me a gown for the event. Wardrobe fittings have always been very stressful for me; I am not a "*standard size that fits a standard dress*" (from *Funny Girl*). I have a thirty-five-inch inseam, a small waist, and a wide-ish ass. Finding clothes to fit me can be a nightmare, and the generally frustrating process can really bring me down. Before arriving, I knew Ali was offering to make me a custom-fit dress, which should have allayed my concern. But I'd had clothes custom-made before, dropping thousands of dollars over the years, and have never been satisfied. So it was with dread, in anticipation of another shameful wardrobe failure, that I walked into Ali's salon on La Brea Avenue in Hollywood. My eye went right to a gorgeous olive green taffeta gown on a dress form in the corner of the room.

"You want to try that one on?" Ali asked me, in his elegant Iranian-via-London accent, as he saw me eyeing the beautiful dress. It looked tiny on the mannequin. "It would never fit me, you see, I'm really hard to fit . . ."

"I actually made it this weekend for you. I'm pretty sure it will be just beautiful on you." His voice was so reassuring I felt myself soften a little.

I sighed deeply as I took the dress into the fitting room. I slapped on some Spanx, put on the dress, and it zipped up effortlessly. I walked out stunned and delighted as I modeled it for Gabrielle in the sitting room. It looked gorgeous and it fit me beautifully. The hard part was over. I had a dress. Now I could relax and look forward to the event.

In January of 2010, at the Beverly Hills Hotel, while sitting with Lara at the *Glee* table in my olive green Ali Rahimi original gown, I heard Chloë Sevigny's name called and not mine. And I was fine. I was actually a bit grateful not to have to wind my way around the tables to get to the stage and accept in front of a live audience. I received several *you were robbed* texts and appreciated the support. I didn't need it, though, as I really was just pleased to be there in a gorgeous dress with Lara (who looked stunning in a deep red silk gown).

Glee took the Golden Globe that night for best comedy or musical, and I was happy as a clam to rush the stage with my

Lara and Jane at the Golden Globes, 2010.

cast mates. As Ryan accepted the award for us all, I stood in the back, just one of the group. Just the way I liked it.

When I was nominated for a supporting actress Emmy the following August, I was able to accept the nomination without having it rock my sense of self. I was even excited, and looked forward to going to the show. Then I was invited to be in the opening number, and I was over-the-moon thrilled. Jimmy Fallon was hosting, and the show was to open with a *Glee*-inspired song-and-dance number. The assembled actors were such a great and talented bunch of people that I was tickled to be included. I adore Jimmy and have found him to be one of the most gracious and lovely people in show business. Of course, the number also featured several of the *Glee* kids, including Lea, Cory, Amber, and Chris. The group was also blessed with Tina Fey (one of my comedic idols and my favorite actress on TV) and Jon Hamm (not only drop-dead handsome but a real goof). We pre-shot a premise piece about getting a group together to win a singing contest to raise enough money for the *Glee* kids to go to the show. Then on the night of the Emmys, we would perform Bruce Springsteen's "Born to Run" on stage live, with Jimmy as Bruce. The fun of filming and practicing for the show completely distracted me from any anticipatory anxiety.

In fact, I was so engaged that I didn't really even contemplate what I would do if I won. The night of the show, after the triumph of our opening number, while I was getting back into my gown, I came up with some talking points in my head, "just in case." It turned out to be a good thing to have thought about, because Stephen Colbert called my name as the winner of the award for best supporting actress in a comedy. I remembered to thank my parents, appreciate my incredibly talented fellow nominees and the fantastic ensemble I am fortunate to be a part of, and to give a shout-out to my wife and Haden. It was also my opportunity to tell the world how proud I am to be an actor.

Back at work, post-Emmy, Ryan gave me another piece of good news: Olivia Newton-John had agreed to do a guest spot on *Glee*, and she and I would remake the "Physical" video. I immediately asked Ryan, "Are you trying to make *all* of my dreams come true?"

I am not often privy to how our guest stars make their way onto the show, other than the usual scuttlebutt about who knows who and how, but this time I was there when it happened. It had started back in August, after our summer hiatus, at that dinner with the whole cast and Fox executives where they told us our lives were about to change. I had been talking with Ryan when he pointed out a distinguished gentleman having dinner with his large family in the restaurant. "That's John Farrar," he said. He didn't need to tell me that this was the guy who'd written "Hopelessly Devoted to You" and several other hits for Olivia Newton-John. Ryan and I were both huge fans of Olivia; in fact, he credits her with teaching him how to sing, from listening to his mother's copy of Olivia's *If You Love Me, Let Me Know* album. (I knew the LP in question quite well, having had that raging crush on her back in high school. At that time, I'd also replaced my boy-crush Ron Howard with John Travolta, so when I heard Olivia and John Travolta were doing *Grease*, I almost imploded.) Ryan suggested we get ourselves over to John Farrar's table to "commence our campaign to get Olivia Newton-John on *Glee*."

John Farrar couldn't have been more gracious and welcoming. He was also shocked we knew who he was; Ryan and I were *very* up on our Olivia Newton-John, so of course we knew who he was; he'd also written "If Not for You," "Let Me Be There," and who could forget "Physical"?

We told him all about our new show, and then Ryan asked, "Do you think Olivia would be interested in being on *Glee*?" John replied that she was living in Florida now and very busy with her charitable work, but we should approach her. He said she would be thrilled that we were such big fans. I asked if he

Mission accomplished.

thought it might help if I told her I had named my dog after her. (On this, he was noncommittal.)

Ryan sent Olivia every episode of *Glee* to date and a letter asking her to honor us with her talent and her presence.

She was a living doll, that Olivia Newton-John, and indeed, she was very moved that I had named my Lhasa after her. She delightfully took part in our making all sorts of fun of her humanitarian work, and we giggled our way through the "Physical" video.

. . .

IN DECEMBER OF 2010, I WAS NOMINATED FOR ANOTHER Golden Globe, and this time they gave it to me. As my category was announced, my fear of snaking my way through those star-studded tables to the stage caused me to plead silently, *Please don't say Jane Lynch, please don't say Jane Lynch.* But when they said "Jane Lynch," I thought, *You're damn right, Jane Lynch!*

I took that opportunity to thank the brilliant Ian Brennan, the creator of Sue Sylvester and the man responsible for every heinous line that comes out of my mouth. He is an incredibly nice and sweet guy who just happens to have a really cruel, supremely mean sense of humor. Of my and Ian's relationship, the *New York Times* said, "Behind most great comedic actors, the saying goes, there is a great comedic writer. Will Ferrell has Adam McKay. Jack Lemmon had Billy Wilder. And Jane Lynch, who won an Emmy Award last month for her portrayal of Sue Sylvester, the acid-spewing, narcissism-redefining cheerleading coach on 'Glee,' has Ian Brennan." I feel so lucky to be able to deliver his deliciously brutal lines. I am forever in debt to this fellow Chicago boy who is eighteen years my junior (I realized that he had been born on the day I performed *Godspell* in high school). Among my favorites so far are:

> *"So you like show tunes. It doesn't mean you're gay.*
> *It just means you're awful."*

Sue Sylvester's better half.

*"I'm going to ask you to smell your armpits.
That's the smell of failure, and it's stinking up my office."*

*"You think this is hard? I am passing a gallstone as
we speak, that's hard!"*

*"I don't trust a man with curly hair. I can't help
picturing small birds laying sulfurous eggs in there,
and I find it disgusting."*

*"I never wanted kids. Don't have the time.
Don't have the uterus."*

I thank the comedy gods every day for putting us together.

In this run of celebratory fun for the success of *Glee*, there have been some events that have really emphasized to me how bizarre fame is. Foremost among them was my invitation to be replicated in wax as Sue Sylvester for Madame Tussauds museum. It was a high honor for me—and a tribute to the popularity of *Glee*—that Sue had become a television icon in one season, and I am not too humble to give some of that credit to myself.

In July of 2010, Lara, Haden, and I were driven in a black limo to the back door of Madame Tussauds museum on Hollywood Boulevard for the big unveiling ceremony. I had gone through the meticulous measuring session a few months before; using ancient tools that looked like instruments of torture, they calculated every part of my face in relation to every other—e.g., the distance of my ear to my cheekbone, cheekbone to the tip of my nose, etc. They matched the exact shade of my eye white and photographed me from all angles as I was slowly spun around on a lazy Susan for humans. I was curious as all get out to see my person captured in wax. They ushered us very quietly into a meeting room where people were already assembled. I saw my agents Gabrielle and Mark, Ian Brennan, some *Glee* fans, and the well-dressed, lifelike, but completely still wax figures of Morgan Freeman, Halle Berry, and Tom Hanks, which just completely freaked me out. For some reason, everyone was speaking in hushed tones. When the museum representative requested gravely that "the family come this way, please" and led us into a waiting area, it suddenly hit me that I felt like we were at a wake. This feeling would only intensify when I finally viewed the wax image of myself. All I could think was *This is how I will look in a coffin when I'm dead*. Though I was grateful that they had made my ass look good, I was also glad that my own last will and testament specified cremation for my remains.

As they led us back inside after the unveiling, I saw two museum workers getting on an elevator with my wax figure, one guy carrying my red tracksuited body while the other one had my decapitated head in his armpit. Minutes earlier, I had wondered if there was anything stranger than standing next to your own lifelike wax figure. The answer is: *yes*.

Luckily, these surreal fame-driven experiences were more than balanced by the really wonderful family and work relationships that formed the core of my life. By the end of July 2010, Lara and Haden were all moved in and happily ensconced in Los Angeles. Haden was due to start Wonderland Elementary in Laurel Canyon in the fall. We set up a temporary home in West Hollywood and started rebuilding my Canyon home to accommodate my new family. I had started working with an architect and designer a year before I even met Lara, as my little house was bursting at the seams with just me. It took an entire year to get the permits, so we were just about to break ground when the girls moved to LA. We would be adding a second story in addition to reworking the entire floor plan. Though I had no idea I would soon be married with children when I was initially designing my new home, I had accommodated for them beautifully. I wondered if this was a case of "if you build it, they will come."

Though still in our West Hollywood rental, I can't tell you how great it was to wake up every day with the people I love in my house, and the license to call them mine. My oldest niece, Megan, moved in with us as well. At twenty-five years old, my sister's oldest child had become an exceptional human being with a terrific sense of humor. She also just adores kids and really embraced her new cousin Haden. I got a kick out of it every time she took Haden on an outing to Yogurtland and they came back giggling. Once, when Lara and I were coming home, we saw them walking down our block, holding hands. There was so much love all around, and I felt so at home.

One of the biggest surprises in my life has been the great joy I have gotten from becoming a mom. It didn't take long before I pretty much had the hang of it. After all, I have a kid who loves to read lines and laugh with me. Our current favorite scene to reenact is the 1960s game show scene I did with Kristen Wiig when I hosted *Saturday Night Live*. Haden is obsessed with Kristen (so am I) and embodies her part in that bit to a tee. And just like me, Haden will work on a moment over and over again to get the timing just right.

The most challenging part so far has been remembering that she needs to eat with some regularity. Lara loves to cook and is usually in charge of this activity, but once a month she travels back to Florida to see her other daughter (she and her ex are

Me and Kristen Wiig on Saturday Night Live.

now working together to repair and unite the family) and meals are left up to me. One Friday when Lara was in Sarasota and Haden had the day off from school for Cesar Chavez Day, I was in the midst of writing this very book you have in your hands. We arose at 8 A.M., and I sat her in front of the TV on one couch and myself with my computer on the other, and we both proceeded to lose ourselves in our activities.

Now, when Haden watches TV, she goes away and becomes completely disconnected from anything in the room other than what's on the screen; I have had to literally "wake" her from this all-consuming stupor. When I write, I go away, too, and I don't mean that I drift off peacefully into a land of creativity and inspiration. It's more like exercise: I grunt and sigh, slap my head trying to find the right word. I growl when the thread of an idea gets away from me, typing furiously with two index fingers. It was 1 P.M. when I looked up to find Haden standing at the foot of my couch. She said, "I'm *sooo* hungry." I was, too, and neither of us had gone to the bathroom for hours, either. We took care of that first, and then I microwaved a piece of leftover pizza for her. The most amazing part is that when this sort of thing happens (and we both know it will again), she eats her pizza, and forgives me.

When I went back to work for the second season of *Glee* late that summer, I felt like I had finally found my work home. To be able to return to the same cast and crew for the second season was wonderful. I was more than ready to get into my comfy tracksuit and menacingly destroy the glee club.

The cast and crew of *Glee* is filled with talented, funny, and hardworking people. The *Glee* kids are all very sweet and professional and really seem to be enjoying the roller-coaster ride of a lifetime that is our show. They work so much harder than me; when they are not shooting, they are rehearsing or recording. They are up at the crack of dawn, and it's not uncommon for them to work fifteen-hour days. It tickles me when I see them work together as a creative group getting through any differences for the good of the whole. Just like the glee club at McKinley High, in real life these actors support one another and allow one another to shine. They are loyal friends to one another both on the soundstage and off. My niece Megan was a production assistant on last season's *Glee* tour, and she has become a part of their group, and I couldn't be more pleased with her new friends.

In particular, I have become a fan of Chris Colfer, our fashionable boy soprano. I not only admire Chris the actor but also Chris the human. When we shot the pilot, Chris was a mere

Chris Colfer and me.

nineteen years old and just fresh out of high school. His coming of age and coming out of the closet has mirrored that of his character, Kurt, and it has played out in full view of the public eye. I couldn't be more proud of him, as he has walked his own path with such grace and dignity. He has become an inspiration not only to gay and lesbian kids all over the planet but to all kids who feel less than "normal" and fear exposure. Even as adults, and I'll speak for myself as a fifty-year-old one, we're all still in high school in that regard. I am so happy we have a courageous and fashion-forward role model to look up to. It's a lot to put on his young shoulders, but luckily Chris has an inner grandma that helps him keep his feet on the ground and his eye on his work. He's already writing and producing his own projects, and I fully expect to be begging him for a job in the future. I will be sure to bring along this paragraph of praise when I do, hoping it will net me something.

I've worked most with Matt Morrison, our steadfast glee club director, Mr. Schuester, and my affection for him runs deep. The extent of his gift as a singer and dancer just floors me, and his sex appeal is off the charts. But what I value most of all in Matt is that he is kind. When he talks, all of his impressions and thoughts are first filtered through his compassionate heart. His sense of humor is still off-color and can be as crude as I like it, but cynicism is not his thing and I love him for that. When-

Matt and I find something very amusing that Cory does not.

ever I'm tempted to engage in gossip and pettiness, all it takes is one look into Matt's soulful eyes (complete with the fullest set of lashes ever given to a person) to get me right back into my heart.

On-set, he has claimed Will Schuester's school office as his own, and I often see him in there during downtime, on his computer, with his headphones on, working on his own music. He always seems completely content with his own company; he loves to travel and go off on adventures all by his lonesome, doing things like jumping out of airplanes. The thought of doing anything like that, much less by myself, terrifies me, but I greatly admire his wanderlust and his need to try new things. I count myself lucky that when we work together he often hangs out with me and talks; I appreciate so much that he lets me into his private world. He also has genuine affection for Lara and Haden. He lights up when he sees them and gives them huge hugs. In this way, he feels even more a part of my family, and working with him hardly feels like a job at all. It really *is* my work home.

The second season of *Glee* also brought me the gift of another amazing guest star. Soon after we all returned, Ryan told me he'd gotten Carol Burnett to agree to play Sue Sylvester's mother. My first thought was *God, I love this job*.

This wasn't the first time that I'd had the chance to work with Carol. I'd first met her back in 2007 when we did a movie together called *Post Grad*. Except for Carol playing my mother-in-law, and Michael Keaton my husband, the film was unremarkable. As Carol would say much later, it could only be seen on Airbuses bound for New Zealand. But for me the experience was magical. My childhood dream to work with the great lady of comedy came true, and I didn't even have to go through

Vicki Lawrence. I was in my trailer, having just arrived for my first day on the movie, when I heard an exuberant, "Jane?" and up the steps bounded Carol Burnett. She greeted me with a hug and I thought my heart would burst. She is one of the loveliest people I've ever met, and we had a great time getting to know each other. No one tells a story like Carol, and because of my childhood fascination with *The Carol Burnett Show*, I couldn't have been a more willing ear. And in the male-dominated world of television, she was a true pioneer; no woman in television since Lucille Ball had been as powerful. I ate it all up, and she took great delight in reliving those heavenly days with me. By the end of that shoot, I barely had to cue her for a good anecdote. I did, however, have to occasionally step outside of myself to remark, *I'm hanging with Carol Burnett*.

I'm also proud to say I made Carol Burnett laugh. It was in between takes, and we were all sitting in the car in which the scene was set. I was in the driver's seat, and Carol was in the backseat. Killing time, I said, "Carol, look at my backing-up face." Pretending to put the car in reverse, straining to see what was behind me, I looked over my shoulder with the most ridiculous and horrific face I could make. She howled with laughter.

Now I would have the chance to work with her again, as Sue Sylvester. She had signed on to play my mother, who was a Nazi hunter. We both had to wait awhile to find out what the story would be.

If you look at the staff of most TV shows, you will find anywhere from ten to twenty writers. On *Glee*, we have three—Brad Falchuk, Ian, and Ryan—making the task of getting each hour-long episode written on time a herculean one. It also means that the scripts sometimes arrive the night before the scene is

shot. Brad has said that the three of them together make one very good writer. I've figured out that if you laughed at something, Ian wrote it; if you cried at something, Brad wrote it; and if you said "What the —— was that?" Ryan wrote it. Judging by the Nazi hunter business, Carol would be in an episode featuring Ryan's touch.

Because of that eleventh-hour arrival of scripts, Carol hadn't read anything about the episode she would be in when Lou Eyrich, our costume designer, called her to discuss the different looks she'd be dressing Carol in for this episode.

"I'll be getting you a dress for Sue's wedding," Lou told her.

"Oh, Sue is getting married! Who is she marrying?" Carol asked.

"Herself," said Lou.

". . . What's that, dear?"

She listened as it was explained that Sue Sylvester would be marrying herself in this episode, and she and my sister, Jean (played by the wonderful and sweet Robin Trocki), would be the only guests at the wedding. Carol Burnett is nothing if not game, so she embraced the role's outlandish story line.

As the writers were working, Ryan asked Carol for a song suggestion for her character. Carol's musician husband, Brian, suggested Carol should sing "Ohio" from the 1950s musical *Wonderful Town* (*"Why, oh why, oh why, oh—why did I ever leave Ohio?"*), and Ryan thought it was a perfect fit. It was, in fact, the very question Sue had wanted her mother to answer for years: Carol's character had left Ohio and a very young Sue

OPPOSITE: *Mother and daughter.*
Carol Burnett and I sing "Ohio."

all alone to raise her handi-capable older sister, and Sue had never understood why. We shot the scene with Carol's character rehearsing the number on the bare auditorium stage. As she began the second verse, Sue reluctantly joined her in harmony. Mother and daughter shared a very touching and poignant moment. But at the end of the song their moment of togetherness was cast aside, and Sue was again rejected by her mother. I, on the other hand, was overjoyed to be singing with Carol and having a wonderful week pretending she was my crazy, Nazi-hunting mother.

In our funny mother/daughter scenes in *Glee*, her character's guilt and shame for having abandoned her children were always just below the surface, creating some lovely and bittersweet laughs. I walked away from that episode impressed with the way Carol Burnett's work has stayed genuine throughout the years. I am honored to call her my friend.

Very soon after we finished shooting with Carol, as I was still reflecting on her career-long commitment to mining the truth for its laughs as opposed to relying on a bag of old tricks, I had a very quick encounter with Alec Baldwin at the *Vanity Fair* party after the Oscars. He grabbed my arm and said, "You know that big laugh you got at the SAG Awards just looking into the camera when they announced your nomination?"

I remembered and said, "What about it?"—trying not to sound defensive.

"People *expect* you to be funny, and from now on, everything you do will get a laugh. That's the good news and the bad news." Great advice that I took to heart; what's funny and works for me today may not be funny and work for me tomorrow. I have to allow my work to evolve and grow. Which in the future will hopefully mean that I won't be throwing a new generation of kids into the lockers with an adult diaper under my trackie.

Honestly, though, I am not overly worried about this, and for one reason in particular. I thoroughly enjoy the people I get to work with, and can't wait to see what they bring to the scene. Indeed, the happiest accidents I have experienced throughout my life are the words and feelings that have almost popped out of my person as I kept myself open to the influence of the people around me. As long as I stay present, and in my heart, I trust that my acting, as well as my life, will not become stale.

Epilogue

I HAVE TO THINK THAT IF ANYONE HAD TOLD THAT younger version of me who wrote letters to Hollywood casting agents from her dining room table in Dolton, Illinois, that I would one day be on a hit television show, and working with Carol Burnett no less, I probably would have believed every word of it. I was practically delusional . . . or maybe I was just prescient. Either way, I knew what I wanted, and (almost) in spite of myself, I got it.

What I did *right* was to be über-prepared and ready to pounce. After I'd walked away from *The Ugly Duckling* my freshman year in high school, I would never let fear overtake me again. Not that I wouldn't ever *feel* fear again, I just would do my best to ignore it or use it. I grabbed at almost every opportunity, maybe even some I should have left by the wayside. I went full-pelt and balls-out, never coming up for air for a good bunch of years. I don't know that this would work for everyone, but it worked for me.

While I was all go, go, go, anxiously looking for the recipe for success, hoping for someone to hand me the keys to the kingdom, Providence was able to sneak in there and lead me to exactly where I needed to be next. In this way, my life really has been a series of happy accidents. I became a comedic actress at The Second City, after being picked out of a large group audition that I wasn't even that keen on doing. I ran into Chris Guest in a coffee shop and was cast in *Best in Show*. Steve Carell's wife told him he had too many guys in his movie, and I got to do *The 40-Year-Old Virgin* and meet a great group of people. The mediocre pilot I was committed to failed and I was released to do *Glee*. I could go on and on.

And of course, I met my wife through an unlikely coincidence of timing in a city in which neither of us lived. The way I see it, these accidents of fate were actually my life taking care of me.

I would love to be able to go back and tell that young girl sitting at the dining room table in Dolton, Illinois, pen in hand, to trust herself in the world. I'd tell her, "You don't have to drink, and you don't have to be anxious. You just have to be you, and everything will be fine." I can say that I do finally trust and have faith in my life.

I would never presume to give anyone advice on how to walk their own path, as I have no desire to deprive anyone of their unique journey; as you can see, my own has been customized to fit my needs and my particular brand of humanness. But I will offer this in the way of counsel (and I defer to the infinite wisdom of Carol Brady when I do): find what it is you do best and do your best with it.

Acknowledgments

To my friend, Lisa Dickey; thank you so much for the rock-solid outline you provided me for this book. Your great suggestions complete with clever turns of phrase have been invaluable.

Thank you, Mel Berger, my literary agent at William Morris Endeavor, for making this first time out in the literary world an exciting and fun-filled one for me. Your support throughout this process and your many kind words of encouragement as I sent you chapter after chapter have meant the world to me.

I give heaps of gratitude to Elizabeth Mikesell. I will always be in debt to you for your wonderful editorial assistance, your encouragement, and your "can do" attitude.

Big thanks to my agent Gabrielle Krengel at Domain. You make everything easier and better. I would be lost without you.

Thank you, Jill Schwartzman, my editor at Hyperion/Voice. Along with being a fabulous editor, you have been most patient and kind with me while I navigated this brand-new terrain as a first-time author. Like Lara, you're a Smith-y, and like me you couldn't get enough of *The Brady Bunch* as a kid; a match made in heaven.

I am so impressed and in debt to the fabulous and fashion-forward president and publisher of Hyperion/Voice, Ellen Archer. You head up a wonderful staff of amazing folks who deserve a big round of applause: Elisabeth Dyssegaard, Kristin

Kiser, Marie Coolman, Kristina Miller, Bryan Christian, Sarah Rucker, Mike Rotondo, Maha Khalil, Claire McKean, Rick Willett, Shubhani Sarkar, Karen Minster, Ralph Fowler, Laura Klynstra, and Sam O'Brien.

Special thanks to the following folks for letting me use your personal photographs in this book: Beth Gilles Whitehead, Stacey K. Black, Guy Shalem, Joan and Mike Zerebny, Aunt Marge, Mom, Sue, and Julie.

And finally, thank you, Lara. You are my partner on every level, but especially so when it comes to the writing of this book. Thank you for making sense of my rambling and disconnected thoughts. I learned so much from you writing this book together. It's also a tribute to your sticking power that after all this, you still want to be married to me. I love you more than I can say.